JESUS: MYTHING IN ACTION

VOLUME I

The Complete Heretic's Guide to Western Religion,
Book Two:
Jesus: Mything in Action (vol. I)
Copyright (c) 2016 by David Fitzgerald
All Rights Reserved

Printed in the United States of America

Published by Create Space

ISBN-13:
9781542858885

ISBN-10:
1542858887

 The Complete Heretic's Guide to Western Religion

JESUS: MYTHING IN ACTION

By

David Fitzgerald

VOLUME I

Other Books by David Fitzgerald

Nailed: Ten Christian Myths That Show Jesus Never Existed At All

Books in *The Complete Heretic's Guide to Western Religion* Series

Book One: The Mormons

Book Two: Jesus: Mything in Action (vol. I)

Book Three: Jesus: Mything in Action (vol. II)

Book Four: Jesus: Mything in Action (vol. III)

Forthcoming:

Sex & Violence in the Bible

The Jehovah's Witnesses

Christmas

Satan!

Dedicated with love to all the people who over the years have said to me:

> "Oh, I know he wasn't the Son of God, but I'm sure there really was a Jesus…"

and all the people who confided in me that they always suspected there wasn't…

Praise for *Jesus: Mything in Action*

My new favorite book! David takes the reader on a (de)mystifying journey into and then out of the dreamscape I once held as "reality." Every page is yet another step up and out of the modern-day-evangelicals' very own Platonian cave. My only disappointment is that he didn't write this book thirty years ago! It would have saved me half a lifetime of chasing shadows and searching for someone who still remains 'mything in action.'
—Jerry DeWitt, Author of *Hope After Faith*

A brilliant read. *Jesus: Mything in Action* is *the* definitive guide to Jesus's historicity. It's a masterpiece of scholarship that will be studied for decades to come.
—Peter Boghossian, Assistant Professor of Philosophy at Portland State University and author of *A Manual for Creating Atheists*

It's not hard to convince atheists that God doesn't exist, but denying the existence of *Jesus*? Most of us have never even considered that possibility. David Fitzgerald walks us through why that's such an important question and then makes a strong case for why biblical scholars – and casual church-goers – should take a second look at an assumption they've long taken for granted.
—Hemant Mehta, Editor of FriendlyAtheist.com

A thorough and entertaining survey of what's wrong with secular scholarship on Jesus, why most scholarship on Jesus isn't really secular, and why the possibility that Jesus was mythical needs to be taken seriously. Every Jesus-myth enthusiast will want to read and reference this one. His demonstration that an alarming number of Jesus scholars are actually contractually required to deny mythicism is alone worth the price of admission. His also revealing the embarrassing truth of how historicist scholars contrive even more flawed or ridiculous theories than mythicists is just gravy.

—Richard C. Carrier, Ph.D., author of *On the Historicity of Jesus*

David Fitzgerald: one of our liveliest, wittiest writers and a scrupulously thorough researcher. As entertaining as *The Mormons* – and as carefully, scholarly, detailed and truthful. And that's well deserved high praise.

For the rest of my life, when Christians challenge me on my criticisms of the truth of their tales and the worth of their piety, I will just say, "Read David Fitzgerald's *Jesus: Mything in Action* and then get back to me."

Fitzgerald has provided us with the most readable, engaging, scholarly, and utterly thorough dismantling of biblical Christianity – and both the Jesus of faith and Jesus of history – I could've ever even imagined. My fellow citizens of Heretic Nation (as Fitzgerald fondly calls us) and I now have all we need for giving the Christian apologists reasons to backpedal – and plenty to apologize for.

—Ed Buckner, Former President of American Atheists (retired)

With this book, Fitzgerald brings forth his best work yet, targeting an audience that is generally open-minded, smart, educated, skeptical, and evidence based. Yet, there are atheists, non-believers, freethinkers and overall believe-in-god-challenged people who are still convinced Jesus was a real historical person. On this I say the author is mistaken – this exceptional book should target all those who care about what is true – yes, including Christians. This outstanding book provides a remarkable amount of evidence that clearly exposes the myth of a historical Jesus and it backs it up with a great

wealth of references giving the reader little option but to be a "militant agnostic" about Jesus' historicity. Even with a treasure-trove of information, this book is an easy read for anyone high school and up. The detailed approach to each piece of evidence and their link to each other, as well as the right amount of pages to present such evidence, its compelling logic, and the brilliant presentation makes *Jesus: Mything in Action* one of the best books I've read in recent years.
—David Tamayo, President & Founder Hispanic American Freethinkers, Inc.

As Charles Darwin drew upon the evidence in the natural world around him for the conclusions presented in *The Origin of Species*, so does David Fitzgerald with regard to history. In *Jesus: Mything in Action*, he reviews the evidence we have as well as the evidence we should have but don't, how we ended up with what we do have, and what that all might mean for the myth of Jesus. With a high-level overview followed by meticulous examination on each point, David's writing is conversational, fun, and accessible to laypersons and academics alike - while providing a veritable treasure map of resources for anyone looking to dig deeper.
—Lyz Liddell, Executive Director of Reason Rally 2016

For many years now I have said, "I am a 50% mythicist." I have read, studied and observed the debate and scholarship for decades; however, I wasn't quite there yet and still had a lot of questions. After reading *Jesus: Mything in Action*, I am now a 172% mythicist. However, this is not just a book on the mythicist debate, David Fitzgerald turned my view of the New Testament and early Christian writings upside down. A view and understanding that I have had since my studies began as an undergraduate. If you have read Ehrman, Price, Carrier, or any number of other authors, this book brings them all together and clears away the fog.

—Darrel Ray, Ed.D., author of *The God Virus*, and *Sex and God*

Jesus: Mything in Action, David Fitzgerald's follow-up to *Nailed*, asks piercing questions that won't go away. If Christianity began with a historical Jesus, then where is he? Why is he a no-show in every written work outside of the gospels? And if we can trace the literary and theological antecedents of every gospel story, is the historical Jesus even necessary? David takes us on a gripping journey through time to show where the myths of the heavenly Christ as well as the legends of the historical Jesus came from. But no matter where or when we look, Jesus of Nazareth himself is the man who wasn't there. Don't myth it!
—Tim Widowfield of Vridar.org

Who was the real Jesus? There is no consensus. There is the Catholic Jesus, the Orthodox Jesus, the Muslim Jesus, and many more. They can't all be right. What if they are all wrong? In *Jesus: Mything in Action*, David Fitzgerald explores the "Jesus of Faith" and the "Jesus of History" which ultimately leads him to ask the question, "Did Jesus really exist?" With wit, insight, and an immense amount of research, this startling book makes a compelling case to support the Jesus Myth theory. I really enjoyed this book and think you will too.
—Dr. Karen Stollznow, linguist, author of *Hits & Mrs., Language Myths, Mysteries and Magic, God Bless America, Haunting America* and *Would You Believe It?* and host of the *Monster Talk* podcast

David Fitzgerald's latest may have supplanted *Nailed* as my go-to resource regarding Jesus. *Mything in Action* makes a compelling case against the long-calcified academic assumptions that Christ's legend is based on a literal person, but much more usefully, it provides a thoroughly-sourced and navigable journey around and over the huge cracks in Jesus' supposedly pristine persona. *Mything in Action* deftly dissects the conflicting and often nonsensical New Testament Jesus tales, exposes the perilous holes in Jesus "history," and reveals a curiously confused Christ portrait that - very possibly - was drawn straight from imagination.

—Seth Andrews, broadcaster, author, host of thethinkingatheist.com

Brilliant, very readable and comprehensive. A wide-ranging discussion of the evidence for Jesus demonstrating that it is exactly what we should expect if Jesus began not as a historical figure but as a theological and literary invention. David Fitzgerald's opening chapters are especially noteworthy as a wonderful breath of fresh air for anyone who has read the diatribes of scholars hostile to the Christ Myth hypothesis. Partly with the assistance of some original research Fitzgerald exposes just how self-interested, strained and nonsensical those attacks have been.

—Neil Godfrey of Vridar.org

In his latest book, David Fitzgerald asks all the right questions about Jesus. He does not try to 'prove' any preconceived notions; rather, he follows the evidence. I was indeed surprised and absolutely captivated by what followed – a real page turner, full of interesting and entertaining facts, many 'impossible to argue' conclusions, a time travelling tour – exceptionally imaginative, brilliantly coordinated and hugely informative. This outstanding work is a must read for anyone who is questioning their faith or seeking confirmation that their atheistic leanings are indeed well founded. They say the quickest way to become an atheist is to read the Bible; this book could be an even faster route (it is shorter); so I would also recommend it to those who believe but are willing to put faith aside for a moment and 'check the facts' with an open mind. If you have the courage, then just as Fitzgerald promises, you really will "never look at Jesus the same again."

—Jim Whitefield, author of *The Bible Delusion: 101 'Hang on a Minute' Moments; And God's Mysterious Ways* and *The Mormon Delusion* series

The genre of history is underpinned by scientific discipline. Although history involves telling stories about the past, the aim is that these should be stories based on evidence, not on prejudice or fancy or the wish to convey a moral. Stories that are told against the facts, especially those told with moral intent, are very likely to be myths. David Fitzgerald's objective, well-researched, and clearly expressed book correctly consigns Jesus firmly to that latter genre.
—Andrew Copson, Chief Executive, British Humanist Association

I am often shocked by the number of non-believers who accept the Jesus myth unquestioned. Now, with *Jesus: Mything in Action*, David Fitzgerald removes all doubt that the history of Jesus is nothing but folklore and mythology. This is a welcome addition to any library of those interested in seeking out the truth with fact based logic and reason.
—Dan Arel, Author of *The Secular Activist* and *Parenting Without God.*

Take your book off the shelf, Tom Aquinas, your *Summa Theologica* is being replaced by David Fitzgerald's *Summa Mythologica*! *Jesus: Mything in Action* is the most nearly exhaustive synthesis of evidence indicating the non-historicity of Jesus of Nazareth ever written. Best of all, it's written in breezy English prose—not the labyrinthine Latinate crime so often committed when discussing "sacred subjects." The organizational logic of the book is impressive; it reminds me of Euclid's *Elements*. Historical Jesus scholars should not be fooled by the ease with which this book can be read by the educated layperson: this book is a must-read for Jesus specialists also *Mything in Action* is a milestone along the long path to progress in Mythicist studies.

—Frank R. Zindler, American Atheist Press

A very handy and entertaining popular-level reference guide to the topic. Loved the H. G. Wells themed section that creatively reveals how the faith could have started without the Historical Jesus and how little even the earliest Christian authors knew about Jesus!

—Raphael Lataster, author of *Jesus Did Not Exist* and Teaching Fellow (Studies in Religion) at the University of Sydney.

Preface

Jesus: Mything in Action is the follow-up to my 2010 book, *Nailed: Ten Christian Myths That Show Jesus Never Existed at All*. In *Nailed*, I pointed out the top ten ways the traditional story of Jesus simply doesn't hold up, and how our evidence for Christianity's origins point to a Jesus who is an allegorical figure, a theological and literary construct, in other words, a purely mythical Christ.

In the concluding chapter of *Nailed*, I asked "Can Jesus be Saved?" and discussed how different our evidence would need to be if there was even just a merely mortal Jesus. That was all that needed to be said – or so I thought. But it soon became apparent that there were still many questions left unanswered. Where did Christianity come from if there was no Jesus? Why do so many biblical scholars – even secular ones – oppose Jesus myth theory? Are all Jesus myth theories viable? What is our evidence for Jesus?

So here to help with those and more questions is *Jesus: Mything in Action*. I planned this to be both a follow-up to Nailed and the second book in *The Complete Heretic's Guide to Western Religion* series. But four years, nearly a quarter of a million words and several discussions with my audiobook engineer later, it became apparent that at around 900 pages, *J:MIA* would have to be three books instead. I'm just as surprised as you are to discover I just gave birth to triplets, and I thank you in advance for your understanding at why a three-part book has been shoe-horned into on ongoing series.

Here's what you're in for:

In vol. I (chapters 1 – 12), we look at the myths of Jesus Mythicism: what it is and isn't; what biblical scholars are saying about it and why; and critically examine our oldest "biographical" source for Jesus – the Gospel of Mark.

In vol. II (chapters 13 – 18), we discuss the construction (and deconstruction) of the Gospels; how Jesus is presented in the rest of the New Testament; and examines the historical sources for Jesus outside of the Bible.

In vol. III (chapters 19 – 25), we engage in a bold thought experiment: a multi-chapter time travel expedition through the origin and evolution of Christianity. I call it "The Gospel According to H.G. Wells."

Hope you enjoy it!

—David Fitzgerald San Francisco, CA October, 2016

TABLE OF CONTENTS

Preface 17

Introduction: Every Jesus but Yours.....................21

Part One: Myths of Mythicism 33

Chapter One: Of Dinosaurs and Deniers 35

Chapter Two: Bias Cut 57

Chapter Three: Who Do Men Say that I am? 99

Chapter Four: The Hole Truth and Nothing But 125

Chapter Five: Embarrassing Jesus 149

Part Two: The Sources for Jesus 177

Chapter Six: The Source of our Problems (and the Problems of our Source) 179

Chapter Seven: The Gospel Truth 201

Chapter Eight: Jesus Gets a Life...................................227

Chapter Nine: The Kiss of Death...................................255

Chapter Ten: Crucify Him!...273

Chapter Eleven: The Crucial Moment............................297

Chapter Twelve: Jesus is Dead 313

Index 335

About the Author 353

David Fitzgerald

"Together we are at risk before the mysteries of life. The quest for the historical Jesus is a small piece of the great adventure. Minor though it may be, it requires the same devotion to truth as all our other pursuits, the resolute willingness to confront the facts, and the unblinking determination to tell all."

– Robert W. Funk

"I therefore claim to show, not how men think in myths, but how myths operate in men's minds without their being aware of the fact."

– Claude Levi-Strauss

"Heresy makes for progress."

– Hypatia Bradlaugh Bonner

Introduction:
Every Jesus but Yours

"In any genuine attempt to recover the historical Jesus, everything is at stake."
—Robert W. Funk

Two billion or so people on this planet claim to be on a first name basis and in constant psychic contact with Jesus of Nazareth. This book is not for them. Instead, I want to talk to *you* – those of you who have weighed the claims of religions like Christianity and found them wanting; or perhaps never even took them that seriously to begin with: you, the atheists, the agnostics, the secular humanists, the unbelievers – the complete heretics, if you will. Here is my question to you, Heretic Nation: Did Jesus exist?

What a silly question! Fifteen-plus years ago, it had never even crossed my mind that Jesus might not have been a real figure. Sure, he was probably the most over-rated figure in history, but *of course* there had to have been a Jesus (or even several of them) wandering around first-century Galilee and Judea, preaching and teaching until he was crucified and became revered by his followers as the divine Son of God. How could a major world religion start without a real person at its core to found it?

Or so I thought. What made me change my mind? Ironically enough, all of those presumptions started to come apart the moment I became curious to know what Jesus really said and did, and how much of his story was simply legendary embellishments piled on later. Only when I began looking into the historical evidence for Jesus did I begin to realize how shockingly sparse it is. And not just sparse; every word of what little we do have is complete hearsay – and also seriously problematic, contradictory and suspiciously reminiscent of older writings... Still, I soldiered on, comfortably certain there was a real Jesus to be found somewhere. But long story short, after two years of pulling on that thread, it became increasingly apparent that there was no sweater left. I was stunned and baffled, but I couldn't shake the conclusion that there had been no Jesus of Nazareth at all – a conviction that has only grown stronger since.

But here's a second question for you: Does it matter if Jesus was real or not? Don't answer just yet; because first we need to ask a different question: *Which* Jesus?

What do I mean when I ask which Jesus we are talking about? Well, even that simple question is more complicated than it looks. That's because the truth is, there are (and as we'll see, always have been, even right from the beginning) *lots* of Jesuses[1], each as individual as a snowflake. For the purposes of our discussion, let's concentrate on two in particular. In reality, both are placeholders for two huge family trees of competing Jesuses, but for the moment we can pretend there are just two of them: The "Jesus of Faith," and the "Jesus of History." Let's start with the "Jesus of Faith."

The Jesus of Faith

Christianity had a good, long run. But it is not too big to fail. We are long past the point where it's reasonable to be agnostic about the so-called "Jesus of Faith." It's ridiculous to pretend the lack of historical corroboration of the spectacular Gospel events, let alone the New Testament's own fundamental contradictions, aren't a fatal problem for Jesus the divine Son of God.

For example:
- Why does Philo of Alexandria, a Jewish aristocrat and leading scholar with close ties to Jerusalem (and who made pilgrimages there[2]), discuss the contemporary state of various first century Jewish sects in his writings, but not a word on the multitudes who followed the miracle-worker and bold, radical new

Jesus: Mything in Action

teacher Jesus throughout the Galilee and Judea? Why does he have nothing to say about the spectacular events that rocked Jerusalem (literally, as they include a pair of major earthquakes), including all the long-dead Jewish saints who emerged from their freshly opened graves and wandered the streets of Jerusalem, appearing to many (Matt. 27:50-54; 28:2) For that matter, why doesn't any other contemporary Jewish historian, like Justus of Tiberias, or Herod's court historian Nicholas of Damascus?[3]

- If Jesus was really found guilty of blasphemy by the Sanhedrin, why was he not simply stoned to death, as Jewish law required (*Mishnah Sanhedrin 6:4 h & i*)? Why is the original trial account of Jesus so full of other unhistorical details and just plain mistakes that could never have actually happened as portrayed?[4] How can each successive gospel continue to overload the original story with their own additional layers of equally unrealistic details that are mutually incompatible with the others? And why can none of them provide a reason for why Jesus wasn't simply freed when Pontius Pilate (and Herod Antipas, as Luke claims) acquitted him?

- Why does Seneca the Younger record all kinds of unusual natural phenomena in the seven books of his *Quaestiones Naturales,* including eclipses and earthquakes, but not mention the Star of Bethlehem, the pair of earthquakes in Jerusalem that were strong enough to split stones, or the three hours of supernatural darkness that covered "all the land" – an event he would have witnessed firsthand? Why didn't every astronomer in the whole world, or indeed, *any* other astronomer in the world, take notice at the time?

- Why can't the Gospels agree on so many basic, fundamental facts about Jesus' life and ministry, such as what his relationship to John the Baptist was – and why was John the Baptist's cult a rival to Christianity until at least the early second century?

- Who were Jesus' disciples, and why is it no Gospels agree on who they were? Why do the disciples disappear so quickly in the New Testament after the Gospels, only to pop up again centuries later when churches start spinning rival legends that they were busy founding Christian communities all along? If any were martyred for their faith, as Christians frequently insist, why don't we have any details of any of the disciples' deaths in the bible?

- When his skeptical Roman opponent Celsus asks the early church father Origen what miracles Jesus performed, why can Origen only respond lamely that Jesus' life was indeed full of striking and miraculous events, "but from what other source can we can furnish an answer than from the Gospel narratives?" (*Contra Celsum*, 2.33)

- Why can't the Gospels agree on where and when the events in Jesus' life and ministry took place? For instance, if he was born during the reign of Herod the Great – or over a decade later, during Quirinius' tenure? Or where he traveled during his ministry? Or when he drove the moneychangers from the Temple? Or whether he raised Lazarus from the dead or not? Or what he was doing during the final weeks of his life? Or why he was arrested? Or on which day he died: Friday afternoon the day *before* Passover, or Friday morning the day *of* Passover? Or where and when he appeared alive again, and to whom, and for how long – just a single day? More about a week? For forty days?

- Why are there so many anachronisms and basic mistakes and misunderstandings about first century Judaean Judaism?[5] Why are the Gospels all written in Greek, not Aramaic? Why do Christians insist that they are eyewitness accounts when none claim to be, or even

read as if they were, and when all contain indications that they were written generations later?[6]
- Why is Paul – and every other Christian writer from the first generation of Christianity – so silent on any details of Jesus' life? Why do they display so much ignorance of Jesus' teachings and miracles, even when often, simply citing Jesus would clinch the argument they are trying to make?
- Despite the frequent boasts in the New Testament of Christianity spreading like wildfire, attracting new converts by the thousands with every new miracle or inspired sermon, why does Christianity remain a struggling, obscure cult of feuding house churches on the fringe of Roman society for two centuries or more?[7]
- Why was early Christianity so torn apart over doctrinal issues that in the gospels, Jesus had already settled long ago?[8] How could Paul accuse the Jerusalem church of harboring false believers and opposing its leaders so viciously if they were supposedly Jesus' own disciples and family?
- Who are all the *other* Christs and gospels being preached by rival sects in the first century?
- Why is there not a single historical reference providing outside corroboration for Jesus in the entire first century; two problematic and obviously interpolated snippets in the decades-later works of Flavius Josephus notwithstanding?

We could pose similar thorny questions all day and never run out of them. Every one of these points stops being a puzzling mystery if we just suppose that Jesus must have been a relative nobody who made little to no impact on his time and that none of the spectacular events of the Gospels ever really happened. But seriously, how is anyone supposed to take the Gospels at face value? It's embarrassing to have to dignify any of the obvious mythological elements of the Gospels, and yet the better part of 2.1 billion people seem unaware of how ludicrous any of them are. We don't even have to rule out whether or not miracles even *can* occur, or point out that stories, delusions and lies are all too common while verified miracles are few if any – we merely have to ask: if they *did* happen, *why didn't anyone else notice them?*

Of course Christians are perfectly free to opt out of skepticism, forgo evidence and place their faith in whichever messiah they please; though it will take more than blind faith and selective hearing to convince the rest of us that their Christ is anything more than a Jesus of their own making. But it's no coincidence that the Christians who study the Bible the hardest are also the most likely to become ex-Christians. Sooner or later, anyone who earnestly strives to be both intellectually honest *and* a Christian will realize he's doing a bad job at one of them.

In the meantime, whatever else the rest of us may think about who Jesus *really* was (or wasn't), every devout heretic can agree on this: Jesus the Christ of Christianity, the divine, only-begotten Son of God, announced by angels, virgin-born babe in a manger; the water-into-wine-turning, loaves-and-fish-multiplying, leper-healing, storm-calming, demon-expelling, water-walking, temple-cleansing, miracle-working savior; the sinless Lamb of God who died on the cross for our sins as a perfect sacrifice, rose from the dead on the third day and ascended to heaven to sit at the right hand of God until he returns one day (soon – very soon!), riding down from the clouds of heaven at the forefront of the whole heavenly host with power and great glory – to most impartial observers, it's perfectly obvious that *that* Jesus never existed.

The Jesus of History

For your standard unbeliever, that verdict on the so-called "Jesus of Faith" is an easily reached and relatively uncontroversial conclusion. Most of us comfortably presume that the *real* Jesus, the "Jesus of History," was at the very least

Jesus: Mything in Action

an inspired preacher or teacher (or an amalgam of several of them) and at best, the most overrated man in history – a merely mortal, flesh-and-blood human being like the rest of us. A Jesus who was 98.5% chimpanzee. A Jesus who happened to become cocooned in layers and layers of pious legendary accretion before emerging as a beautiful, divine messianic butterfly. This would appear to be a perfectly reasonable conclusion. What more needs to be said?

Maybe nothing. Then again, in reality, it seems there is a great deal more to be said. For instance, when some joker tries to justify this or that moral absurditrocity[9] by assuring us that Jesus vouchsafed his opinion, maybe it would be helpful to know if in fact, Jesus really *had* said any such thing. Is it possible to know?

The real question remains, when you strip away all those layers of legends and myth, what does that human being at the core look like? Is there anyone there at all? Increasingly over the last fifteen-plus years, our confidence in knowing what Jesus' opinion was (let alone boldly asserting it!) has eroded away to virtually nothing – arguably, it has been completely obliterated. What's more, the same is true for our ability to verify *even a single basic fact of his existence.* As we'll soon see, anyone who tries to convince you they know the first thing about what Jesus really said or did, should be shocked to learn the current state of Historical Jesus studies and the number of faulty assumptions the entire field has been operating under for decades, if not centuries.

Accordingly, our view on Jesus and early Christianity is badly overdue for a shakeup. I tried giving the matter a few shakes myself with my 2010 book *Nailed*, which took on the top ten ways Christianity's official story fails to pass the reality check, and made the case for what's called Jesus Myth theory or Christ Myth theory: the position that argues that Jesus was never a real person at all. I was pleased by the enthusiastic reception *Nailed* received (and continues to receive) from many freethinkers. I didn't even mind its inevitable dismissal by Christians, who regard it as ridiculous, poorly written, shoddily researched garbage – honestly, what else *could* they say? – though it's been interesting to see how many Christians think my research skills and writing dramatically improved when I wrote my next book about Mormonism[10] ... What did surprise me, however, was the number of my fellow atheists who were openly contemptuous of the idea that there may never have been a historical Jesus.

The H Word
Is there an atheist Jesus? You might think so, from how vehemently some of my fellow heretics defend him. I've long since gotten used to their usual charges: this doesn't matter; this is all old stuff; this was long since discredited by all reputable scholars. Charitable critics call it just minority opinion; the less so call it nothing more than historical revisionist nonsense, fringe pseudo-scholarship, junk history, crackpottery, the atheist equivalent of creationism, etc. That's fun to hear.

Again, I never expected everyone to agree with me, and I received my share of good, fair criticism, too; points I've responded to in this book – but I was also taken aback to see otherwise sensible freethinkers taking up some of the most brazenly fallacious barbs in the Christian apologetic arsenal to defend the "real Jesus." It's ironic that many atheists (even more than one secular biblical historian) have been infected with an unwarranted sense of certainty about the reality of a Jesus – a nasty syndrome they've caught from uncritically relying on the rhetoric of Christian apologists who have long spread the old egregious lie that mythicism was a heresy done away with ages ago.

Robert Price, as usual, answered this crowd best when he asked: The Jesus Myth theory has been debunked? When did that happen? The truth is, the arguments of the mythicist camp have never been rebutted – they've rarely even been debated. Instead, they've been sniffed at, mocked, declared to be mistaken, outdated or simply irrelevant, and more often than not, simply ignored; in short, they've only ever been, in a word, *Harrumphed*.[11]

Honestly, I completely understand that even for many atheists, this radical notion is a tough sell and sets off all their well-honed skeptic alarms – as well it should. All Christ Myth theory is not created equal; there are plenty of half-baked crackpot mythicist notions that are just as crazy wrong as anything in mainstream Christianity. Those cranks and their asinine pet theories just make the work of serious myth scholars harder, so they need to go away, too.[12] And please believe me when I say if I am wrong about any components of my own precious pet theories (and I have been, often), I will cheerfully withdraw that claim when shown to be wrong (and I have done, often). My ego isn't invested in this theory; or at least, I've certainly tried to be mindful to not let that happen. As I said in *Nailed*, if I am wrong about any of this, *I want to know*. That said, after over a decade and a half of seeking out and researching scholarship, innumerable long discussions with historians, hammering out thoughts on Jesus Myth theory and putting them through the crucible, the hardy ideas and facts that made it through that refining fire appear well supported.

Still, let me first assure you of one thing: Yes, I am indeed a big bad atheist who wants Christianity and all the other religions to stop being ridiculous and just go away already. However… *that has absolutely nothing to do with my thoughts on the historicity of Jesus.* While I may indeed have an atheist axe to grind, I have no ideological allegiance to Jesus Myth theory, and will be just as happy an atheist if it turns out there really *was* a wildly overrated first century Judaean preacher named Jesus. I'd be extremely surprised, but I'd be perfectly fine with it, should enough new evidence turn up to change my mind. Until then, I continue to argue for the Jesus Myth position for just one reason: because I think it's the correct one.

And so, here is this book. If you are an unbeliever who remains skeptical of the theory that Christ may never have existed at all, this book has been written especially for you. My goal is not to convince you that Christ Myth theory is the sole key to unlocking the true origins of Christianity – though, personally, I remain convinced that it is. Rather, it's simply to point out some of the serious problems with dismissing the theory outright, discuss its strengths and weaknesses, suggest some reasons why it has been so maligned by the majority of historians, shed light on some troubling facts about the current state of Jesus Studies in general, and draw attention to the work of far better mythicist scholars than I to make a case for why Christ Myth theory remains the strongest answer to the question of who and what Jesus really was and how Christianity actually originated and evolved.

So while I don't blame anyone for being skeptical of the idea that Jesus was never a real historic individual, I hope you'll consider looking into the question, whether you are on a first name basis with him or think he was probably just another failed apocalyptic prophet from first-century Judea. No matter where you are on the spectrum now, or where you wind up on it after you finish reading this book, I promise you'll be surprised by what you find in this book – and you will never look at Jesus the same again.

Inasmuch as I have an agenda at all, here it is: I'm not out to necessarily convert you to atheism on the Jesus question (an ajesusist?), but I *do* hope that after reading this book, you'll recognize the need to be at least an agnostic on the issue. No, strike that; I want you to be *militant agnostics* on the issue; so when people ask where you stand, you'll poke their chest and say: "I don't know if there was a Jesus – *and neither do you!*"

***

Note: Increasingly, historians no longer use the terms B.C. (*Before Christ*) and A.D. (*Anno Domini*) to label years; instead they (and this book, except when quoting from other sources) use BCE (Before Common Era) and CE (Common Era).[13]

¹ Riddle: How is Jesus like an octopus? If group of octopus is composed of octopi, not octopuses, then likewise the plural of Jesus should actually be "Jesi," shouldn't it? As it turns out, no. Octopi/Octopuses are both accepted usages; but as a Semitic word without a second declension, the plural of Jesus would never be *Iêsoi* (as in Greek) or *Jesi* (as in Latin); so "Jesuses" is indeed the correct term. For more discussion on both topics, see: http://grammarist.com/usage/octopi-octopuses/ and https://en.m.wiktionary.org/wiki/Jesuses#English (which includes this usage note: "Care should be taken to establish context when using this term, as some Christians find the notion of more than one Jesus to be blasphemous.")

² Philo, *On Providence* 2.64

³ Nicholaus of Damascus was a Gentile in the court of Herod and his successor Herod Archelaus and wrote a history of the reign of both kings. His histories stop before 20 CE, but he would have recorded (or at least defended) Herod the Great's slaughter of the innocents had that actually occurred.

⁴ See "Jesus' Trial on Trial," etc., in *Nailed*, pp. 92-99

⁵ See *Nailed*, ch. 4 for details

⁶ As we'll see later; but also see *Nailed*, ch. 4 & 5 for details

⁷ See "Christianity on the Fringe," in ch. 10 of *Nailed*

⁸ See ch. 8 and "Can Jesus Be Saved?" in *Nailed*

⁹ "Absurditrocity" copyright David Fitzgerald

¹⁰ *The Complete Heretic's Guide to Western Religion, Book One: The Mormons* (2013)

¹¹ Rbt. M. Price, e-mail to the author, 12/18/13

¹² For instance, by the time the book is done, you'll see why I'm unconvinced by any theory that claims Christianity was an invention of Flavius Josephus or a Roman invention to placate the Jewish masses (à la Joseph Atwill).

¹³ Although for an entertaining counterargument, see Richard

David Fitzgerald

Carrier's article "B.C.A.D.B.C.E.C.E." in *Hitler Homer Bible Christ*, pp. 25-27

Part One: Myths of Mythicism

Chapter One:
Of Dinosaurs and Deniers

"Whenever you find yourself on the side of the majority, it is time to pause and reflect."

- Mark Twain

I'm not a young earth creationist, flat-earther or holocaust denier. I have no time or respect for 9/11 truthers, Kennedy assassination conspiracy buffs, or Obama birther types. There's no way in hell the Moon landings were faked, and climate change denial absolutely drives me up the wall – seriously, don't get me started.[1] I despise all manner of bogus pseudoscience, pseudomedicine or pseudohistory. So why would I want to be a Jesus mythicist? Isn't that just another brand of pseudoscholarship? A fringe position in biblical studies, thoroughly debunked by all reputable scholars long ago?

Well, that's half right, anyway. Absolutely, mythicism is a minority position in biblical studies – and I have no doubt it always will be, for as long as that particular field of study exists. And who wants to be in the scholarly minority? Not me. Some people seem to revel in being contrarians, but personally, I find no pleasure in being on the outside of the scholarly consensus. So why do that to myself? The truth is, it's not because of any "fundamentalist atheist" agenda I harbor, or because I haven't studied the evidence enough that I put up with the aggravation (and believe me, it can be extremely aggravating).

Honestly, it's not much fun to be the kid on the edge of the crowd pointing and murmuring "Hey... the Emperor has no clothes..." – but if the invisible, undetectable and by-all-indications-nonexistent shoe fits... what else *can* you say? I choose to remain relegated to the minority for just one reason:

because I think it's the only position that best explains the problematic evidence for Christianity's origins. Period. And as I've said before, I'll gladly change my mind if some new evidence overturns everything – but honestly, I don't think that's going to happen. But then again, who cares what I think – what about the experts? The real question is:

Why Aren't More Historians Mythicists?

It's an excellent question. We *should* pay attention to what the experts in the field think. So why aren't more of them mythicists? As it so happens, there's an excellent answer to this question: Most historians aren't biblical historians; so when the question of Jesus' historicity comes up, it's only natural that they'll turn to the majority opinion of bible scholars. Who are the majority of biblical scholars?

Biblical history has always been an apologetic undertaking in the service of Christianity. Even today it remains the only branch of history still overtly dominated by believers. In fact, many biblical history scholars are not historians at all; they are ministers, theologians, or strong believers with specific denominational affiliations.[2] Some critics of my book *Nailed* questioned these claims; but the field's apologetic origins are certainly no secret to historians. Hector Avalos observes: "Most standard histories will grant that biblical studies began as an apologetic enterprise. Few biblical scholars will admit it is still just that."[3] Yes, there are also a considerable number of important secular biblical scholars (and we'll be talking more about them in chapter three) but that doesn't change the fact that, like evolution, right from the start the very notion of Jesus Myth faces stiff resistance from the majority of the field. This is not an unfair *ad hominem* slam on them; I'm not even trying to be mean – it's simply an acknowledgment of a serious, and realistically nigh-insurmountable, bias.

On the Bias

We all have our own biases, of course; that's no crime. The problem is that in this case their particular bias is a deal killer. Ask yourself: how many Christians do you suppose are open to entertaining the idea that the lord and savior they depend on for their salvation – not to mention their salaries – might never have existed?

As nonbelievers, we don't *need* Jesus to be a myth. If it turns out the mythicists are wrong, and one day some good evidence for a real Jesus gets uncovered, it's not as if Christianity will suddenly start making sense. We'll still be perfectly happy heretics. It's no skin off my atheist nose if it turns out there *was* a Jesus after all, but Christian biblical scholars sure as hell can't say the same if their situation is reversed. Christians can't even enjoy a relaxed agnosticism about the *mere possibility* of mythicism. They need Jesus NOT to be a myth.

Unfortunately, he is a myth.

As we'll see through the course of this book, that is true, no matter whether it's the mythicist camp or the historicist camp that ultimately comes out on top. The "Jesus of Faith" gets debunked either way. What's important about the historicist/mythicist argument, and what makes it worth arguing about, is that it shows what we can and can't know about who or what Jesus really was. Everything we learn from the back and forth of this historical argument on both sides, helps us call the bluff of anyone who says they know how Jesus wants you to behave, or think – or vote.

Theologian William Wrede cautioned us in the nineteenth century that facts are sometimes the most radical critics of all. Jacques Berlinerblau notes in *The Secular Bible*,

> The problem with modern biblical research it that it has not gone far enough. Too often, it has deferred to tradition, censured itself, and refused to pursue the delectably blasphemous implications of its own discoveries.[4]

Arguably, it's gotten to the point where now secular biblical historians are the only ones who are actually making any real progress in the field at all. The majority is too busy circling the wagons to protect their own sects' cherished doctrines and dogma from dangerous new knowledge. Yet even among secular biblical scholars, it is difficult to find one who doesn't come out of a religious background. Rabbi Jon D. Levensen, one of today's most prominent Jewish biblical scholars, observes, "It is a rare scholar in the field whose past does not include an intense Christian or Jewish commitment."[5]

What's more, religious scholar Timothy Fitzgerald (no relation) points out in his *The Ideology of Religious Studies* that theological assumptions are a pervasive difficulty in the field, not merely among practicing believers, but for the formerly religious as well: "even in the work of scholars who are explicitly non-theological, half-disguised theological presuppositions persistently distort the analytical pitch."[6] So of course this is minority opinion – and I fully expect mythicists like me will remain on the scholarly periphery for as long as biblical studies continue.

Bucking the Consensus?

Although, despite their status as academic pariahs, it isn't as though mythicists are actually opposing the field. Most of the arguments advanced by serious mythicists aren't controversial at all – on the contrary, as we'll see, many of the pillars supporting Christ Myth theory have been the majority opinion for over a century; long-established matters including the Synoptic Problem, Markan Priority, and the actual authorship of the Gospels and Pauline epistles. To a great extent, it's only the tip of the iceberg that separates mythicists from the consensus. The final conclusion reached by mythicists may be controversial, not the evidence cited and the methodology employed to get there.

Not that consensus is always an ironclad guarantee of certitude. It's certainly reasonable for laypeople to appeal to the consensus, and in most cases, the consensus is a very fine thing, built upon a good, solid foundation – at least, it is until enough experts begin to disagree with the prevailing opinion and point out problems until a paradigm shift occurs. But it's begging the question to simply allow the brute fact of consensus itself to dismiss dissenting experts. As Richard Carrier has pointed out, that would become circular, and then we would have dogma, not a quest for knowledge.

Another less obvious consideration is when scholars are *afraid* to go on record with what they really think, a particularly alarming concern in Jesus studies. Historicists can't count agnostics on their side when reckoning the consensus; but as we'll see in the next chapter, there are many more agnostics on Jesus' historicity than feel safe to go on record saying so. Still, is it reasonable to think *an entire field* of experts could be wrong? Ask your phrenologist. Or your pastor.

From Blasphemy to Consensus

As it turns out, biblical studies have already set many excellent precedents for just such radical paradigm shifts. All great advancements in science begin as challenges to commonly held theory; every great advance in the history of biblical scholarship has begun as blasphemy. Take the Old Testament: It's no longer taboo for historians to declare that Adam, Eve, Abraham, Isaac, Jacob, Job, Jonah, Joseph, Joshua, Moses, Noah, Sampson, Ruth and Boaz, and a sizable portion of the Old Testament's other most prominent major characters never existed.[7] They are purely literary creations. The first historians to argue the Patriarchs were mythical had to square off against a firm and broad consensus; now, far from being some fringe notion, the patriarchs' nonhistoricity is the most widespread mainstream view among scholars.[8]

Richard Carrier takes this to its logical conclusion, showing that what's good for the Moses is good for the Messiah:

> ... Moses is now regarded as fictional, yet like Jesus he performed miracles, had huge numbers of followers, gave speeches and had travels, and dictated laws. No mainstream historian today believes the book of Deuteronomy was even written in the same century as Moses, much less by Moses, or that it preserves anything Moses actually said or did – yet it purports to do so, at extraordinary length and in remarkable detail. No real historian today would accept as valid an argument like 'Moses *had* to have existed, because so many sayings and teachings were attributed to him!' And yet if this argument is invalid for Moses, it's invalid for Jesus.[9]

The same is true for the 6th century BCE prophet Daniel. The Old Testament book named for him records his life in great detail, beginning in 606 BCE, in the third year of the reign of Judaean king Jehoiakim, when four young Jewish nobles including Daniel are carried off to Babylon to be trained as advisers to the Babylonian court. There, Daniel has a stellar career filled with spectacular accomplishments, and thanks to his prophetic wisdom, rises to the rank of "third ruler" of the kingdom. After the Persian conquest of Babylon in 539 BCE, he remains one of three senior imperial administrators under Darius the Mede, before finally dying at a venerable age, probably some time during the reign of the Persian king Ahasuerus (Xerxes in Greek) and most likely being buried at Susa, in what is today Khuzestan, Iran. The book of Daniel is impressive, replete as it is with rich historical details of momentous events and famous people from the 6th century BCE. The only thing is – funny story – it's a fake.

Even in ancient times scholars like the 3rd century Neoplatonist philosopher Porphyry could identify the signs that the book was a forgery from much later than the time it depicts. For one, whenever "Daniel" talks about his own time in the sixth century BCE, he is vague and inaccurate; unable to keep even his basic facts straight.

For example, he claims "Darius the Mede" conquered Babylon (Dan. 5:30), when it was actually Cyrus the Persian (as per Ezra 1:1). In fact, there never was a King "Darius the Mede;" he is thinking of Darius the Persian (who succeeded Cyrus' son Cambyses 18 years later).[10] But strangely enough, when talking about events four hundred years in his future, his accuracy and attention to details markedly improves...

Today, modern critical scholars are unanimous in their conviction that the book of Daniel is a complete fiction, actually written in the second century BCE.[11] Historians have even pinpointed that it was written between 171 and 164 BCE; the point at which the perfect track record of Daniel's "prophecies" abruptly flatlines, suddenly going from uncannily accurate to epic fail.

To make matters worse for your Sunday school teacher, today historians doubt that Daniel existed in the first place. And as Carrier points out, even if he did, historians are certain the book of Daniel does not contain anything he authentically said or did:

> "Rather, this Daniel, and everything he is supposed to have said and done, was all invented to create a historical authority for a new vision of society, to inspire a new unity and a new moral order against the immoral rule of dominating foreigners. We must accept that the same is at least possible for Jesus."[12]

Again, Daniel's story is replete with real-life details of actual events and involves known historical personages. Daniel is considered a major prophet in all three Abrahamic faiths, with at least six tombs claimed to be his, scattered from Iraq to Iran to Uzbekistan. As we'll see, the prophecies attributed to him were a major contributing factor to the very emergence of Christianity. And yet, Daniel is a complete myth.

Despite the smug dismissiveness of Christian apologists and secular scholars alike, the fact is, Jesus shares many parallels with Old Testament figures like Daniel, and still others like Joshua and Moses and more (and not just older biblical characters; see chapter 13) – completely fictitious, completely legendary figures. So why should the suspicion that Jesus might be just as fictitious as any of them raise eyebrows? If the quantity and quality of evidence that Jesus really existed was markedly superior to the evidence for any of these other beloved biblical figures, then we would be justified in comfortably dismissing it as a crackpot notion.[13] But it isn't, and we can't.

Mythicism: Creationism for atheists?
Some of my Christian friends (and the occasional frenemy) find it funny that a staunch evolutionary advocate like myself, who blasts Creationists for their denial of the overwhelming scientific consensus, is promoting a position opposed by the majority of biblical scholars. What's the difference between mythicists like me and the creationists I oppose?

Ironically enough, the creationism analogy boomerangs. Comparing Jesus-myth theory with creationism is exactly 100% backwards for starters. Consider: There was an age, scarcely a century and a half ago, when creationists ruled the earth like dinosaurs; when the Christian scriptural view of Genesis was dominant, entrenched, dogmatically privileged and safeguarded from criticism – just like the caricature that creationists try to sell their flock today of a "Big Science" racket cramming evolutionary theory down their tender Christian throats.

Evolution didn't arrive by Darwin coming like Moses down the mountain with *Origin of Species* carved on stone tablets. Evolutionary theory first emerged from the primeval waters while higher education was completely under the thumb of Christianity. And yet it completely vanquished creationism – at least, in the scientific community. How did *that* happen? Contrary to popular belief, it did not begin with Darwin. His bombshell, the explanation of the mechanism of evolution, was the mass-extinction event, but pernicious faults had already started eroding away at the foundations of Creationism's official story long before him.

A century before the publication of *On the Origin of Species*, the rising Industrial Revolution demanded metals, which in turn demanded new geological research to find them. A growing field of mineralogy professors and mining experts across Europe sought out metal and coal deposits. The more successful ones noted relationships between fossils and geological strata.

Increasingly and astonishingly, the fossils being discovered included the bones of previously unknown giants; what we today know as megalosaurs, mammoths, plesiosaurs, pterodactyls, ichthyosaurs, and more. Using comparative anatomy, biologists showed these were extinct antediluvian animals; that is to say, animals that had lived and completely died out before the biblical flood of Noah. Some thought that meant there had to have been more than one cataclysmic flood... but even with that attempt at explanation, biologists couldn't explain how Noah's flood could have killed these prehistoric fish and enormous marine creatures too!

To make matters worse, ancient human remains and flint hand axes were found in the bed of the river Somme in France - at the same layer as extinct elephants and rhinoceros. From their position in the strata, it was clear they were considerably older than the bible's chronology allowed. Geologists like James Hutton and Charles Lyell went further, demonstrating unmistakable signs of what came to be called *Deep Time*: the realization that slow, inexorable geological processes had been changing the face of the Earth – and still were – for far longer than anyone had ever dared guess.

And once Darwin arrived and published his theories, the

jig was up. But it wasn't just him, or course. Discoveries in biology, anatomy, zoology, geology, geography, paleontology, and other fields of science had all been building up a steady pressure on beloved, long-accepted biblical 'facts' of the Flood of Noah, the Garden of Eden, the heavenly Firmament, The Tower of Babel and the like, until the contrary evidence reached such a critical mass that finally, however much it displeased the clergy and their flocks, no intellectually honest academic could deny it. And so the great paradigm shift began - an exodus from Genesis.

Once Darwin laid bare the workings of Natural Selection, the old biblical worldview simply couldn't hold up to the truth, and so creationism went extinct in most environments – almost all. But... who would be foolish enough to deny evolution today? Exactly. As you probably realize by now, the last defenders of creationism are also the most strident opponents not of Jesus mythicism, but all the other modern secular historical views of Jesus, as well – the biblical literalists.[14]

And let's face it: Jesus Myth is even *more* dangerous to their beliefs than evolution. It's kryptonite for Christianity. If you're a believer, you can find ways to twist your faith to make room for evolution; Christians do it all the time, and in increasing numbers these days. But you can't very well pull off that same trick to accommodate Jesus Myth...

Not that I'm necessarily comparing Jesus Myth theory to a concept as earthshaking as Natural Selection, but consider the parallels for a moment. Like evolution, the concept of Christ Myth didn't appear out of nowhere, but was the result of many advances in scholarship, over hundreds of years, from different lines of evidence exposing the crumbling foundation of the old traditional view. And the initial response to both was exactly the same: *That's ridiculous. All serious scholars disagree. The evidence is overwhelming.* And the cracks in the New Testament are every bit as potentially disastrous for the traditional origins of Christianity as the cracks in the Old Testament were for the traditional origins of the earth.

What sort of cracks? Here are a few of them, lurking behind questions such as: Did eyewitnesses write the Gospels? Were Matthew, Mark, Luke and John really the authors of the books attributed to them? Did they copy from each other? Do their Gospels contradict one another? Did Jesus (or any of the other characters in the Gospels) really say and do everything as presented in the Gospels? Are any of Paul's letters forgeries? Are there interpolations in his undisputed letters? Was Paul's Jesus different from the Gospels' Jesus? Was there more than one Christ? Was John the Baptist's sect part of Christianity, or was it a rival cult? Are any of the other epistles in the New Testament really by the authors whose names they bear – or even written during their lifetime? How did our New Testament become canonized? Is our New Testament the same as that of the early Christians? How certain are we that the texts of our biblical books have been preserved accurately?

As we'll see, the answers to questions like these don't bode well for Christianity, *whether there was a real Jesus or not* – and they certainly erode our confidence not just in Christianity's official story, but in any hope of finding the very man himself. Jesus studies have long been showing worrisome fractures like all these and still more. In his devastating book *The End of Biblical Studies*, Religious Studies professor (and former evangelical preacher) Hector Avalos has convincingly demonstrated that similar fissures are rife throughout the entire biblical studies field.

Field of Dreams

But really, is it fair for me to denigrate Creationists for ignoring the overwhelming scientific consensus on Evolution, when my fellow mythicists and I are at odds with virtually the entire field of biblical studies? Absolutely.

And this is why. Trying to equate mythicism and anti-evolutionism is comparing apples to oranges – fossil Neanderthal oranges. There is not a single fact in Historical Jesus studies that has been established with anything remotely like the multiply attested, consistently confirmed weight of concrete physical evidence, accumulated worldwide across a range of scientific disciplines, that supports the facts of evolutionary science. In fact, while evolution has withstood over a century and a half of challenges with unparalleled success, precisely the opposite can be said about Jesus Studies. Do you want to see a theory in crisis? Sorry, creationists, it's not Darwinian evolution – it's Jesus Studies. Richard Carrier explains:

"The quest for the historical Jesus has failed spectacularly. Several times. Historians now even count the number of times. With the latest quest (numbered "the third") and its introduction of criteria, the concept of Jesus we're supposed to believe existed is actually getting more confused and uncertain the more scholars study it, rather than the other way around. Progress is supposed to increase knowledge and consensus and sharpen the picture of what happened (or what we don't know), not the reverse.

"Instead, Jesus scholars continue multiplying contradictory pictures of Jesus, rather than narrowing them down and increasing their clarity – or at least reaching a consensus on the scale and scope of our uncertainty or ignorance. More importantly, the many contradictory versions of Jesus now confidently touted by different Jesus scholars are all so very plausible – yet not all can be true. In fact, as only one can be (and that at most), almost all must be *false*. So the establishment of this kind of "strong plausibility" has been decisively proved *not* to be a reliable indicator of the truth. Yet Jesus scholars keep treating it as if it were.

"This has left us with a confused mass of disparate opinions, vast libraries of theories and interpretations essentially impossible to keep up with, and no real attempts at improving or criticizing the worst and gathering the best into any sort of coherent consensus view of what actually happened at the dawn of Christianity, or even during its first two hundred years."[15]

This scholastic mess has been an open secret in biblical history circles for decades. Over forty years ago, professors like Robin S. Barbour[16] and Cambridge's Morna Hooker[17] were complaining about the naïve assumptions underlying the criteria being used to gauge the "authentic" elements of Jesus. She added, "Every scholar likes to produce assured results. To say, as I am doing, that there are none, and can be none, may seem like a counsel of despair. But assured results are dangerous things."[18] And even then, it was obvious that other scholars were also losing confidence in the methods being employed by their colleagues. But it wasn't difficult to see why their criticisms fell on deaf ears; as Hooker noted,

> "the various criteria seemed to offer a way forward in a field where progress had previously proved impossible. Searching for the 'real historical Jesus' in the 1960s and 1970s appeared as hazardous as trying to make one's way across a bog, jumping from one tuft of grass to another, while in constant danger of sinking. (theologian and historian Ernst) Käsemann's famous suggestion that we might be able to find 'more or less safe ground under our feet'[19] was enormously attractive…"[20]

But no matter how enticing it may have appeared, Käsemann's "more or less safe ground" has proven to be sinking sand after all. Forty years after Hooker, Barbour and others began to raise the alarm, a steady and growing stream of historians after them have reached the same conclusions: the methods that have been devised and employed to tease out hints of the "Real Jesus" from the tangled mass of myth, legend and pious fraud simply cannot do the job. In fact, *every* expert who has since seriously examined the issue has also reached the same conclusion.[21]

Anthony Le Donne and Chris Keith's book *Jesus, Criteria, and the Demise of Authenticity* (2012) gathers biblical historians with a range of opinions on the future of Jesus studies. Some hope that new criteria can be found or current ones refined. Others conclude that the criteria approach is completely bankrupt and needs to be completely abandoned. But across the board, all the contributors agree the traditional criteria of authenticity used by Jesus historians do not work.

Many scholars have since agreed with Gerd Theissen's description of a common opinion in the field: "There are no reliable criteria for separating authentic from inauthentic Jesus tradition."[22] Stanley Porter was one of them; he attempted to fix the problem by developing new criteria – only to run into all the same problems[23] – as even Porter himself had to concede.[24] As Dale C. Allison Jr. says, "It is time to quit making excuses for them, time to move the standard criteria from the center of our discussion to the periphery."[25]

Christians in Lab Coats?
Why has it taken so long for historians to admit that the methodology of Jesus Studies has been so fatally flawed all along? A considerable part of the unwillingness to give up on the criteria is the anxiety arising from the raw uncertainty inherent in Jesus studies. Christians want faith, but Christian scholars want a faith bolstered by facts. But to get that, they needed scientific tools capable of providing them with assured results – and neither methods nor results have panned out. Hooker described biblical historians' desperation for hard scientific validation of their methods:

> "For many, the pursuit of this goal was fuelled not only by the desire to discover the truth about Jesus, but by the determination to prove that those engaged in it were not influenced in their decisions by religious belief, but were motivated by the same scholarly impartiality shown by those working in other disciplines."[26]

Unfortunately for them, scholarly impartiality isn't Christian scholarship's strong suit. Conservative New Testament scholar Nick Perrin provided an inadvertent example after being commissioned to write a book[27] to counter Bart Ehrman's *Misquoting Jesus.* Perrin first chides his evangelical readers that biblical faith ought not fear historical inquiry:

> "When people succumb to that temptation of ignoring challenges to their faith, they are in the end demonstrating that they are more committed to the feeling of having a lock on truth than they are to truth itself."[28]

Amen to that. But after this admirable start, Perrin goes on to display the standard posture of unflappable apologetic confidence in scripture, and assures us his Christian faith is *not* a faith willfully oblivious to historical realities:

> "Nor is biblical faith to be afraid of historical inquiry; rather, it seeks out such inquiry. If faith and history collide, it might make a pretty mess for a time. But the only worse mess is a stillborn faith that insists on fleeing history and, ultimately, the world in which we live."[29]

Again, kudos; this is just the sort of thing we *want* to hear from historians – and from Christians in general. More encouraging (if unsubstantiated) declarations follow: Perrin tells us Jesus Christ doesn't want blind acquiescence; he demands that believers ask questions when they've come to realize, once again, that they don't yet fully understand the fine points of divine revelation, etc.[30] But when it's time to put his money where his mouth is, Perrin's tough talk about not fearing history doesn't hold up to the tough questions; as he puts it, "being Christian does not also require us to be rationalists."[31]

Perrin's certainly right about one thing: when faith and

history collide, it does indeed make a pretty mess. And it's messier than he seems to realize:

> "My point in the book is to disabuse readers of the notion that Jesus scholars are scientists wearing white lab coats. Like everyone else, they want certain things to be true about Jesus and equally want certain others not to be true of him. I'm included in this – I really hope that I am right in believing that Jesus is both Messiah and Lord. Will this shape my scholarship? Absolutely. How can it not? We should be okay with that."[32]

Should we now? Or is this precisely the problem?

And there is further cause for concern. John Meier has let the cat out of the bag when he basically admitted that "quest for the historical Jesus" is, in effect, a theological quest for academic credibility in disguise.[33]

Avalos describes the entire infrastructure of biblical studies as an "ecclesiastical-academic complex," an arrangement that has allowed a potent mix of theological, economic and political agendas to contaminate scholarship.[34] This troubling condition isn't just confined to the haunts of mainstream Christianity. Whether consciously or unconsciously, Christian influence and bias creep in even at secular academic institutions, which often have roots in religious institutions, and in any case, can't escape their culturally Christian background.

Huffalumps and Woozles

It is not only mythicist historians who are sounding the alarm, either. Though Donald Akenson of Queen's University in Kingston, Ontario believes there was a Yeshua of Nazareth (if not a Jesus-the-Christ), he has also recognized the methodology problem. In *Surpassing Wonder: The Invention of the Bible and the Talmuds* (1998), he admits that some criteria are problematic, and goes even farther; arguing that with very

Jesus: Mything in Action

few exceptions, specialists in Jesus Studies have not followed sound historical practices, despite all their best efforts. There is an unhealthy reliance on consensus for propositions that ought to be based on primary sources or rigorous interpretation. He illustrates the situation with an apt parable from Winnie-the-Pooh entitled: "Pooh and Piglet Go Hunting and Nearly Catch a Woozle."

One fine winter day, with snow on the ground and frost in the air, Pooh finds himself walking reflectively, through the woods. To his friend Piglet, the bear seems to be deep in thought, rather like a Victorian clergyman collecting thoughts for a sermon. He joins Pooh and asks him what he is doing. "Hunting," Pooh replies; adding mysteriously, "tracking something." Trouble is, Pooh doesn't know quite what he is tracking. "I shall have to wait until I catch up with it," he says.

Fretful but ever helpful, Piglet wonders, "Oh Pooh! Do you think it's a- a- woozle?" Pooh thinks it may well be, and the two follow the trail of this mysterious beast. As they circle the thicket they find more and more woozle prints, as one woozle track is joined by another and then another, and still another – a whole herd of woozles! They are ready to abandon the hunt when a voice from the sky (Christopher Robin, who has been observing the pair from high in an old oak tree) explains that they have been going in circles around the copse, and the growing number of tracks in the snow is none other than their own.[35]

Akenson is quick to add that this is not an allegory for Jesus studies or a slam on his colleagues, but you can't help but think his analogy may be more apt than he realizes, especially as he goes on to admit,

> "However, the more one immerses oneself in the continually-growing literature concerning the historical Yeshua, the more one realizes how dependent emotionally and cognitively the scholars are on each other, and how comforted they are by the ever-growing band of footprints

that fill their path. Certainly their quarry must be just ahead."[36]

Akenson also blasts the thousands of biblical scholars in the last century who "claim (either explicitly or implicitly as evidenced by the methods they employ) that the rules of proof which apply in secular historical scholarship are all very well, but that there are special evidentiary by-passes when it comes to Jesus-the-Christ."[37] He praises those scholars who do endeavor to apply rigorous historical method and avoid such special pleading, but notes they are in difficult circumstances.

How difficult? Let's see…

***

For further reading:

Hector Avalos, *The End of Biblical Studies*, 2007
    Richard Carrier, *On the Historicity of Jesus*, 2014
Chris Keith & Anthony Le Donne, *Jesus, Criteria & Demise of Authenticity*, 2012

Incidentally, for a look at how Old Testament studies is on no better footing archeologically than New Testament studies, see:

Israel Finkelstein and Neil Asher Silberman, *The Bible Unearthed: Archaeology's New Vision of Ancient Israel and the Origin of Its Sacred Texts*, Touchstone, 2001

[1] Even when it comes from one of my favorite biblical scholars (looking at Robert M. Price...)
[2] Avalos, p. 292
[3] Ibid., p. 15; also p. 29 where Avalos also lists several of these standard biblical histories.
[4] Berlinerblau, p.11
[5] Levensen, p. 30
[6] T. Fitzgerald, p. *x*
[7] See, for example, Israel Finkelstein and Neil Silberman, *The Bible Unearthed: Archaeology's New Vision of Ancient Israel and the Origin of Its Sacred Texts* (New York: Free Press, 2001) and Israel Finkelstein and Amihai Mazar, *The Quest for the Historical Israel: Debating Archaeology and the History of Early Israel* (Atlanta, GA: Society of Biblical Literature, 2007); Thomas Thompson, *The Mythic Past: Biblical Archaeology and the Myth of Israel* (New York: Basic Books, 1999), *Early History of the Israelite People: From the Written and Archaeological Sources* (New York: Brill, 1992), and *The Historicity of the Patriarchal Narratives: The Quest for the Historical Abraham* (New York: W. de Gruyter, 1974); William Dever, *What Did the Biblical Writers Know, and When Did They Know It? What Archaeology Can Tell Us about the Reality of Ancient Israel* (Grand Rapids, MI: William B. Eerdmans, 2001); Hector Avalos, *The End of Biblical Studies* (Amherst, NY: Prometheus, 2007). See also *The New Interpreter's Bible: Old Testament Survey* (Nashville, TN: Abingdon Press, 2006).
[8] For more discussion, see Carrier, *On the Historicity of Jesus*, ch. 5, element 44 (pp. 214-22)
[9] Ibid., p. 10
[10] For still more of "Daniel's" historical blunders, see Randel Helms, *Who Wrote the Gospels?* pp. 20-21
[11] *ABD* II, p. 33
[12] Carrier, op cit.

[13] Again, this is not to say there aren't far too many truly ridiculous, crackpot Jesus myth theories stinking up the place – as we'll see – but serious mythicists oppose them just as strongly as do the rest of the field.

[14] Christians aren't the only ones opposed to Christ Myth theory, of course, but we'll be talking about the others presently – and needless to say, Christianity has always been the driving force behind all biblical studies.

[15] Carrier, *Proving History*, pp.12-13

[16] See Barbour, *Traditio-Historical Criticism of the Gospels*

[17] Hooker, "Christology and Methodology," pp. 480-87

[18] Hooker, "Wrong Tool," p. 581

[19] See footnote in Keith and Le Donne, *Jesus, Criteria & the Demise of Authenticity*, p. xiii

[20] Ibid.

[21] Carrier, op. cit., pp.11

[22] Porter, p.115

[23] See Avalos, pp. 203-209 and Bird, pp. 55-67

[24] Porter, *Journal* p. 69-74

[25] Allison, p.9

[26] Keith and Le Donne, p. xiii-xiv

[27] Nick Perrin, *Lost In Transmission? What We Can Know About the Words of Jesus* (2008)

[28] Perrin, p. xxi

[29] Ibid., p. 42

[30] How Perrin knows this is an open question, since he doesn't tell us where Jesus ever says anything remotely like this.

[31] Trevin Wax interview with Nick Perrin; available online at: http://www.thegospelcoalition.org/blogs/trevinwax/2009/04/01/jesus-lost-in-transmission-an-interview-with-nick-perrin/

[32] Ibid.

[33] See Neil Godfrey's Vridar post, "The Historical Jesus Quest Is Theology in Disguise," available online at: http://vridar.org/2013/12/07/the-historical-jesus-quest-is-

theology-in-disguise/
[34] See Avalos, *The End of Biblical Studies,* Prometheus Books, 2007
[35] Cited in Akenson, pp. 539-40
[36] Ibid.
[37] Ibid., pp. 538

Chapter Two: Bias Cut

"It is difficult to get a man to understand something, when his salary depends upon his not understanding it."

- Upton Sinclair

If I haven't made it sufficiently clear yet, let me say it outright: Biblical Studies, and in particular, Historical Jesus Studies, is in crisis. Some readers of *Nailed* seem to think I was trying to paint most Jesus scholars as dishonest; all part of a conspiracy in smoke-filled back rooms of theological seminaries to suppress any dissent on Jesus. Am I saying this is a conspiracy theory? Of course not. Am I saying Christian biases and presuppositions pervade the entire field? Of course I am. And how could it be otherwise?

We don't need to invent conspiracy theories to recognize that the field is in genuine trouble – and largely of its own making. Of course the vast majority of biblical scholars are sincere and committed to seeking out the truth. But as many of them have discovered, when their research sometimes leads them to uncomfortable conclusions, theological (and political, and economic) truths can trump historical realities, even at the most well-meaning evangelical institutions, as an increasing number of Christian biblical historians have been complaining for decades now.

Theologically Correct

Like Avalos, Carrier, Hooker, and many others, Donald Akenson finds it seriously problematic that the vast majority of biblical scholars are employed in institutions rooted in a theological or denominational or political ideology (however vestigial). But the problem goes beyond scholars having a personal Christian bias. More than any other group in present day academia, biblical historians are under immense pressure – sometimes overt, sometimes subliminal, but virtually omnipresent – to theologize their historical work. He adds: "These institutional affiliations inevitably involve pressures upon the scholars, or limits on what they can think. It is a hard business to be in."[1] As he sees it, all the biblical historians that have managed to maintain the scholarly integrity of their work have done so through considerable individual heroism.[2]

Which brings us to yet another serious problem, and another difference between biblical studies and any other field of history – and yet another way the false mythicism-as-creationism analogy boomerangs. Consider the tired Creationist complaint about "Darwinism" being entrenched by their imagined "Big Science." All the evidence for Intelligent Design theory never gets a fair shake, they insist, because the cold-hearted scientific cabal that runs the show locks them out and declares them pariahs, all because their creationist "theories" are blasphemy to the dogmatic Darwinist orthodoxy of the scientific establishment. Which is just as asinine as, well, as Intelligent Design itself.

Scientists are skeptical. Scientists can be biased. Scientific opinion can be slow to change. But make no mistake: Science *loves* a paradigm shift. If anyone really did come up with a smoking gun that proved Evolution was fatally flawed, and the evidence checked out, they wouldn't be outcasts; they would be rock stars. Every scientific journal would scramble to be the first to break the news; every major university would offer them tenure; they would be interviewed on every network; they would make the headlines across the globe; they would be a dead cert to win the Nobel Prize. And that would be just for starters. They would be lionized for making such an epochal leap for science, and rightly so. Not that it will ever happen, because Evolution is a fact – though I'll be happy to change my mind should anyone prove otherwise.

But here's what "Big Science" would never do: Start out with some predetermined conclusion, and then demand that all scientists must swear allegiance to that idea, regardless of what evidence became uncovered in the future. Can you imagine?

Who would *ever* think that was a good method to discover the truth... about *anything?*

Survey Says
And yet, look what we find throughout Christian academia: the majority of biblical historians are Christian believers. Increasingly, biblical studies departments, academic positions and degrees are only to be found being offered by religious institutions. And a considerable number (if not the majority) of religious institutions require a confession of faith from their scholars. When I began writing this book, I was somewhat surprised to discover that there were no studies substantiating these three simple facts. So I set out to confirm or deny them. A crack team of volunteer researchers, led by their tireless team leader Susi Bocks, spent months investigating all 4,726 schools, colleges and universities in America. Like news of Ted Haggard's furtive extramarital sex life or Bill O'Reilly's non-existent military service record, the results were simultaneously surprising and yet no surprise at all.

While not strictly impossible, it's fairly problematic to identify, locate and contact every biblical scholar in the country in order to confirm their professed religious self-identification. It's also problematic to parse out how many self-identified "biblical historians" included in the consensus are those whose degree is actually in theology or divinity or Christian education, not history.

However, it *is* possible to not merely survey a representative sample, but in fact conduct a complete census on every American learning institution that offers studies and/or degrees relating to biblical studies, Jesus, New Testament, Early Christian History, etc. Susi Bock's research team proceeded to do just that.

Here's what they found: Out of the 4,726 degree-granting institutions of higher education in the United States, 1,417 of them offer some form of relevant Biblical/Jesus/NT Studies (see figure 1). Of these, the majority do indeed have a religious

David Fitzgerald

affiliation; nearly a perfect 60/40 split, with 814 (57.44%) religiously-affiliated versus 603 (42.55%) non-affiliated (see figure 2).

It's not surprising that schools with a religious affiliation would prefer that their employees share their faith. But how many actually make that mandatory? Things get quite interesting when you ask that question. The research team's initial attempts at finding that answer discovered that a third (273 total, or 33.53%) of the religiously-affiliated learning institutions required their employees to hold the same beliefs as the school as a condition of their employment; as set down in a statement of faith or similar religious commitment they were required to sign/verbally confirm, and adhere to. One university (which shall go unnamed) lays out the penalty for failure to abide by the faith statement with this pronouncement, in language typical of all these schools:

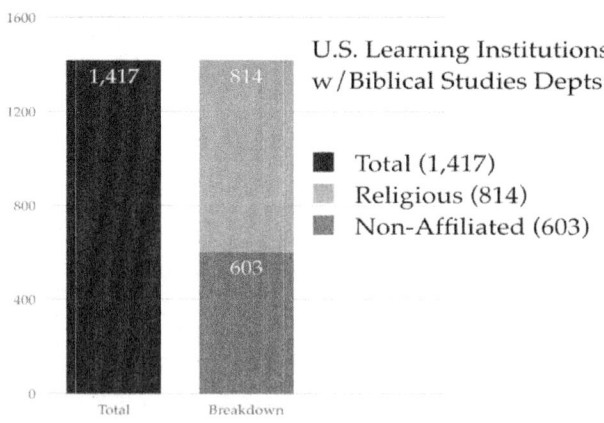

Figure 1. Total no. of U.S. degree-granting institutions offering Biblical Studies with breakdown between religious and non-religiously affiliated campuses.

"Whenever a member of the Board of Trustees, administrative officer, professor, teacher or instructor is not in complete accord with the foregoing Doctrinal

Statement, he or she shall forthwith withdraw from all connections with the University, and his or her failure to do so shall constitute grounds for immediate removal from such positions by the Trustees."

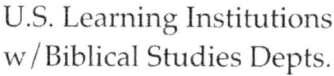

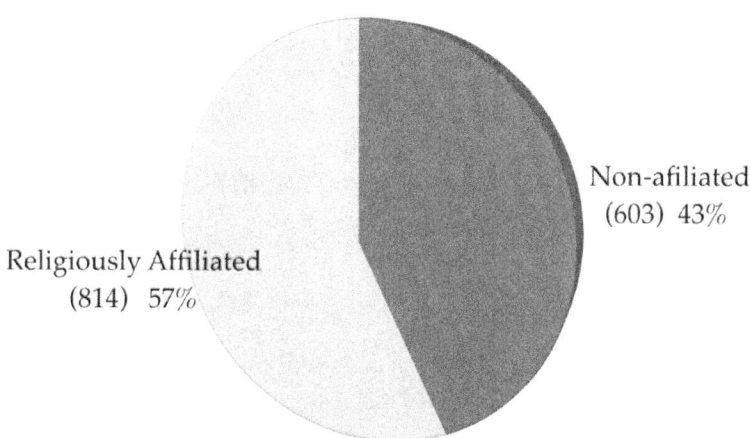

Figure 2. Breakdown of religious and non-religiously affiliated campuses.

However, the research team quickly discovered that this 33% was much lower than the actual percentage. In reality, the 33% only represented the number of schools that would *openly* acknowledge that they required a signed statement of doctrinal compliance. The breakdown of the remaining 2/3rds was:

197 (24.2%) No Response
344 (42.26%) No Statement Required.

Both of these figures warrant further breakdown. Of the 197 institutions tabulated as "No Response," the majority by far (192 schools) gave no response to repeated e-mail and telephone queries. This included schools whose representatives gave researchers the run-around: not returning calls, shuffling inquiries "to the legal dept.," and other forms of passive-aggressive stonewalling. The remaining five campuses simply declined to answer (In one case, the representative of the school asked the researcher what group was conducting the census. When told it was research for my new book, she responded I was a notorious atheist author and they would not cooperate in any way. I cannot adequately express how deeply touched I am by this.).

As for the remaining subset, 344 campuses claimed they did not require any statement of faith from their instructors or employees. However, for 38 of these schools, this was flatly untrue. In fact, further investigation showed their statement of faith and/or doctrinal requirements could be located on their school website. By the same token, 25 of the schools declining to answer turned out to have a statement of faith online as well. So that 1/3 of religiously affiliated schools requiring proof of doctrinal adherence as a condition for employment is actually at the very least 41%. Short of an actual nationwide investigation of all 814 religiously affiliated campuses (and I would welcome any efforts to conduct such a feat) there is no easy way to determine the exact number, but we know it must certainly be much higher. Indeed, the actual number could well be as high as… all of them.

What does all this mean? These numbers have staggering ramifications. First, it's official: the majority of biblical historians in academia *are* employed by religiously affiliated institutions. This fact alone explains much of the resistance to Jesus Myth theory even among scholars who personally identify as secular. Furthermore, of those schools, we can quantify that at least 41% (if not 100%) require their instructors and staff to publicly reject Jesus Myth or they will not have a career at that institute of higher learning. So the question shouldn't be: "How many historians reject mythicism?" but "How many historians are *contractually obliged* to publicly reject mythicism?"

Despite much lip service given to academic freedom, the sad truth is that for religious institutions (and by extension, the majority of all biblical history positions), academics have only as much freedom as can fit comfortably within the school's theological constraints. Any scholar whose findings threaten to step over that line – no matter how innocent or innocuous the doctrine in question may seem – is in danger.

Christianity does not play well with others
There are a number of tactics that religious institutions and individual academics use to coerce scholars to stay within those rigid lines. By coincidence, they all begin with a "B," as in bullshit. These are: Bullying, Bluster, Besmirching Critics, and Bagging on Qualifications.

1. Bullying
Yes – bullying. Think I'm exaggerating? Here are half a dozen cases (and there are more) of sincere, devout Christian biblical scholars who have found themselves in hot water over issues that may seem fairly innocuous to the rest of us:

CASE ONE: Mike Licona

CRIME: Daring to admit something in the bible might not be true

PUNISHMENT: Lost his job and speaking engagements

Mike Licona is a well-known Christian apologist who specializes in defending the resurrection of Jesus in debates and in print. He was also the Apologetics Coordinator for the Southern Baptist Convention's North American Mission Board - that is, until he dared suggest one of the wiggier events in the Gospels might not be literally true.

David Fitzgerald

In his 2010 book, *The Resurrection of Jesus: A New Historiographical Approach*, Licona briefly questioned the historical reality of this unique incident that immediately follows Jesus' death on the cross – an event found nowhere else but in Matthew's gospel:

> "... and the graves were opened; and many bodies of the saints which slept arose, and came out of the graves after his resurrection, and went into the holy city, and appeared unto many." (Matt. 27:52-53)

Many Jewish saints arose from the dead, came out of their graves, walked into the streets of Jerusalem and appeared to many.[3] What's not to believe? Despite being a specialist in defending the resurrection, a mass grave exodus of reanimated saints strolling down downtown Jerusalem – completely unnoticed by anyone else in history – was just a little too hard for even Licona to accept. So he made the modest suggestion that this "strange little text," as he called it, might – *might* - only be metaphorical apocalyptic imagery.

Naturally, such blasphemy triggered a paroxysm of outrage from fellow evangelical apologists like Norman Geisler, who accused Licona of denying the full inerrancy of Scripture and insisted that he should recant a view that was "unorthodox, non-evangelical, and a dangerous precedent for the rest of evangelicalism."[4] The president of Louisville, Kentucky's Southern Baptist Theological Seminary, Albert Mohler, praised Licona's book as a masterful defense of the historicity of the resurrection; yet spent most of his review criticizing what he called Licona's "shocking and disastrous"[5] questioning of Matthew's mass resurrection.

At least two Southern Baptist entities, including the New Orleans seminary and the Southern Baptists of Texas Convention, rescinded invitations for Licona to speak at their apologetics conferences. And a year later in 2011, Licona resigned from both as a research professor at Southern

Evangelical Seminary and as the apologetics coordinator for the North American Mission Board. Licona said he offered to resign rather than cast a shadow over the mission board and its president, and the NAMB swiftly eliminated Licona's position.

A few leading evangelical scholars such as William Lane Craig, J.P. Moreland, and Gary Habermas tried unsuccessfully to come to Licona's defense, but most scholars feared showing their support openly. Apologist Paul Copan, president of the Evangelical Philosophical Society, admitted, "I know a good number of evangelical seminary professors who have privately expressed support for Mike Licona, but cannot do so publicly for fear of punitive measures."[6]

In *Christianity Today*, New Testament professor Craig Blomberg complained of "the tragedy of 'witch hunts' of this nature" and accused Licona's critics of "going after fellow inerrantists with whom they disagree and making life miserable for them for a long time in ways that are unnecessary, inappropriate, and counterproductive to the important issues of the Kingdom."[7]

CASE TWO: Peter Enns

CRIME: Claiming that scripture is divinely inspired and inerrant ... and yet produced by fallible humans, contradictory, part myth, and similar to other, older ancient Mesopotamian religious texts

PUNISHMENT: Lost his job

Professor Peter Enns set off a two-year inquisition at Westminster Theological Seminary for the theological equivalent of trying to have his cake and eat it too. In his book *Inspiration and Incarnation: Evangelicals and the Problem of the Old Testament* (2005), Enns delved into three dangerous topics for traditional biblical studies: biblical similarities with other ancient Near Eastern religious texts; "conflicting theologies" in the Old Testament (i.e., places where the Bible contradicts itself); and finally, the ways the New Testament authors employed the Old Testament to craft their own writings.

He emerged from these particularly treacherous hinterlands of orthodoxy with an unusual way to defend biblical inerrancy: by proposing that there are no errors of contradictions in scripture... because God put myths, "seemingly-contradictory" passages and irreconcilable perspectives in the texts *on purpose*. As Enns saw it, the Lord was perfectly fine with a "messy" scripture. That is, even though the ancient writers of the Bible had limited worldviews, long-discarded attitudes and fallible understandings of how reality worked, God used such flawed tools to hammer out his divine revelation. God apparently writes in mysterious ways, too...

Not many of his colleagues were happy with his theory of scripture created via a divine Rube Goldberg contraption. After over two years of meetings, debates and special reports discussing whether or not Enns was in violation of acceptable theology, in 2008 the majority of the seminary's board of trustees ruled that Enn's book was incompatible with Westminster's required beliefs and voted to suspend him. In September 2011, Enns also lost his job with BioLogos Foundation, a Christian advocacy group who tries to breach the gap between science and Christianity.[8]

CASE THREE: Christopher Rollston

CRIME: Criticizing the marginalization of women in the Bible

PUNISHMENT: Lost his tenured position

"To embrace the dominant biblical view of women would be to embrace the marginalization of women. And sacralizing patriarchy is just wrong... So, the next time someone refers to 'biblical values,' it's worth mentioning to them that the Bible often marginalized women and that's not something anyone should value."

The author of these incendiary words (in an online article for the Huffington Post's religion section[9]) was not some firebrand atheist feminist, but Christopher Rollston, professor of Old Testament and Semitic Studies at Tennessee's Emmanuel Christian Seminary – which wasted no time threatening disciplinary action against him in response. Word spread rapidly among the historian community. The school's (possibly self-appointed) faculty representative, Dr. Paul Blowers, repeatedly insisted this wasn't censorship or a heresy trial, and that Emmanuel championed open and free dialogue. However, Blowers soon let it slip that the seminary had in fact *immediately* begun termination proceedings against Professor Rollston after the article ran. Despite widespread condemnation from the field and questionable motives, Emmanuel fired Rollston a few months later.

Historians were outraged: The firing of a tenured professor is no small matter, let alone when the prof in question is the most prominent and well-respected member of a school's faculty. As Tom Verenna noted:

"Had this been just an academic disagreement, no one would have blinked an eye towards Dr. Blowers, Emmanuel, or this situation. Academic disagreements happen all the time and are the staple of credible, critical scholarship of which Dr. Blowers believes to be so vital to his institution and to himself. But this has not been a simple matter of disagreement, or a friendly sparring match between two colleagues over nuance... No, Dr.

Blowers may be displeased with Dr. Rollston's HuffPo article, but he took it from a general disagreement to something much more scandalous."[10]

The scandal grew even more sordid. In documents obtained by *Inside Higher Ed*,[11] it appeared the seminary's president, Dr. Michael Sweeney, began the termination process in part because of an acute financial crisis. The fretful president feared offending prospective tuition-paying students, and also hoped for a "six-figure" donation that could bail out the seminary – from a donor who disliked Rollston. That this new revelation came *written in the notice of termination to Rollston* – let alone that it listed multiple *economic* reasons – was outrageous in itself. Historian Robert Cargill was one of many who expressed their shock:

> "An institution simply cannot fire a tenured professor who broke no rules (and who happens to be the most credible scholar at Emmanuel) just because the institution wants a donation. Tenure is designed to protect freedom of thought. If Emmanuel wants to fire its professors for thinking outside of Emmanuel's predetermined theological constraints, why offer tenure in the first place? In my professional opinion, Emmanuel has committed a grievous violation of academic integrity, and one that will not only cost them financially, but one that will ruin the reputation of the institution for years to come."[12]

Biblical Studies professor Jim West was even more blunt, in a post entitled, "So for Emmanuel 'Christian' Seminary, Money is the Determinative Factor, Not Scholarship, Education, or Academic Integrity":

> "The fact that the school is acting as it is purely for the sake of money shows beyond any shadow of a doubt that Mr. Blowers and his cohorts are more interested in money

than truth. And that means Emmanuel has ceased to be an institution of higher learning and is now simply a money-collecting agency. How sad. Congratulations Mr. Blowers, you and your ilk have managed to destroy a school and turn it into a gathering of greedy televangelists telling the ignorant flock what it desperately wishes to hear just to make a buck."[13]

CASE FOUR: Bruce Waltke

CRIME: Speaking out in favor of not denying evolution

PUNISHMENT: Lost his job

Dr. Bruce Waltke was a big name in evangelical theology; he has often been called the preeminent Old Testament scholar in the field. But, like so many other conservatives before him, a video led to his downfall. Only in his case, it was not for closet homosexuality or any sexual shenanigans. His crime took place during a video interview at a 2009 workshop for the BioLogos Foundation (the Christian non-profit founded by Francis Collins to promote the idea of harmony between science and religion), where, according to several accounts by those who have seen the video, he said this:

> "If the data is overwhelmingly in favor of evolution, to deny that reality will make us a cult ... some odd group that is not really interacting with the world. And rightly so, because we are not using our gifts and trusting God's Providence that brought us to this point of our awareness."[14]

As it turned out, warning Christians that burying their heads in the sand would only marginalize them further was completely intolerable to those Christians with their heads buried the deepest. Waltke's evangelical employers, the

Reformed Theological Seminary, promptly went ballistic. Dr. Waltke's suggestion that perhaps Christianity needed to acknowledge basic tenets of science so upset the seminary that he was pressured to ask BioLogos to first remove his interview from their web site, and then to post a clarification where he dutifully reaffirmed his support for creationists and his belief that Adam and Eve were real. BioLogos obliged in all this, but it still wasn't enough backpedaling to save Waltke; and RTS soon announced it had accepted his resignation. (Incidentally, that same year, Tremper Longman III, another noted Old Testament scholar, was "disinvited" from RTS for doubting the historicity of Adam.)

The uproar over Waltke's comments in more retrograde evangelical circles was matched by his scandalized academic evangelical colleagues who were greatly disturbed to see such a distinguished Christian scholar first bullied so harshly, and then fired – not for casting doubt on any basic Christian dogmas, but for merely recognizing the need for religion *to acknowledge established scientific facts.* BioLogos' response pulled no punches:

> "The fact that Dr. Waltke felt he was unable to leave the video in place, despite the fact that he still agrees with its contents, is an extremely important statement about the culture of fear within evangelicalism in today's world. Leading evangelicals who support evolution are rightly fearful of personal attacks on the integrity of their faith and character... There are countless people, especially young people, who are discovering that the world of science is not out of touch with reality. Data emerge every day that makes this even clearer... When young people discover that neither the science they've been taught in their churches nor the theology that undergirds it are credible, many will feel they have to throw out their faith."[15]

Beliefnet columnist (and Christian) Rod Dreher agreed with the seminary that Waltke's remarks were controversial and overstated, but even he expressed his shock at their treatment of Dr. Waltke, saying:

"...It is all but incomprehensible that in 2010, any American scholar, particularly one of his academic distinction, could be so harshly bullied for stating an opinion consonant with current scientific orthodoxy. Doesn't Waltke at least have the right to be wrong about something like this? Don't mistake me, I believe that any and every religion, and religious institution, has the right, and indeed the obligation, to set standards and to enforce them. But is this really the hill these Reformed folks want to die on?"[16]

He added:

"I spoke with an ex-Evangelical friend about this today, telling her how mysterious Waltke's bullying was to me. She said it's not the least bit surprising to her. 'You didn't grow up with it, so you have no idea how central biblical literalism on this stuff is,' she said. 'It's all about biblical inerrancy. If Genesis is not literally true in every respect, in their minds the whole thing falls apart. They can't give an inch on this.'"[17]

CASE FIVE: Tom Thompson

CRIME: Establishing the ahistoricity of the biblical patriarchs

PUNISHMENT: Years of constant and unwavering attempts to destroy his career from a variety of antagonists

David Fitzgerald

In the 1970s and 1980s, Thomas Thompson's *summa cum laude* PhD dissertation and subsequent book, *The Historicity of the Patriarchal Narratives: The Quest for the Historical Abraham* triggered a vicious 20+ year backlash that very nearly destroyed his career before it began.[18]

After his dissertation was accepted by the Catholic Theological faculty in Tübingen, Thompson worked as a research fellow in Israel doing archaeological research, developing maps on Bronze Age settlements for both Palestine and the Sinai and Negev, and giving series of seminars and lectures at the British School of Archaeology and the Hebrew University. His career in academia seemed off to a fine start.

Troubles began when he was assigned to take his PhD examinations in dogmatic theology from a certain Joseph Ratzinger. The future Pope Benedict was not pleased with Thompson's findings. Thompson recalls:

> "When I spoke with him concerning bibliography for the upcoming examination, he explained to me that a Catholic could not write such a dissertation as I had and that I would not be receiving my PhD from their faculty in Tübingen. I must point out that the shock with which I met this statement, at the time, caused me to fixate my thoughts on the first phrase: that a Catholic could not write it ... but I had! ... and what then was I, if not a Catholic? ... and then: why couldn't a Catholic write it?"[19]

Thompson soon sensed the coming alienation from friends and colleagues in the Catholic faculty with whom he had worked and shared his life with for nearly ten years. Copies of his as yet unpublished dissertation began to be sent back. The Catholic Biblical Monograph Series editor returned his manuscript unread; on the grounds he had submitted the work to them unsolicited. The Society of Biblical Literature monograph series rejected it on the basis of what they called its inadequate academic standards and "irresponsible" historical reconstructions.

After considerable, further delays in preparing the manuscript for the press, the dissertation was finally published early in 1974, but not before a long period of conflict and disagreement, culminating in the rejection of his PhD candidacy and his finally leaving Tübingen in 1975. Although several compromises and alternatives were sought, he finally had to receive his PhD from another school, in 1976.

Response to his book *Historicity* was open hostility. The first salvo came from the president of the Catholic Biblical Association, who warned of "a new hypercriticism" in biblical studies at the 1974 annual meeting. In early 1976, at a SBL meeting, Yale prof Dean McBride gave a detailed and blistering lecture critiquing his dissertation. Even though Thompson had been explicitly invited by the meeting's coordinator to attend the lecture and to give his response, he was repeatedly denied a chance to respond to either McBride or any of the other criticisms raised during the lengthy discussion period. No one protested the procedure of the meeting.

At the oral defense of Thompson's dissertation at Temple University, a Virginia Union Theological Seminary professor asked the faculty to be invited as a special opponent, in order to debate and challenge Thompson's thesis. The heated debate lasted some 2 hours, during which the guest adversary became very antagonistic and strongly opposed acceptance of the thesis. Temple's faculty, however, unanimously granted the PhD degree, *summa cum laude*.

Reaction to his dissertation continued to be consistently negative from both the Catholic Biblical Association and the Society of Biblical Literature, with a large number of review articles criticizing and rejecting his work, competence and integrity. Although he applied for some 45 teaching positions over a two-year period, he never received a single response to any of his applications. An application letter for an assistant professorship at Harvard was returned to him unopened. He failed to get *even an acknowledgment his application was received at all* in virtually all cases, except for a letter from the head of a search committee at the University of Arizona, making a "friendly" request that he withdraw his application for an open position.

By the 1980s, Thompson had lost track of the public debate, which had been so harsh and relentless it crushed every conceivable contribution he could possibly make. He had become an unemployable, highly vulnerable scholar. At the few local and national CBA and SBL congresses he was able to attend, his papers were consistently rejected without explanation, even when no other topics competed. Meanwhile, in Europe his applications to speak at international meetings were accepted – but he could not obtain travel grants to honor the invitations.

Thompson nearly threw in the towel. He had gone through a divorce, had taught high school for three years, and had become a handyman and journeyman house painter. Just as he had begun his own business in the fall of 1984, he received a letter from Jerusalem's École Biblique, telling him he had been awarded their annual professorship for a semester. He nearly refused the appointment, but in the end could not resist and left for Jerusalem in the late summer of 1985.

There it was not long before he discovered that his conclusion on the ahistoricity of the Old Testament patriarchs that had been so viciously opposed in the States was now on its way to becoming mainstream opinion, not least because it had been so strongly supported in Germany, Holland, Denmark and England. His happiness at this news was diminished by the heavy criticism aimed at the École, now openly accused of anti-Semitism for appointing him to their annual professorship.

Although ostracized by the Albright Institute[20], at the end of his tenure at the École Biblique, Thompson was appointed director of a UNESCO-sponsored Palestinian toponomy project dealing with the integrity of ancient place names in modern Israel. The historical geography project was controversial;

among other things it criticized the Israelis for de-Arabicizing Palestinian place names and doing damage to the region's cultural heritage. When the project was accused of "anti-Semitism," Saudi funding was withdrawn and UNESCO dropped their support.

Unemployed once more, Thompson returned to the States and resumed house painting. A few years later, he was recommended for a teacher replacement job at Lawrence and from there moved to the Jesuit University of Marquette in 1989. There he continued writing a new book, *Early History of the Israelite People*. Though a popular instructor and the best-known scholar in a faculty of 31 members, he did not have tenure – Marquette was an extremely conservative faculty. Tenure review had been set for the spring of 1992 and he expected the votes for tenure were 30-1 in his favor. But in a cruelly ironic twist of luck, a long - and very favorable! - review of *Early History* appeared on the front page of a London newspaper and was quickly picked up by countless others. Suddenly the pride of Marquette University put the entire school under fire from conservatives up in arms about their greatest horror: a critical historian. Votes shifted and Thompson was out of a job yet again.

Prior to this change of fortune, a friend had suggested he apply for an open professorship in Copenhagen. Fifty-three years old and facing an almost certain future of bleak unemployment, he inquired about the post and before the year was out received two dozen red roses and a request to join their faculty as professor in Old Testament Exegesis. He arrived in Copenhagen in May, 1993 and lived happily ever after. His conclusion that the Old Testament patriarchs were not historical figures is now more or less the mainstream opinion even in many evangelical institutions.

CASE SIX: Anthony Le Donne

David Fitzgerald

CRIME: Scholarship offended certain donors and university staff

PUNISHMENT: Lost his job

Lincoln Christian University's Anthony Le Donne was a young up and coming Evangelical New Testament scholar – until his book. *Historical Jesus: What Can We Know and How Can We Know It?* (2011) cost him his job. Why? Hard to say – the book was well received by biblical historians and there was nothing in it particularly new or scandalous to his fellow evangelical New Testament scholars. Nonetheless, his views of memory theory and how it related to Jesus traditions so disturbed certain donors and university staff that after a year the university president bowed to pressure and terminated his employment.

Scholars were swift to express their support for Le Donne and their indignation over his treatment. University of Edinburgh's Larry Hurtado pulled no punches when he called the incident shameful and cowardly, and openly asked why some Christian institutions treated their academic staff in a manner so harsh, so paranoid, and so unchristian - not just in Le Donne's case, but across the field of biblical scholarship:

> "Over the last few months I had more reports of academics being let go by Christian-aligned academic institutions, and for what seem to be very minor differences of view on any one of a variety of relatively minor matters. These are degree-granting institutions, supposedly committed to academic excellence (or so says their publicity), yet behaving in a paranoid manner toward their own academic staff, because on some matter arising from their scholarly work they say or write something that bothers some high administrator.

"These are all also putatively Christian institutions (making as much of this in their publicity as well), which, if anything, actually makes this behavior even more troubling. Typically, no due process, no hearing, no opportunity to explain or give warrants for the offending action, or to correct allegations made, no fair consideration of matters at all: Just a dismissal.

"And, as I've stated, in all the instances I've in mind (all of which concern biblical scholars), the offending matter was truly trivial: Maybe the supposed date of a given biblical writing, maybe some judgment about the genre of a writing or passage, maybe the exegesis of a particular passage or set of passages. No major doctrine called into question, no denial of any item of historic Christian faith, no moral lapse, no criticism of teaching effectiveness, just a charge of having stepped out of the party line on any one of a number of matters undifferentiated as to importance.

"What kind of "academic" institution handles matters in such a disgracefully unfair, unreasonable and unreasoning, and dictatorial manner? What kind of "Christian" institution is so narrow, so ungracious, so unkind, so Stalinesque as to handle things this way? What does it say about the "faith" held, how nervous, uncertain, jittery, and reactionary it must be? (As someone once said about such matters, "With 'friends' like these, Jesus doesn't need enemies!")"[21]

These are just a few recent case studies (others include Fr. Thomas L. Brodie, Tremper Longman III, Gerd Lüdemann, Michael Pahl, and still others[22]). As you can see, there are troubling similarities about all these cases. None are examples of mere scholarly arguments. Scholarly disagreements, even quite vicious ones, occur all the time; that's not special.

What makes all these (and other similar cases) so heinous is the blatant violation of basic principles of scholarship:

touting academic freedom while covertly quashing it, abusing tenure – especially to score financial donations (!), the petty, dogmatic level of overreaction to scholarly conclusions one doesn't like, the attempted suppression of such findings, and the underhanded ways in which the retaliation is carried out: secrecy, arbitrary dismissals, alarming levels of vindictiveness, and a pervasive atmosphere of fear among colleagues who are afraid to speak up in their defense lest they be attacked too.

It's also important to note that bullying of this kind doesn't just affect individual scholars. As Thomas Thompson's case showed, even entire schools can be punished for supporting an unpopular scholar, to the point where they are intimidated against hiring them... even when Thompson's view later becomes mainstream! In the peculiar world of biblical studies, yesterday's blasphemy often becomes tomorrow's reigning consensus; but that may not do the blasphemer any good today.

What's more, in every instance here, all the vicious retribution has been over relatively minor matters, nowhere near as potentially faith-shattering as the Jesus historicity issue. If devout Christian scholars are afraid to lend their support over "truly trivial" biblical issues for fear of their careers being destroyed, what chance is there they will be willing to risk weighing in on (or even looking into) big-ticket crucial issues – like questioning Jesus' very existence?

If you've been paying the least bit of attention so far, you know the answer already: a number of biblical historians are afraid to go on record with what they really think. When discussing the scholars who have openly come out in support of Myth theory, Carrier has found there are many more agnostics than will go on record saying so, including several major figures in the field who have confided in him that: "they do not touch this topic with a ten foot pole, precisely because they fear the kind of thing Ehrman is doing and threatening. They do not want to lose their jobs or career prospects and opportunities. They do not want to be ridiculed or marginalized." But as they don't feel safe coming forward with these views publicly, he has continued to protect their anonymity.[23]

This is not a new situation, nor is it limited to America. The late Rudolf Augstein, respected German journalist and author of *Jesus Menschensohn* ("Jesus the Son of Man")[24] exposed more of the process. He revealed what quite prominent theologians and biblical scholars had told him privately: the party line of there being no doubt that Jesus was a real historical figure, as real as Julius Caesar or Otto von Bismarck, did not convince them. That they had doubts. But they kept their doubts private, and so the party line thrived, and dissenters continued to be relegated to outsider status and routinely mocked by the mainstream…[25]

2. Bluster

Maybe it's just me, but when you've spent over a decade reading them, it becomes fascinating to watch Christian apologists in their efforts to tout Jesus' existence as an incontrovertible, unassailable, established fact of history, like a sweatshop of Rumpelstiltskins desperate to spin insistence into ironclad certitude: "It is beyond doubt…" "No serious scholar disagrees…" "Despite all this, of course Jesus *did* exist…" They seem to believe that if they just say magic incantations like these loudly enough, often enough, and with enough unshakable confidence, they can transmogrify wisps of flimsy evidence into solid gold. "I wish" becomes "I think" becomes "I know."

And this attitude even gets passed down to secular scholars along with other evangelical presuppositions.[26] But given what we can and can't know about Jesus, and the problematic nature of the sources for *all* our data on Jesus (as we'll see in part two), even if a single founder of Christianity really had existed in first-century Palestine, we have nowhere near the weight of evidence to justify that level of assurance on any single fact concerning him.

As Carrier observes in *On the Historicity of Jesus*, this isn't how objective scholars behave in the first place: "If it is realistically possible that Jesus didn't exist, then it is not longer possible to argue that we *know* he existed. We can only argue that he may have existed, or probably did. This would not be an unusual result in the field of history."[27]

And as we'll also see later, so many of our "facts" about Jesus come from historians conflating what we know about Jesus with what we know about first century Palestine (see ch. 4). But facts like those are actually a function of our current understanding of historical or archeological contexts; they don't mean any knowledge about Jesus has gained a secure footing. This trend is noticeable in nearly every book that purports to solidify reliable new information on the "Real Jesus."

What's more, if Jesus does turn out to be completely mythical, he'll be in good company. Besides the majority of the Old Testament patriarchs and virtually every ancient Christian martyr[28], we could add Aesop, Homer, the founder of Taoism Lao-Tzu, Swiss patriot William Tell, and Ned Ludd (the leader of the "Luddites" movement) to the list of famous figures who have turned out to have been completely unhistorical – and as one Buddhist scholar recently admitted to me, many in Buddhist scholarly circles would add Prince Siddhārtha Gautama, a.k.a. the Buddha himself, to the list.

Not even seemingly well-established figures like Socrates[29] and Confucius have been above suspicion. Scholars continue to debate whether Marco Polo ever really traveled to China. Incredibly, at least one Islamic theologian has left his faith after publicly doubting Muhammad's historicity,[30] and even the prophet's presumed genuine writings are vastly eclipsed by false *hadith* (traditional sayings attributed to the prophet), as Muslim scholars have recognized for centuries.

A *sīra*, that is, one of the various traditional biographies of Muhammad, relies upon the Qur'an and collections of *hadith* as resources. Muslim tradition holds that the *hadith* were compiled by Muhammad's followers shortly after the prophet's death in 632 CE and these eyewitnesses completed the task within two decades. In reality, the evidence demonstrates this process actually began roughly a century after that time – and continued for generations.[31]

Ostensibly, each of these *hadith* must come with an *isnād* (a chain of named authorities who vouchsafe its testimony) to authenticate its claims about the prophet. Unfortunately, it was all too easy to forge either one as needed. One could simply invent names freely to create an *isnād* out of whole cloth; or even better, just tack on an existing one that had already won the approval of the *ulama*.

Even the earliest Muslim scholar to investigate the traditions, the 8th century Shu'bah ibn Al-Hajjaj, known as the 'King of *Hadith*,' declared that roughly two-thirds of them were fabrications – and modern researchers are even more skeptical.[32] It wasn't unusual for the judgment of a Muslim jurist, even one living as much as a century after Muhammad, to be retroactively attributed to the prophet, complete with an authoritative and completely fictitious *isnād* securely attached.[33]

All this means that Muhammad's biography – just like that of Jesus – first emerges decades or more after the fact, grows more elaborate with time, spawns a tremendous number of forged teachings in his name; and none of the supposedly impeccable eyewitness sources vouching for him can be verified, let alone taken at face value.

It's nothing short of astounding to realize that the historicity of *all* these venerable religious figures – the Buddha, Moses, Abraham, Lao-Tzu, and Muhammad – has also come into question. Could this suggest that having a purely mythic founder may actually be the normal pattern of development for major world religions?

3. Besmirching Critics of Biblical Studies Methodology

When Butler University's James McGrath recently insisted that historical Jesus scholars use the same methods as any other historians, he dismissed *Vridar*'s Neil Godfrey as some sort of bigoted idiot for saying otherwise[34]. But Godfrey did not have to look far to find several other evangelical biblical scholars (such as Jens Schröter, Chair and Professor of Exegesis and Theology of the New Testament and New Testament Apocrypha at the Humboldt University) who plainly admit that the methodology used by Jesus scholars was not only a peculiar 20th century development, but didn't appear in any other strands of historical research, either.[35]

Schröter is not the only evangelical biblical scholar pointing out that Biblical Studies has critical problems with methodology, special pleading and other flaws. A number of his fellow Christians raise the same complaint in *Jesus, Criteria and the Demise of Authenticity* (2012). These aren't the only problems.

Jesus Studies is in crisis – because Christianity is in crisis. Both are under tremendous pressure to show that all is well and under control – even while their evidentiary foundations are crumbling. Likewise, all the other subfields of Biblical Studies are also dying out in secular academia; which first of all means there are fewer and fewer jobs for current and future biblical historians. What's worse, it also means that increasingly, the *only* institutions offering positions in Biblical Studies will be the religious institutions. Which makes it that much more difficult to espouse blasphemous theories…

4. Bagging on Qualifications

Another weapon in the apologetic arsenal (but one that has been taken up by secular scholars as well) is the credentials game. It's perfectly fine to be concerned whether someone making a historical claim is qualified to do so. Amateur armchair historians abound, and in the interest of full disclosure, despite a degree in history and over a decade and a half of serious research, I certainly count myself as one of these amateurs.

As I mentioned in *Nailed*, very little of the information and opinions I present are my own insights. I regard myself as a combat reporter, not a front-line soldier of the Jesus historicist/mythicist war. It's an important distinction to make, especially considering that amateurs have been responsible for cooking up some of the worst crackpot Jesus myth theories (though the worst crackpot *historical* Jesus theories continue to be made by professionals).

The problem is when critics go too far in the other direction, and become *hyper*-skeptical about their opponent's qualifications. Bart Ehrman has been especially prone to dismissing mythicists this way of late; alleging that they can't do competent work because they don't have degrees "specifically" in early Christian history – though in fact both Richard Carrier and Robert Price do. When Ehrman insinuates that no one is qualified to talk about this unless they have an extremely hyper-specific degree major and a specific kind of appointment at a university, at best all he is doing is committing the No-True-Scotsman fallacy; his worst examples are no better than *ad hominem*.

In fact, Carrier, Robert Price, and Thomas Thompson are all more than adequately qualified to evaluate the evidence for and against the historicity of Jesus, and there are many qualified and insightful amateurs like Neil Godfrey, Tim Widowfield and Earl Doherty (who actually does have a classics degree), as well as impressive post-grad PhD candidates like Tom Verenna and Raphael Lataster, all of whom have done remarkable work on the historicity issue. The game goes something like this:

"What are your credentials?" the apologist demands to know.

"Well, I studied history in school..." says the mythicist.

"Yes, but was this in college?"

"It was."

"Yes, but was it a major university?"

"That's right."

"Yes, but did you graduate?"
"I have a degree..."
"Yes, but do you have any advanced degrees?"
"I have a PhD."
"Yes, but do you have a *relevant* PhD.?"
"I do, in history."
"Yes, but is it in ancient history?"
"It *is* in ancient history."
"Yes, but is it in ancient Christian history?"
"It is, actually."
"Yes, but is it in ancient Roman Christian history?"
"As a matter of fact, it is."
"Yes, but are you employed as a historian?"
"I am."
"Yes, but is it at a major university?"
"It certainly is."
"Yes, but do you have tenure?" (grilling continues, *ad infinitum…*)

You can never win this game. I'm exaggerating slightly, but not really; I see variations on this conversation pop up all the time; though it's interesting to note in most cases, it's never occurred to the apologetic interrogator to ever ask their pastor/authority figure what *their* credentials are… (And though I use a Christian apologist in the example above, secular critics certainly play the same game, too).

John Dickson, a founding director of the Centre for Public Christianity, has made repeated promises online to eat a page of his Bible if someone can find just *one* full Professor of Ancient History, Classics, or New Testament in an accredited university somewhere in the world who thinks Jesus never lived. Please feel free to encourage him to keep his promise, since he already owed us a few pages when he first made his boast. Even with his caveats, there *are* full history professors at accredited universities – Arthur Droge, Kurt Noll, and Hector Avalos are all historicity agnostics. And they won't be the last. The first peer reviewed pro-mythicist article has already been published in an established academic journal,[36] by doctoral candidate in religious studies Raphael Lataster (so that'll be at least one more page for Dickson to eat).

An End to the B's: Burying the Hatchet
At the end of the day, this isn't a war between those scholars who think there was a real, albeit non-divine, Jesus and those who think he was only a myth; scholarly disagreements are what drive historical research. The only real antagonism here is between those scholars who think mythicist positions deserve to be engaged seriously and those who reject them without examination – well, those, and also those Christian higher educational institutions that continue to intimidate their scholars from even openly expressing agnosticism on the issue...

Even though they don't realize it, often even Christian scholars have contributed to mythicist theory, albeit usually accidentally (and often not realizing how they are contradicting themselves). For example, in *Nailed* I showed how some of the apologetic arguments of esteemed Christian bible historian Bruce Metzger were shown to be completely false, calling as my witness the findings of ... esteemed Christian bible historian Bruce Metzger.[37]

In fact, let me speak briefly to my fellow Bart Ehrman fans, since Ehrman has become one of the louder voices on the side of the beshmirchers. I'm with you, Bart fans: I have a tremendous amount of respect, admiration and affection for Bart. Arguably, he's single-handedly done more to dispel long-standing misconceptions and outright myths of biblical scholarship and sweeping out the dusty cobwebs obscuring the results of centuries of biblical research than anyone. Yet for such a staunch historicist, for years I've been saying that Bart Ehrman's research has inadvertently made him also one of the best mythicists scholars out there.

Mythicists like me weren't disappointed with Ehrman's 2012 book *Did Jesus Exist?* because we expected him to agree with us; we were disappointed because we were expecting Ehrman would provide the best defense of historicity, and the best critique of bad mythicism. But instead of clearing out the deadwood, he actually only piled on more. Even worse, he phoned in a book far below his usual standard, and his testy reaction to the critics who pointed out *DJE*'s many errors and shortcomings – in particular Richard Carrier[38] – was another disappointment.

I was pleased to see that with Ehrman's more recent books, like his excellent *Forgery and Counterforgery*, he's returned to the high caliber of work that we've come to expect from him, and that in his most recent books *How Jesus Became God* and *Jesus Before the Gospels*, he recognizes that much of what the field relies on as established facts aren't so established after all, and corrects some of the mistakes he made in *DJE*. What's more, in *HJBG*, Ehrman increasingly turns to the same arguments as mythicists. He acknowledges that the earliest believers "knew" Jesus was raised from the dead; not because (as apologists argue) no one would make such a claim unless they knew the tomb was empty (pp. 7, 174), but because they had visions of Jesus from heaven (pp. 194-96). Ehrman also now sees that ancient Judaism was not an example of monolithic groupthink (p. 50), but just as rife with alternate opinions and heresies (i.e., p. 69, 75 and more) as anything in Christianity. This is an important admission, as it corrects (and nullifies) the basis of many of the arguments he gets wrong in *DJE*. And there are other examples[39]

It's my hope that feuds like this current one can be avoided by honestly engaging with the criticism of the ideas and focusing on the quality of the arguments raised instead of taking criticism personally as a personal attack. Tom Dykstra has brought to my attention[40] two apt comments from historians. Michael Goulder recalled that it took time for colleagues to accept his arguments that the gospel authors created parables and nativity stories in line with their own doctrinal concerns: "Scholars who have assumed a position over many years do not quickly recant it and publicly admit their error; nor can a novel hypothesis expect to carry the day at once in a conservative profession. It may be particularly difficult to shift opinion over texts which are fundamental to the faith of the critic."[41] He believes in the long run his arguments will persuade a new generation of scholars – but it will take time. Paradigm shifts don't come from the professors in the consensus; they come from young scholars on the margin of the subject.[42]

Dennis R. MacDonald, remarking on the response to his own scholarship, concurs: "As is the case with all paradigm shifts, one must expect resistance from those who have benefitted from business as usual. I no longer expect scholars of my generation to accept my work with open arms; if acceptance occurs at all, it will come from future generations."[43]

Allied Forces
However, there's good reason for mythicists to be optimistic: Increasingly, scholars are open to the idea without feeling any need to fully commit to myth theory. This is not a fight between mythicists and historicists; it is a fight between those that take myth theory seriously and those that reject it out of hand. Many more scholars are fine with privately taking an agnostic stance on the matter (and would be willing to share their true feelings publicly if it wouldn't endanger their career). And there are historicist scholars who are happy to be allies with mythicists – figures like MacDonald and Mark Goodacre, both who have done groundbreaking work in biblical scholarship. Another is Philip Davies, Emeritus Professor of Biblical Studies at the University of Sheffield, England, whose thoughts on the controversy are worth hearing.

In the online journal *The Bible and Interpretation*, Davies responded to Bart Ehrman's book *Did Jesus Exist?* Like Ehrman, Davies accepts the historicity of Jesus. But he is alarmed both by Ehrman's rhetoric and his implied threats against the professions of anyone who would dare question the historicity of Jesus[44], especially in light of the shameful treatment Thomas Thompson received, despite his final overdue vindication. Davies not only defends Thompson's work on this matter, he acknowledges that Thompson and Thomas Verenna have amassed a great deal of evidence demonstrating that whether he was real or mythical, the profile of Jesus in the New Testament is composed of stock motifs drawn from all over the Mediterranean and Near Eastern world.

Though a historicist on the Jesus issue, Davies argues this whole debate should be taken seriously and can't be snubbed outright or dismissed as the work of amateurs. He fully recognizes that the evidence for Jesus' historicity is no slam-dunk, and that in light of how weak and extremely problematic it actually is, nothing warrants the degree of rhetoric coming from critics like Ehrman. On the contrary, Davies counters that acknowledging the possibility that Jesus didn't exist is *the only way the field can maintain any academic respectability:*

> "Surely the rather fragile historical evidence for Jesus of Nazareth should be tested to see what weight it can bear, or even to work out what kind of historical research might be appropriate. Such a normal exercise should hardly generate controversy in most fields of ancient history, but of course New Testament studies is not a normal case and the highly emotive and dismissive language of, say, Bart Ehrman's response to Thompson's *The Mythic Past* shows (if it needed to be shown), not that the matter is beyond dispute, but that the whole idea of raising this question needs to be attacked, ad hominem, as something outrageous. This is precisely the tactic anti-minimalists tried twenty years ago: their targets were 'amateurs,' 'incompetent', and could be ignored. The 'amateurs' are now all retired professors, while virtually everyone else in the field has become minimalist (if in most cases grudgingly and tacitly). So, as the saying goes, déjà vu all over again.

"I don't think, however, that in another 20 years there will be a consensus that Jesus did not exist, or even possibly didn't exist, but a recognition that his existence is not entirely certain would nudge Jesus scholarship towards academic respectability. In the first place, what does it mean to affirm that 'Jesus existed,' anyway, when so many different Jesuses are displayed for us by the ancient sources and modern NT scholars? Logically, some of these Jesuses cannot have existed. So in asserting historicity, it is necessary to define which ones (rabbi, prophet, sage, shaman, revolutionary leader, etc.) are being affirmed—and thus which ones deemed unhistorical. In fact, as things stand, what is being affirmed as the Jesus of history is a cipher, not a rounded personality...

"Let's abandon fatuous reasoning such as accepting miraculous stories because no-one would make them up (Wright, the con man's dream mark), or placing faith in 'eyewitness' accounts while actually admitting how unreliable they are (Bauckham). Sophistry of this sort betrays an already accepted dogma looking for rationalization: *fides quaerens indicium*[45]. There are reasonable ways of setting out the historical problem, even if there is no satisfactory solution.

"So what do we have here by way of evidence for Jesus? No certain eyewitness accounts, but a lot of secondary evidence... Am I inclined to accept that Jesus existed? Yes, I am. But I am unable to say with any conviction what he may have said and done, or what his words and deeds might tell us about who or what he thought he was. Even what his followers thought about him is highly colored with hindsight, embellishment, rationalization and reflection."[46]

David Fitzgerald

All of these considerations are important to realize how much hidden bias affects the majority opinion on the historicity issue, and to reverse the all-too-common trend of poisoning the well – but none of it matters when it comes to actually analyzing our evidence for Jesus. So now time to stop talking about the problems in the field of biblical research, and actually talk about biblical research. Time to put mythicism to the test. Will Jesus Myth theory be the final dinosaur killer for Christianity? Or does it need to be discarded as just one more theory of Christian origins that ultimately didn't pan out (such as, say, taking the gospels as inerrant)? Let's see.

***

For further reading:

Raphael Lataster, "It's Official: We Can Now Doubt Jesus's Historical Existence," in *Think* (by The Royal Institute of Philosophy), Vol. 15.43 (Summer 2016), pp. 65-79

Philip Davies, "Did Jesus Exist?" in *The Bible and Interpretation,* August 2012, available online at: www.bibleinterp.com/opeds/dav368029.shtml

Hector Avalos, *The End of Biblical Studies,* 2007

Chris Keith and Anthony Le Donne, eds., *Jesus, Criteria and the Demise of Authenticity,* 2012

Steven Bollinger, "I Accuse You, You Cowardly Closeted Academic Mythicists!" in *The Wrong Monkey,* March 23, 2012. Available online at:
http://thewrongmonkey.blogspot.com/2012/03/i-accuse-you-you-cowardly-closeted.html

Tom Dykstra, "Ehrman and Brodie on Whether Jesus Existed: A Cautionary Tale about the State of Biblical Scholarship," *Journal of the Orthodox Center for the Advancement of Biblical Studies,* vol. 8.1, 2015. Available online at:

http://ocabs.org/journal/index.php/jocabs/article/viewFile/80/47

Neil Godfrey's (and frequent contributor Tim Widowfield) *Vridar* blog is one of the finest sources of reports on relevant issues in bible studies and Jesus historicity. Here are just three posts worth reading for our discussion here:

"Unrecognized Bias in New Testament Scholarship over Christian Origins." Available online at:
http://vridar.org/2015/04/17/unrecognized-bias-in-new-testament-scholarship-over-christian-origins/

Neil Godfrey, "'Partisanship' in New Testament Scholarship." Available online at:
http://vridar.org/2010/03/17/partisanship-in-new-testament-scholarship/

Neil Godfrey, "How Open To Radically Fresh Ideas Are New Testament Scholars Really?" Available online at:
http://vridar.org/2014/08/04/how-open-to-radically-fresh-ideas-are-new-testament-scholars-really/

For a revealing look at how early Christian fathers fabricated an entire tradition of Christian martyrdom (a fact that was largely uncovered and debunked by later Christian scholars), see:

Candida Moss, *The Myth of Persecution*, 2014

For examinations of the historicity debates on the founding figures of other religions (where many of the same questions have also been raised), see:

ibn Warraq, The Quest for the Historical Muhammad, 2000
Israel Finkelstein and Neil Asher Silberman, The Bible Unearthed, 2001

Two essays from Buddhist scholar Eisel Mazard questioning the historicity of the Buddha:

"Dissent from the Top: Reading Ancient Buddhist Texts as Historical Evidence." Available online at: https://medium.com/@eiselmazard/dissent-from-the-top-reading-ancient-buddhist-texts-as-historical-evidence-9cabf2ad32bf

"Problems of "Canon" and "Reason" in Theravāda Studies: Cultural Anthropology Encounters the Pali Canon (巴利文大藏經), From Cambodia to Yunnan." A more detailed article, formally peer-reviewed and published in an academic journal, dealing with the questions of how the source texts are known (and how, in a sense, they've remained unknown). Available online in English and Chinese at: http://a-bas-le-ciel.blogspot.ca/2014/03/canon-and-reason-complete-chinese.html

Incidentally, I'm not a dogmatic Jesus myther. For a handy list of a few of the things it would take to turn me agnostic on the Jesus historicity issue (or even convince me there really *was* an historical Jesus), see the chapter "Can Jesus Be Saved?" in David Fitzgerald, *Nailed: Ten Christian Myths That Show Jesus Never Existed at All,* 2010

---

[1] Akenson, pp. 539-40
[2] op cit., pp. 541
[3] Incidentally, some Christian critics of *Nailed* accused me of creating a straw man for simply repeating what these verses say *exactly as given in the Bible*. Hey, it's *your* book...
[4] Bobby Ross, Jr., "Interpretation Sparks a Grave Theology Debate" *Christianity Today,* November 7, 2011. Available online at: http://www.christianitytoday.com/ct/2011/november/interpretation-sparks-theology-debate.html
[5] Ibid.

6 Ibid.
7 Ibid.
8 For details, see "Theologian Peter Enns talks about why BioLogos did not renew his contract," available online at: http://www.uncommondescent.com/intelligent-design/theologian-peter-enns-talks-about-why-biologos-did-not-renew-his-contract/
9 Christopher Rollston, "The Marginalization of Women: A Biblical Value We Don't Like to Talk About" *Huffington Post*, 8/31/2012
10 Tom Verenna, "In Support of Christopher Rollston (and a Reply to T.M. Law)," October 10, 2012. Available online at: http://tomverenna.wordpress.com/2012/10/10/in-support-of-christopher-rollston-and-a-reply-to-t-m-law/
11 Robert Cargill, "Inside Higher Ed Exposes Emmanuel Scandal: Christian Seminary To Terminate Professor in Exchange for Donation?" October 15, 2012. Available online at: http://robertcargill.com/2012/10/15/inside-higher-ed-exposes-emmanuel-scandal-christian-seminary-to-terminate-professor-in-exchange-for-donation/
12 Ibid.
13 Jim West "So for Emmanuel 'Christian' Seminary, Money is the Determinative Factor, Not Scholarship, Education, or Academic Integrity." Available online at: http://zwingliusredivivus.wordpress.com/2012/10/15/so-for-emmanuel-christian-seminary-money-is-the-determinative-factor-not-scholarship-education-or-academic-integrity/
14 Available online at: http://www.beliefnet.com/columnists/roddreher/2010/04/evolution-defense-behind-theologians-ouster.html - sx8J5UQzTzefkarW.99)
15 cited in ibid.

[16] Read more at:
http://www.beliefnet.com/columnists/roddreher/2010/04/evolution-defense-behind-theologians-ouster.html - sx8J5UQzTzefkarW.99

[17] Ibid.

[18] Taken from Thomas L. Thompson's "On the Problem of Critical Scholarship: A Memoire," in *The Bible and Interpretation,* April 2011

[19] Ibid.

[20] The Albright Institute of Archaeological Research in East Jerusalem.

[21] "Academic Injustice and Shameful Cowardice." Available online at:
http://larryhurtado.wordpress.com/2012/04/27/academic-injustice-and-shameful-cowardice/

[22] For example, see more details here:
- Fr. Thomas L. Brodie
http://www.irishcentral.com/news/irish-priest-disciplined-after-claims-jesus-never-existed-in-controversial-book-187717531-237560221.html
Temper Longman:
http://euangelizomai.blogspot.com/2010/04/end-of-reformed-evangelical-ot-scholars.html
Gerd Lüdemann: Gerd Lüdemann, "The Decline of Academic Theology at Göttingen," *Religion* (2002) 32, 87–94
http://www.tandfonline.com/doi/abs/10.1006/reli.2002.0411
Michael Pahl:
http://www.patheos.com/blogs/euangelion/2012/10/michael-pahl-dismissal-from-cedarville-university/
http://euangelizomai.blogspot.com/2010/04/end-of-reformed-evangelical-ot-scholars.html etc.)
Candida Moss: Moss jokes (at least, I *think* she's joking) in *The Myth of Persecution* that she might not have had the courage to see the book through to completion if not for friends who encouraged her to stand her ground and

assured her she wouldn't be fired (p. 261). Despite the overall positive reception of her book, she did get lambasted in reviews like this one: Radner, Ephraim (May 2013). "Unmythical Martyrs A review of The Myth of Persecution: How Early Christians Invented a Story of Martyrdom". *First Things.*

23 See "On Bermejo-Rubio's Dispassionate Plea for a Historical Jesus." Available online at: http://freethoughtblogs.com/carrier/archives/5085

24 Rudolf Augstein, *Jesus Menschensohn,* Deutscher Taschenbuch Verlag, 2001

25 Cited in Steven Bollinger, "I Accuse You, You Cowardly Closeted Academic Mythicists!" in *The Wrong Monkey,* March 23, 2012. Available online at: http://thewrongmonkey.blogspot.com/2012/03/i-accuse-you-you-cowardly-closeted.html

26 I use what I call *the Belfast Analogy* to describe the bizarre nature of Biblical Studies. In Northern Ireland during the Troubles of the 1960s to the 1990s, we had a minority, the Ulster Protestants surrounded by the majority Catholic Ireland. Meanwhile, nested within Ulster was a Catholic minority. Feeling under siege, Ulster protestants in turn made life intolerable for their captive minority-within-a-minority.

Likewise, Christians feel surrounded by the secular world, and this is no less true in academia. But while believers may feel under siege in all other fields of history, in the rarified world of Biblical studies, Christian presuppositions, biases and above all, theological interests still hold sway, making life very hard for any scholars whose findings threaten Christian doctrine. (It occurs to me that Cold War East Berlin is an analogous situation. Nikita Khrushchev reportedly said, "Berlin is the testicles of the West. When I want the West to scream, I squeeze on Berlin.")

27 Carrier, *On the Historicity of Jesus,* p. 14

28 See Candida Moss, *The Myth of Persecution: How Early*

Christians Invented a Story of Martyrdom, 2013
[29] That said, see ch. 13 for evidence for Socrates.
[30] Imam Muhammad Sven Kalisch lost the chair for Islamic pedagogy at the University of Münster after doubting the historical existence of Muhammad (and also Jesus and Moses) in 2008. He later came to the conclusion that the prophet never existed and renounced Islam in 2010. Official Islamic groups in Germany have confirmed him as an apostate. See Katharina Völker, "A Danger to Free Research and Teaching in German Universities? The Case of Muhammad Sven Kalisch" in *The Teaching and Study of Islam in Western Universities*, Morris, et al., eds. (London, Routledge, 2014) pp. 175ff.
[31] See Juynboll, pp. 9-76
[32] See Juynboll, p. 20; and Noll, in Thompson & Verenna, pp. 262-263
[33] Juynboll, pp. 15-16; Cook, M., "The Opponents of the Writings of Tradition in Early Islam," p. 490
[34] See "Historical Jesus Studies Are Different Methodologically from Other Historical Studies," available online at: http://vridar.org/2012/09/20/historical-jesus-studies-are-different-methodologically-from-other-historical-studies/ - more-31935
[35] In *Jesus, Criteria and the Demise of Authenticity*, pp. 51-52
[36] Raphael Lataster, "It's Official: We Can Now Doubt Jesus's Historical Existence," published in *Think* (by The Royal Institute of Philosophy), Vol. 15.43 (Summer 2016), pp. 65-79
[37] See *Nailed*, pp. 120-121; cf. Bruce Metzger, "Important Witnesses to the Text of the New Testament," in *The Text of the New Testament; Its Transmission, Corruption and Restoration* (1992), pp. 36-92.
[38] See Carrier, "Ehrman on Historicity Recap," available online at: http://www.richardcarrier.info/archives/1794
[39] For more, see Carrier's review of *HJBG*, available online at:

http://freethoughtblogs.com/carrier/archives/6923
40 Dykstra, p. 223
41 Goulder, pp. 134-35
42 paraphrased slightly from Goulder (cited in Dykstra, p. 225n331)
43 MacDonald, "My Turn," p. 23
44 See Philip Davies, "Did Jesus Exist?" in *The Bible and Interpretation,* August 2012, available online at: http://www.bibleinterp.com/opeds/dav368029.shtml
45 *Fides quaerens indicium* means "faith seeking evidence;" a play on Anselm of Canterbury's famous phrase *fides quaerens intellectum* ("faith seeking understanding").
46 Davies, op. cit.

Chapter Three:
Who Do Men Say that I am?

"Both history and theology converge on a proper answer to this: the historical Jesus will always be a fabrication, and the search for him antagonistic to true religious belief."
                                           - Phillip Davies

As I mentioned in the introduction, our familiar figure of Jesus is in actuality two: the "Jesus of Faith," and the "Jesus of History." And the strange case of Dr. Jesus and Mr. Christ is even odder than that; since both are composed of still ever more variations of themselves. The "Jesus of Faith" is an umbrella term for the gargantuan number of different saviors that inspire Christianity in all its riotous diversity: The Catholic Jesus and the Orthodox Jesus and those of all the eastern sects in between, the Lutheran Jesus, the Anglican Jesus, the Presbyterian, the Baptist, Methodist, and all the other flavors of evangelical Jesuses, the Snake-Handler's Jesus, the Pentecostal Jesus, the liberal and the republican Jesus, the KKK's angry Aryan Jesus and the southern gospel choir's Black Jesus, the Seventh-Day Adventist Jesus, the family-friendly Mormon Jesus, the Jesus being peddled on your doorstep by Jehovah's Witnesses, the gentle, loving Quaker Jesus and the dour Calvinist Jesus, the Unitarian and Universalist Jesuses, the out-there woo-woo New Age Jesuses, the Jesus who embraces gays and lesbians and the Jesus who sternly demands they be cast out, not to mention the Muslim Jesus impressed into service as a true prophet of Islam. It seems no matter where you fall on the religio-socio-political spectrum, it's as if there is a Jesus made to order just for you – in over 33,000 varieties, according to the *World Christian*

David Fitzgerald

Encyclopedia. Perhaps the real number is closer to 2.18 billion; with no two believers sharing the same Jesus...

And yet, none of the believers of any of these Jesuses of Faith seem overly concerned that there is no evidence for his spectacular miracles or his multitude of followers throughout the Holy Land, or seem to care much that the detailed gospel accounts contradict themselves on even the most basic facts of his life and ministry, or that even devout bible scholars recognize that the gospels are filled with historical difficulties and outright impossibilities.[1] It doesn't even seem to give them pause to consider how many thousands of "false," "counterfeit" Christs outnumber their own personal savior. Fortunately for us, we can leave the unending stream of those competing Jesuses of Faith alone and concentrate on the so-called "real" Jesus.

Apologists love to parrot the old lie that "no serious historians reject the historicity of Christ," but they either fail to realize – or deliberately neglect to mention – that the "Historical Jesus" that all secular biblical historians *do* accept is at best no more than just another first century wandering preacher and founder of a fringe cult that eventually became Christianity. In other words: they don't realize that the "real" Jesus completely debunks their own. They can't have it both ways.

What can we say about *that* Jesus, the 'Jesus of History'? As we saw in chapter two, the majority of biblical scholars are employed by religious institutions and despite broad assurances of academic freedom, those historians don't have the luxury of saying who or what they really think Jesus was, if it might offend the theological sensibilities of their school's administrators or financial patrons. Though it didn't use to be the case, today there are numerous secular biblical scholars who aren't beholden to any doctrinal view of Jesus and happily do have real academic freedom to investigate the matter. These academics are surely our best bet to discover unbiased information about any real historical Jesus, so maybe we should leave it up to the consensus of the experts in the field and ask them what they say. A sound plan – except for one small problem: there *is* no consensus on Jesus…

A Cornucopia of Christs
Just like the plethora of variations on the "Jesus of Faith," there is no single "Jesus of History." Albert Schweitzer, in his *From Reimarus to Wrede: A History of Research on the Life of Jesus* (1906), was already discovering that every scholar claiming to have uncovered the 'real' Jesus seemed to have found a mirror instead. Investigators found Jesus to be a placeholder for whatever values they themselves held dear. Over a century later, the situation has not improved — quite the contrary. To say there is still no consensus on who Jesus was is an understatement. A quick survey (Robert Price presents excellent examples in his *Deconstructing Jesus*[2]) shows we have quite an embarrassment of Jesi:

Cynic philosopher — The many borrowings from Greek philosophy in Jesus' teachings would make sense if Jesus had actually been a wandering Cynic or a Stoic sage, or the Galilean equivalent. Leif Vaage, Burton L. Mack, John Dominic Crossan, Gerald Downing and others have strongly defended this view, citing plenty of Cynic statements with their equivalents in the Gospels.

Liberal Pharisee — Something like his predecessor, the famous Rabbi Hillel. The gospels paint the Pharisees as legalistic bad guys, but in real life, they would have loved someone like Jesus. In *Jesus the Pharisee: A New Look at the Jewishness of Jesus* (2003), historian Harvey Falk argues that virtually all of Jesus' judgments on the *Halakha*, the Jewish law, are paralleled in the Pharisaic thought of that time, as well as later rabbinic thought.

Charismatic Hasid — Similarly, respected Dead Sea Scroll authority Geza Vermes, an expert on New Testament-era Judaism and author of *Jesus the Jew: A Historian's View of the Gospels* (1981), sees Jesus as one of the popular freewheeling Galilean holy men, unorthodox figures like Hanina Ben-Dosa or Honi the Circle-Drawer. Just like Jesus, they had little respect for the niceties of Jewish law, which of course ticked off the religious establishment.

Essene Heretic — Others like J.M. Allegro have pointed to parallels between early Christians, John the Baptist's sect and the Therapeutae/Essenes of Qumran who gave us the Dead Sea scrolls, wondering if Jesus and John the Baptist were members of that radical community.

Conservative Rabbi — On the other hand, Jesus upholds the Torah, insisting, "not one jot or stroke of the Law will pass away" (Matt. 5:17–19). He wears a prayer shawl tasseled with *tzitzit* (Matt. 9:20–22), observes the Sabbath, and worships in synagogues as well as the Temple.

Antinomian Iconoclast — But on the *other* other hand, Jesus then turns around and, point-by-point, dismantles the Torah in verses like Mark 7:15–20 ("There is nothing from without a man, that entering into him can defile him: but the things which come out of him, those are they that defile the man."), Matt. 5:21–22, 27–28, 31 ("It hath been said, Whosoever shall put away his wife, let him give her a writing of divorcement: But I say unto you, That whosoever shall put away his wife, saving for the cause of fornication, causeth her to commit adultery: and whosoever shall marry her that is divorced committeth adultery."), Matt. 5:33–37, 38–42, 43–44 ("Ye have heard that it hath been said, Thou shalt love thy neighbor, and hate thine enemy. But I say unto you, Love your enemies, bless them that curse you, do good to those that hate you, and pray for them which despitefully use you, and persecute you..."), *etc.*, and dismisses the Temple in verses like Mark 13:1–2, Luke 21:5–6 and Matt. 12:6–8 ("But I say unto you, That in this place is one greater than the temple. But if ye had known what this meaneth, I will have mercy and not sacrifice, ye would not have condemned the guiltless. For the Son of man is Lord even of the Sabbath day.").

Magician/Exorcist/Faith Healer — Morton Smith, discoverer (or more likely, its forger — but that's another story[3]) of the *Secret Gospel of Mark* made the argument that Jesus the Christ was actually *Jesus the Magician* (1981) in the book of the same name. Harvard's influential and prolific Helmut Koester has said that Jesus must have been a combination prophet/miracle worker/exorcist.[4] In his *Magic in the New Testament* and *Jesus the Sorcerer*, Robert Conner makes an extensive survey of research on early Christian magical practices as seen in the gospels. Like the pagan miracle workers, Jesus cast out demons and healed the blind, deaf, and mute with mud and spit (Mark 5:41; 7:33–34), using the same spells, incantations and techniques as taught in the many popular Greek magic handbooks of the time.[5]

Violent Zealot Revolutionary — But maybe Jesus was really a political messiah, inciting a revolt against the Romans, like Theudas or "the Egyptian," the unnamed Messianic figure Josephus describes, or the two "robbers" crucified with Jesus (since rebel bandits were commonly referred to as robbers). Why else would it be the *Romans* crucifying him, rather than the Jewish Sanhedrin just stoning him to death for blasphemy, as the law demanded?

There is evidence one can point to: Luke's Gospel lists a disciple called Simon "the Zealot," and seems to hint that Jesus had other Zealots in his entourage: at the Last Supper, Jesus tells his followers to grab their bags and buy a sword (Luke 22:36); they tell him they already have two swords on hand (Luke 22:38); when Jesus is about to be arrested they ask if they should attack (Luke 22:49). In Mark 14:47, one of the disciples does just that and cuts off the ear of one of the High priest's men (the story grows more details in the other Gospels: Matt. 26:51–52, Luke 22:50–51, John 18:10).

Many capable scholars including Robert Eisler, S. G. F. Brandon, Hugh J. Schonfield, Hyam Maccoby, and Robert Eisenman have thought this is where the real Jesus is to be found, and there are many scholarly variations arguing for the 'Jesus-as-*Che* theory.' Most recently this theory was revived by "Zealot" author Reza Aslan, who Fox News infamously accused of the unforgivable crime of weighing in on Jesus while being Muslim.

Nonviolent Pacifist Resister — But then again, as Bruce Malina and others have argued, Jesus isn't called the Prince of Peace for nothing. There's no trace of such political agitation when he instructs his followers "if someone strike you on the right cheek, turn the other also" (Matt. 5:39), or when conscripted by Roman soldier to lug their gear for a mile, to "go with him two" (Matt. 5:41).

Apocalyptic Prophet — This is the Jesus that Albert Schweitzer and many subsequent historians have thought was the real thing: A fearless, fiery Judgment Day preacher announcing that the end was nigh and the Kingdom of God was coming fast. Like Paul (and many other first century Jewish apocalypts) this Jesus did not expect the world to survive his own lifetime. Bart Ehrman makes the case for such a figure in *Jesus: Apocalyptic Prophet of the New Millennium* (1999). Paula Fredriksen, author of *From Jesus to Christ* (1988) argues that the Gospels and the early history of Christianity don't make sense unless Jesus was an apocalyptic visionary.

First-Century Proto-Communist — Was Jesus the first Marxist? Milan Machoveč and other leftists have thought so. You have to admit Jesus has nothing good to say about the capitalist pigs of his day (Luke 6:24, 12:15), repeatedly preaching that they cannot serve both God and money (Matt. 6:24, Luke 16:13), that they should sell all they own and distribute the money to the poor (Matt. 19:21, Mark 10:21, Luke 18:22) and most famously, that it is easier to get a camel through the eye of a needle than for the rich to get into heaven (Matt. 19:24, Mark 10:25, Luke 18:25) — and don't forget his casting the moneychangers out of the Temple with a scourge. Acts not only depicts the early Christians as sharing everything in common, it even explicitly states the Marxist credo: "From each according to their ability, to each according to their need" (Acts 4: 34–35).

Early Feminist — Or was he the first male Feminist? Some scholars like Elizabeth Schüssler Fiorenza and Kathleen Corley point to his role as the "Child of Wisdom" and as a prophet of *Sophia*, the feminine personification of divine wisdom in Jewish tradition. They also point out his unusual attitudes towards women, some of which seem remarkably progressive for the first century. They say not only that some of his closest followers and early church leaders were women, he forgave the woman caught in adultery, and challenged social customs concerning women's role in society (John 4:27, Luke 7:37, Matt. 21:31–32).

Earthy Hedonist — Or was he a male chauvinist pig? Onlookers criticize him for being "a glutton and a drunk" who consorts with riffraff like tax collectors and whores (Luke 5:30; 5:33–34; 7:34, 37–39,44–46).

Family Man — but then again, Jesus is a champion of good old family values when he gets even tougher than Moses, ratcheting Old Testament law up a notch and declaring "Whoever divorces his wife and marries another commits adultery against her, and if she divorces her husband and marries another, she commits adultery" (Mark 10:11–12). He also reminds his followers to honor their father and mother, then sternly warns "whoever speaks evil of father and mother must surely die" (Matt. 15:4).

Home Wrecker — but then when *Jesus* speaks evil of the family, apparently it's okay: "If any man come to me, and hate not his father, and mother, and wife, and children, and brethren, and sisters, yea, and his own life also, he cannot be my disciple" (Luke 14:26). When Jesus is told his mother and brothers have come to see him, Jesus ignores them and asks, "Who is my mother? Who are my brothers?" (Matt. 12:47–48) "Do not think I have come to bring peace to the earth; I have come not to bring peace, but to bring a sword. For I have come to set a man against his father, and a daughter against her mother, and a daughter-in-law against her mother-in-law" (Matt. 10:34–35).

Savior of the World — But despite all that, Jesus loves everyone; he even preached to Samaritans (John 4:39–41; Luke 17:11–18) and Gentiles (Matt. 4:13–17, 24–25).

Savior of Israel (only) — Well, perhaps he loves everyone *except* Samaritans or Gentiles. When a Canaanite woman begs him to heal her daughter he ignores her. After the disciples ask him to make her go away, he first refuses, saying "I am not sent but unto the lost sheep of the house of Israel" (Matt. 15:24). When Jesus sends out his disciples, he commands them not to preach the good news to gentile regions or Samaritan cities (Matt. 10:5–6).

Heir to the Throne/Royal Pretender — Or was Jesus the actual heir of David and attempting to found a new royal dynastic line when he lost the game of thrones? In *The Jesus Dynasty*, James Tabor argues he was David Koresh-like, charismatic but delusional and suicidal, with his own Branch

Davidian-style group of followers who believed he was sent by God to be their king.

Radical Social Reformer — Still others like John Dominic Crossan, Gerd Theissen and Richard Horsley take the opposite tack and see Jesus not as a royal but as a champion for the Jewish peasants suffering under the yoke of the Roman Empire and its rapacious tax collectors; a Jesus somewhat along the lines of Gandhi and his struggle against the British Empire.

And this is by no means a complete list: there is still a range of portraits littering the scholarly landscape. What's more, there are still more uncertainties; even Jesus' historical setting has come into question, with scholars like Israel Knohl, Robert Eisenman, and the late Alvar Ellegård placing him in a completely different time and place than first century Judea. The lack of consensus has only grown more enormous with time, and it has not gone unnoticed. James Charlesworth, director of the Dead Sea Scrolls Project at Princeton Theological Seminary, opened his international symposia on Jesus research by noting "what had been perceived to be a developing consensus in the 1980s has collapsed into a chaos of opinions."[6] After his own survey of the field, even the respected Helmut Koester expressed his bafflement: "The vast variety of interpretations of the historical Jesus that the current quest has proposed is bewildering."[7]

Will the Real Jesus Please Stand Up?
How plausible are any of these hypothetical reconstructions, anyway? As Price notes in *Deconstructing Jesus*,[8] many of those above are quite plausible, make good sense of a number of gospel texts, don't violate accepted historical method, aren't impossibly anachronistic, and are the result of deep and serious scholarship. As far as it goes, all of them have their strengths. None of them are particularly far-fetched. All tend to center on particular constellations of Gospel elements interpreted in certain ways, and reject other data as inauthentic — something

all critical historians do, regardless of the subject. All appeal to solid historical analogies for their new take on Jesus. But, as Bart Ehrman points out, one fatal flaw haunts most if not all of them:

> "The link between Jesus' message and his death is crucial, and historical studies of Jesus' life can be evaluated to how well they establish that link. This in fact is a common weakness in many portrayals of the historical Jesus: they often sound completely plausible in their reconstruction of what Jesus said and did, but they can't make sense of his death. If, for example, Jesus is to be understood as a Jewish rabbi who simply taught that everyone should love God and be good to one another, why did the Romans crucify him?"[9]

Ehrman adds that for most theories, their proposed connections between Jesus' life and his death are at times rather shaky and unconvincing. He's right, but ironically, his own theory also suffers from the same problem, since being an apocalyptic prophet wasn't illegal either! To make his theoretical Jesus work, Ehrman still has to "tack on" additional assumptions, which could just as easily be tacked on to any of the other proposed Jesuses.[10]

E.P. Sanders, who has written several books on Jesus, including *Jesus and Judaism* (1985), acknowledges that one of the embarrassing unsolved questions in the quest for the historical Jesus is that no one has been able to say why Jesus' 'teachings' would have compelled the Romans to execute him in the first place.[11] And what's worse, noted Judaism scholars Geza Vermes, Haim Cohn, and others have pointed out that on top of all the other many historical and legal difficulties with Jesus' trial, nothing he is accused of amounts to blasphemy in the first place![12]

But to be fair, the problem may go deeper than just poor reconstructions. After all, the original source for all of them,

Jesus: Mything in Action

the Gospels, *also* fail to make a credible link between Jesus' life and death — and disagree with each other on just what led to Jesus' death. In Mark (3:6) the Pharisees began plotting to kill Jesus at the beginning of his career, after he heals a man's withered hand in the synagogue (though oddly enough, it will take 11 more chapters to get Jesus arrested, and when that happens, the Pharisees don't have anything to do with it). According to Luke (19:47-48) it's because he cast out the moneychangers from the Temple in the final week of his life. In Matthew (26:3-4) the Jewish priests and scribes meet at the high priest's palace some time after that and plot his death. But for John, Jesus' Temple-cleansing incident has nothing to do with his death: in his story, that happened at the *beginning* of Jesus' career, at least three years earlier. Instead, John's Jesus brings the wrath of the Sanhedrin on his head because he electrifies the whole country by raising Lazarus from the dead (11:43-53), even though Lazarus doesn't even *appear* in the other gospels (unless you count a fictional character from a parable in Luke).

Incidentally, all the hypothetical Christs in our list above are some of the more-or-less reasonably plausible reconstructions. As you descend further, you'll find there some truly absurd, hopelessly crackpot "real" Jesus theories moldering away at the bottom of the barrel. Venerable religious traditions have Jesus spending his youth as a yogi in India and then escaping the cross to live a long life before his death and burial in Srinagar, Afghanistan (as the Ahmadiyya Muslims believe) or appearing in the New World for three days to name twelve new disciples to organize his church among the ancient Israelites in America, as the Book of Mormon tells us (3 Nephi 11-26).

Slightly less venerable traditions hold that Jesus just managed to survive the crucifixion and was nursed back to health by his disciples;[13] or that he fled across Siberia to Japan where he lived to the age of 106 and was buried in Shingō;[14] or that he became pen pals with King Abgar of Edessa;[15] or that his name appears in micro-inscriptions on ancient coins and monuments;[16] or that his entire ministry was staged, including faking all his miracles, his death, and resurrection, all in an unsuccessful effort to set himself up as the King of the Jews;[17] or that Jesus simply suffered from some form of mental health issue such as multiple personality disorder or schizophrenia;[18] or that the Merovingian dynasty of France descended from a royal bloodline tracing back to Jesus and Mary Magdalene.[19]

An Embarrassment of Possibilities
But let's forgo the imaginative for the plausible and return to focus on the more viable historical Jesus theories that have been confidently proposed by respected scholars and accepted by the mainstream. If we restrict ourselves to just those, we still have a surprising number of options. All of them are plausible – but are any of them true? This multiplicity of convincing possibilities *is precisely the problem*: the various scholarly reconstructions of Jesus cancel each other out. Each sounds good until you hear the next one. Price makes this perfectly clear:

> What one Jesus reconstruction leaves aside, the next one takes up and makes its cornerstone. Jesus simply wears too many hats in the Gospels – exorcist, healer, king, prophet, sage, rabbi, demigod, and so on. The Jesus Christ of the New Testament is a composite figure…the historical Jesus (if there was one) might well have been a messianic king, or a progressive Pharisee, or a Galilean shaman, or a magus, or a Hellenistic sage. But he cannot very well have been all of them at the same time.[20]

Many others, including Richard Carrier, Burton Mack, and Jesus Seminar members like Robert Funk and John Dominic Crossan have commented on this exact problem. Crossan has frankly complained that the plethora of historical Jesus reconstructions has turned into a circus. In his *The Historical Jesus: The Life of a Mediterranean Jewish Peasant* (1993), he puts it bluntly:

> But that stunning diversity is an academic embarrassment. It is impossible to avoid the suspicion that historical Jesus research is a very safe place to do theology and call it history, to do autobiography and call it biography.

What's more, despite this overabundance of hypothetical Jesus models, Burton Mack has pointed out yet another problem: no single one of them can account for all of the wildly divergent movements, theologies, ideologies, christologies and mythic figures of Jesus that dot the early Christian landscape.[21] As Thomas Thompson and Thomas Verenna put it in their revealing 2012 book, *Is This Not the Carpenter?* "Jesus is as fluid a figure as is our understanding of early Christianity."[22]

Could Jesus have been a Stealth Messiah?
It's not uncommon to hear our fellow atheists postulate that perhaps the real Jesus was none of these things, but probably just one more itinerant Jewish preacher wandering the Galilee, and that everything else we think we know about him were just later add-ons. Is it realistic to imagine that there could still have been a real Jesus who lies buried underneath centuries of legendary accretion? It's certainly *possible*. Is it plausible? Maybe. Do I think that's what happened? Based on the evidence of the first hundred years of Christianity, not a chance. In the final chapter of *Nailed* ("Can Jesus be Saved?") I observe that:

> There comes a point when it no longer makes sense to give Jesus the benefit of a doubt. Even if we make allowances for legendary accretion, pious fraud, the

criterion of embarrassment, doctrinal disputes, scribal errors and faults in translation, there are simply too many irresolvable problems with the default position that assumes there simply had to be a historical individual (or even a composite of several itinerant preachers) at the center of Christianity.

I go on to illustrate how differently the New Testament and early Christianity would look if even a merely human Jesus had been an actual historical figure. One problem I find with the suggestion that Jesus was a fairly unknown figure in reality has to do with the *other* messianic figures we know about in this period. There was certainly no shortage of saviors then. We know of a surprising number of wanna-be Judaean messiahs from around the time of the early first century. Here are some of them:

John the Baptist — John appears in all four gospels and defers to Jesus, although, interestingly, none of the gospels can agree on if they were perfect strangers, first cousins, rivals, partners, or if they even lived in the same time. While we shouldn't be surprised if John the Baptist turned out to be another mythical religious founder figure, we do have a modest amount of later extra-biblical evidence for John. Josephus mentions John the Baptist briefly (*Antiquities*, 18.*v*.2), and his sect shows up in a second-century apocryphal acts novel, the *Clementine Recognitions* (1.53,60) where they debate their rivals, the Christians; arguing that John the Baptist, not Jesus, was the messiah.[23] (See ch. 20 for more details on John and the Baptist sect).

Apollonius of Tyana — The 3rd-century sophist Philostratus the Elder wrote a biography of this Neopythagorean philosopher and alleged miracle worker with a surprising amount in common with our Jesus, with whom he was often compared in ancient times[24] – though many now question

Jesus: Mything in Action

whether Philostratus' earlier biographical sources, or their subject, ever really existed at all.

"The Egyptian" — In Acts, 'Luke' name-drops three failed messiahs lifted from Josephus. Incidentally, Luke's mistakes in describing these figures are one of the reasons we know he was stealing from Josephus, and not vice-versa.[25] One of these, referred to in Acts 21:37–38, was known only as 'The Egyptian' (possibly as a nod to Moses or Joshua, rather than his actual nationality) and led his followers up to the Mount of Olives so they could watch him command the walls of Jerusalem to fall down (*Antiquities* 20.*viii*.6). For some reason, this otherwise foolproof plan failed. The Romans slaughtered his flock, and he fled.

Judas of Galilee and **Theudas the Magician** — Luke has the famous rabbi Gamaliel mention the failed uprisings of both these messianic pretenders in a speech shortly after Jesus' death (Acts 5:34–37). Unfortunately for Luke, Theudas' uprising wasn't until over a decade *after* this, under the reign of Fadus, procurator from 44 to 46 (see *Antiquities* 20.*v*.1–2). Compounding the anachronistic error, Luke also blunders by reversing the correct order and saying Judas came after Theudas, when in fact Judas came first, predating Theudas by decades! (cf. *Jewish War* 2.*viii*.1; *Antiquities* 18.*i*.1)

Athronges the Shepherd and **Simon of Peraea** — Judas of Galilee's uprising was one of several after Herod the Great's death. Two other failed usurpers mentioned by Josephus were Athronges the Shepherd (*Jewish War* 2.*iv*.3; *Antiquities* 17.278–284) and a slave of Herod's, Simon of Peraea (*Jewish War* 2.57-59; *Antiquities* 17.*x*.7), who was also mentioned by Tacitus (*Histories* 5.9.2).

"An Impostor" (**The *Sicarii* messiah**) — Another unnamed messiah, this time the leader of a gang of *sicarii* (named after their *sicae* daggers) bandits. He promised to deliver his followers to freedom if they would follow him into the wilderness; but only succeeded in getting them and himself slaughtered by troops sent after them by the Roman governor Festus (*Antiquities* 20.*viii*.10).

"The *Taheb*" — An unnamed Samaritan styling himself as the Samaritan messiah the *Taheb* ('the Restorer') led his armed followers to their sacred Mount Gerizim, where he showed them sacred vessels buried there by Moses — or at least, he *would* have, if Pilate and his forces hadn't gotten there first, killing many of them in battle, scattering the rest, and executing the leaders, including the *Taheb* (*Antiquities* 18.*iv*.1–2).

Jonathan the Weaver — yet another Moses-like messiah who convinced a throng to follow him into the wilderness with promises of "signs and apparitions," only to have the Romans come and kill most of them. Jonathan himself was taken into custody and finally burned alive (*Jewish War* 7.*xi*.1–3).

Carabas — Philo of Alexandria relates (*Flaccus* 6.34–40) that in the year 38, an anti-Semitic Alexandrian crowd welcomed newly-minted king Herod Agrippa I by staging an improv coronation starring Carabas, a local madman and vagrant forced to become a mock-king by a street mob in ways that eerily parallel Christ's mockery by the Roman soldiers (and in Luke, also by Herod Antipas's war council) in the Gospels (see Ch. 10 for details).

Yeshua ben Hananiah/Jesus ben-Ananias — In book 6 of *The Jewish War* (6.*v*.3), Josephus mentions another madman, this one from Jerusalem, who also shares some nearly two dozen striking similarities to our familiar Jesus; so much so that like Carabas, his story may well have been an inspiration to Gospel writers. This "very ordinary yokel" one day becomes a doomsday prophet and eventually the Jewish authorities haul him before the Roman procurator, where he is "scourged till his flesh hung in ribbons" before being released. Josephus explicitly notes repeatedly he says nothing in his own defense (see ch. 10 for details).

Simon bar-Giora — Yet another messianic figure with interesting similarities to Jesus, revolutionary Simon was welcomed with leafy branches into Jerusalem as a deliverer and protector from another wanna-be messiah, the Zealot **John of Gischala**, whose faction had occupied the sacred precinct. After this triumphant entry he commenced the cleansing of the temple, "sweep(ing) the zealots out of the city." But Simon ultimately surrendered to the Romans, was tortured, and finally executed as a would-be king of the Jews (*Jewish War*, books IV, V, & VII).

Simon Magus — A Samaritan sorcerer called Simon the Magician, or Simon of Gitta, shows up often as a bad guy in early Christian writings. In Acts (8:9-24) he bewitches all of Samaria into deifying him, until he sees all the amazing true miracles of the apostles and converts to Christianity. But he shows his true colors after being baptized, when he tries to bribe Peter into laying hands on him so he can get the power of the Holy Ghost, too.

Naturally, Christians would never stand for ministers using their God-given abilities just to get rich, so instead all Simon gets is a stern rebuke and the sin of simony named after him. Simon goes on to make more trouble. Church fathers often accuse him of being the father of all heresies. According to several early Christian legends, he finally gets his come-uppance when doing magic in the Forum of Rome. Using his sorcery (or possibly a chariot pulled by demons, depending on who's telling the story) he flies through the air, amazing onlookers until Peter prays him down, at which point he promptly crashes to the ground and dies.

There is some doubt about the historicity of Simon the flying sorcerer, but we know from Christian commentators like Epiphanius, Hippolytus, Irenaeus and Justin Martyr that a messianic cult of Simon Magus certainly thrived in Syria, Rome and various districts of Asia Minor during the second century; not finally dwindling away until the 4th century.[26]

If Jesus' fame was anywhere near the levels depicted in the Gospels — multitudes following him, fame spreading throughout Judea, to Syria, Egypt, the ten cities of the Decapolis league, *etc.* — his achievements were easily on par with even the best of these. But every one of these was able to accomplish something Jesus couldn't. How did loser messianic figures like 'the *Taheb*' and Jonathan the Weaver and the rest manage to leave a historical footprint — but not Jesus? How could everyone outside his own cult fail to notice him, or even his new religion, for nearly a century? Conversely, if Jesus was so forgettable he wasn't even as interesting as any of these (and still others), then how could he inspire a fringe religion of tiny feuding house churches to pop up all across the far-flung corners of the Roman empire?[27]

Other Gospels, Other Jesuses, Other Christs
And there's still another consideration — what about all the *other* Christs of the first and second century that we find in the Gospels, Paul's letters and other early Christian writings? As I mention in *Nailed* (pp. 151–52):

> Paul himself complains about the diversity among early believers, who incredibly treat Christ as just one more factional totem figure, some saying they belong to Paul, or Apollos, or Cephas – or to Christ. Paul asks, "Has Christ been divided?" (1 Cor. 1:10-13). Paul also repeatedly rails against his many rival apostles, who "preach another Jesus."

> In his letters Paul often rages and fumes that his rivals are evil deceivers, with false Christs and false gospels so different from his own true Christ and true Gospel, that he accuses them of being agents of Satan and even lays curses and threats upon them! (2 Cor. 11:4, 13–15,19–20, 22–23; Gal. 1:6-9; 2:4)
>
> Other early Christians were just as concerned as Paul. The *Didakhê*, an early manual of Christian church practice and teachings, spends two chapters talking about wandering preachers and warning against the many false preachers who are mere "traffickers in Christs," or "Christmongers" (*Didakhê* 12:5).[28]

The evidence is clear; there were many different Jesuses and Christs being preached by different groups in the first century (and even into the early second century, when the *Didakhê* was likely written). No single individual Jesus made an impact on history, but many different ones made an impact on theology – at least on the cultic fringe. The 'Stealth Messiah' approach to the problem simply fails to make any sense of the evidence. For me, this central, inescapable paradox was one of the first clues that there was something very wrong with the traditional picture of Jesus. Consider: Either Jesus taught or did a host of amazing, revolutionary things – and no one outside his fringe sect noticed for generations... *or*... he didn't... and yet still managed to inspire a network of tiny communities to arise all over the ancient Mediterranean – although they couldn't agree about even the basics of his life, his ministry, who he was, who his followers were, or what he taught.

Ignorance is Blest

Two thousand years later, we appear to have no better grasp of who or what Jesus was than they did. And increasingly, biblical scholars are coming to the realization that the field of Jesus Studies has failed to verify any single fact of Jesus' life. "The quest for the historical Jesus is an abject failure," concluded Hector Avalos in *The End of Biblical Studies*,[29] in which he further argues that, as a biblical scholar, he can no longer pretend that biblical studies holds any relevance for anyone. Morna Hooker, after decades of harshly criticizing the failed methodology of Jesus historians, openly questions whether the time has come to abandon the whole enterprise of trying to discover the 'real historical Jesus.'[30] Yet academics continue to defend dozens of completely contradictory historical Jesus theories, all accepted as plausible.

Historicists like Hooker and mythicists like Carrier (and many others on both sides of the historicity debate) agree that the state of biblical studies, and in particular Jesus studies, should be a scandal. Hooker thinks we may find that we may be able to know "quite a lot" about Jesus, but we may not reconstruct anything he said or did with certainty. The simple fact that our gospels are in Greek, when Jesus would have spoken Aramaic, means our record is already at least one remove from reality. She asks for:

> "the recognition that all our results are only tentative. We know too little to be dogmatic... All the material comes to us at the hands of the believing community, and probably it all bears its mark to a lesser or greater extent..."[31]

Carrier goes even further, and cautions that even if you believe there was a real Jesus, you should not be quick to assume that his historicity has been well established:

> "Historicists have a lot of work to do before they can claim to have their house in order. Their sins are many. They have far too quickly assumed that various fundamental conclusions in the field are settled, which in fact are not, such as the dating of New Testament documents... They have routinely over-stated what the evidence can actually prove, conflating conjectures with

demonstrable facts almost as often as mythicists do, and they lack anything like a coherent methodology."[32]

"A superbly qualified scholar will insist some piece of evidence exists, or does not exist, and I am surprised that I have to show them the contrary. And always this phantom evidence (or an assurance of its absence) is in defense of the historicity of Jesus. This should teach us how important it is to stop repeating the phrase 'the overwhelming consensus says…' Because that consensus is based on false beliefs and assumptions, a lot of them inherited unknowingly from past Christian faith assumptions in reading or discussing the evidence, which even secular scholars failed to check before simply repeating them as certainly the truth."[33]

Current Jesus scholarship has a dirty little secret; actually a rather large dirty secret. After centuries of scholarly pursuit, we are left with a field of academia in riotous disarray, with a glorious mess of hypothetical reconstructions of a savior-figure who is uncorroborated by any contemporary sources outside his fringe religious movement, and yet somehow simultaneously has rival doppelgangers and competing gospels; whose miraculous deeds are overshadowed by much less interesting would-be messiahs, all of whom nevertheless still manage to beat him in one regard by leaving a footprint in the historical record.

It's a bizarre and underreported situation. Contrary to virtually every other field of science or history, the more we study Jesus, the less we know about him. Carrier again:

"…the concept of Jesus we're supposed to believe existed is actually getting more confused and uncertain the more scholars study it, rather than the other way around. Progress is supposed to increase knowledge and consensus and sharpen the picture of what happened (or what we don't know), not the reverse. Instead, Jesus scholars continue multiplying contradictory pictures of Jesus, rather than narrowing them down and increasing their clarity – or at least reaching a consensus on the scale and scope of our uncertainty and ignorance."[34]

After three grand quests in search of the Historical Jesus and whole libraries filled with theories and interpretations, just what concrete facts can be established about Jesus – or do we have any?

***

For further reading:

Richard Carrier, "Why We Might Have Reason for Doubt: Should We Still Be Looking for a Historical Jesus?" *The Bible and Interpretation*, available online at: http://www.bibleinterp.com/articles/2014/08/car388028.shtml

For still more lists of views of the historic Jesus:

Of Men and Muses: Essays on History, Literature and Religion, by Thomas Verenna (esp. pp. 46-47, where there is an even longer list, with references)
Is This Not the Carpenter? ed. by Thomas Thompson & Thomas Verenna

---

[1] See *Nailed*, esp. ch. 2 & 5, for a sampling of some of the most noteworthy.
[2] Price, DJ, pp. 13-15
[3] See "The Forgery of an Ancient Discovery? Morton Smith and the Secret Gospel of Mark," in Bart Ehrman's *Lost Christianities*, pp. 67-89
[4] Koester, Intro. NT, p.78

⁵ This is reported by ancient writers such as Celsus, *De Medicina* V, 28, 18B; Galen, *On the Natural Faculties*, III, VII, 163; and Pliny, *Nat. Hist.* 28. 7. See also 28. 4, 22. Rabbinical sources also vouch for the use of spittle for healing purposes (BB 126b; Shab. 14.14d; 18; Sotah. 16d,37).

⁶ James H. Charlesworth and Petr Pokorny, editors, *Jesus Research: An International Perspective*, p.1

⁷ ("The Historical Jesus and the Historical Situation of the Quest: An Epilogue," in Chilton and Evans, *Studying the Historical Jesus*, p. 544)

⁸ Price, *Deconstructing Jesus*, p.15

⁹ Ehrman, *Jesus: Apocalyptic Prophet of the New Millennium*, p. 208

¹⁰ For details of Ehrman's reconstructed Jesus, see http://ehrmanblog.org/why-was-jesus-killed-for-members/

¹¹ Cited in Mack, *The Christ Myth*, pp. 32-33

¹² See Geza Vermes *The Passion*, pp. 100-102; for Cohn, see "Blasphemy? What Blasphemy?" in chapter nine.

¹³ Many have proposed variations on this hypothesis over the last 200+ years; more recently, Robert Graves and Joshua Podro in *Jesus in Rome* (1957), and Hugh J. Schonfield in *The Passover Plot* (1965).

¹⁴ Bird, Winifred, "Behold! Christ's grave in Shingo, Aomori Prefecture," *Japan Times*, 25 December 2011, p. 10

¹⁵ Eusebius records this legend in *Ecclesiastic History* I.12, which was widely believed throughout the Middle Ages.

¹⁶ See the very entertaining "Pseudohistory in Jerry Vardaman's Magic Coins: The Nonsense of Micrographic Letters" in Carrier, *Hitler Homer Bible Christ*, pp. 155ff.

¹⁷ Starting at least as far back as the late seventeenth/early eighteenth century German Rationalists; such as Karl Friedrich Bahrdt in *Ausführung des Plans und Zwecks Jesu (Execution of the Plan and Purpose of Jesus)* c.1784-92. It's worth noting that even in ancient times there were

critics like Porphyry and Celsus making similar accusations.
[18] Ted Jeory, "Jesus Christ 'may have suffered from mental health problems', claims Church of England," (express.co.uk) available online at: http://www.express.co.uk/news/uk/341926/Jesus-Christ-may-have-suffered-from-mental-health-problems-claims-Church-of-England
[19] The most infamous recent reheat of this hoary old chestnut was in the 1982 book *Holy Blood, Holy Grail* which in turn inspired Dan Brown's 2003 bestseller *The Da Vinci Code.*
[20] Price, *Deconstructing Jesus*, pp. 15–16
[21] Mack, op.cit., p. 35
[22] Thompson and Verenna p. 10
[23] See ch. 20 for more details on John and the Baptist sect.
[24] Price, *The Christ Myth and its Problems*, p. 20
[25] See Carrier, "Luke and Josephus" (2000) the Secular Web library, available online at: http://infidels.org/library/modern/richard_carrier/lukeandjosephus.html
[26] See Stephen Haar, *Simon Magus: The First Gnostic?* New York: Walter de Gruyter, 2003, pp. 11-15 (for a critique of *this* Simon's historicity: Gerd Lüdemann, *Untersuchungen zur simonianischen Gnosis* (*Studies on Simonian Gnosis*), Göttingen: Vandenhoeck und Ruprecht, 1975).
[27] Incidentally, we could consider the possibility that all these also-ran messiahs are mythical too – perhaps they are all just copies of the Joshua story. But if so, a story-cluster like this can have only two origins: oral lore picked up by Josephus, or Josephus himself (or some other source he's using, such as Justus of Tiberias, or some lost Jewish apocryphon). If they are just the result of first-century urban legend, all these tales and rumors of Judaean saviors still confirm that the zeitgeist was rife with messianic

fever.

The other possibility stretches credibility: that a single Jewish author invented this messianic fever, coincidently enough, precisely when messianic cults like Christianity and the Qumran community arose – and yet the author doesn't mention either of them... See Carrier, *On the Historicity of Jesus,* pp. 70, n25 for more discussion.

[28] Bart D. Ehrman (ed. & trans.). *The Apostolic Fathers,* Volume I, Loeb Classical Library, Cambridge, Mass.: Harvard University Press, 2003:437

[29] Avalos, p. 212

[30] Keith and Le Donne, *Jesus, Criteria & the Demise of Authenticity,* p. xiv

[31] Cited in ibid., p. xv, ixx

[32] Carrier, *On the Historicity of Jesus,* p. 12

[33] Carrier, "Why We Might Have Reason for Doubt: Should We Still Be Looking for a Historical Jesus?" *The Bible and Interpretation,* available online at: http://www.bibleinterp.com/articles/2014/08/car388028.shtml

[34] Carrier, *Proving History,* p. 12

Chapter Four:
The Hole Truth and Nothing But

"...the previous reconstructions of who Jesus was, what he said, and what he did are coming unraveled in the light of new information, new methodologies, and new perspectives."

Are you ready for a switch? Time to turn our investigation inside out. Let's forget this book is arguing that there was no Jesus and approach the question from the other direction. Just for argument's sake, let's say we presume there *was* a real Jesus of Nazareth, if not a divine Jesus Christ, and look for what we can discover about *that* guy (Incidentally, this approach is exactly how I became a mythicist). How much of our biographical data for Jesus is original, and how much is legendary accretion that was piled on later? And how much of any of it, original or not, is verifiable? What facts, if any, can we know for sure about that man?

Question Marks
Over the last 350-plus years, Jesus historians around the globe have been searching for an answer to that question. We can trace back the modern search to as early as Baruch Spinoza in the 17th century, although there were other pre-modern attempts as well[1]. Nevertheless, most in the field have typically identified three major "Quests" in the search for the "real" Jesus.[2] And few historians deny all three have failed.

The first quest began in the 1770s with figures like Reimarus and Lessing; and ended in 1906 – according to Albert Schweitzer's *The Quest of the Historical Jesus*, which both coined the phrase and recognized that the "Quest" had come to a screeching halt. His criticisms of the Quest's epic failure largely put a wet blanket on efforts to craft a biography for the historical Jesus for nearly half a century; the so-called (not entirely accurately) "No Quest" period.

Then in 1953, Ernst Käsemann rekindled hope among German bible historians by suggesting that with the right tools, like the "criterion of embarrassment" or the "criterion of double dissimilarity" to identify the authentic sayings of Jesus[3], historians might just be able to cut through the layers of legendary accretion and reach the real Jesus at last. But by the 1970s, this "New Quest had also stalled out.

In 1988[4] N. T. Wright coined the term "Third Quest" to refer to new approaches to the historicity question, such as recognizing Jesus was Jewish (The "New Quest," driven by a generation of German Christian scholars, is still haunted by charges of academic anti-Semitism). In fact, with each new "Quest," the field has dramatically changed course and pursued the ever-elusive Jesus of history in a new direction, dropping the tools they were using in favor of new historical methods and criteria.

Beyond the Third Quest

We should keep in mind that the entire "Quest" paradigm itself has strong detractors[5], and at best, it is a simplification: like every aspect of early Christianity we've managed to uncover, the real story becomes even more tangled and confused the deeper we dig. If we accept the "Quest" paradigm, we're technically still in the "Third Quest." Which direction is the current quest taking us now?

Neil Godfrey observes that the "Third Questers" are, once again, working under assumptions and methods that are diametrically opposed to those of the previous quest.[6] Today the default consensus for the majority of biblical historians is to presume that the Gospel stories reflect a real (if obscured) historical figure at their core, and then pick away at the elements of the story that they don't think reflect the real facts. How do they decide which ones don't? Primarily it is by gauging them by employing a "criterion of plausibility" – that is, does the event, saying or situation in question fit with what we know about the context of first-century Judea?

As William Arnal notes in *The Symbolic Jesus: Historical Scholarship, Judaism and the Construction of Contemporary Identity*:

> "Plausibility thus serves as both a mechanism for determining historical authenticity and as a hermeneutical device. No serious scholars of ancient Christianity accept the historicity of everything in the canonical gospels. But it appears that "third quest" scholars most often assume that, barring clear evidence to the contrary, the material in the gospels does reflect actual historical events. **In other words, the burden of proof rests with those *denying* the authenticity of the material**; exactly the opposite approach is normally taken by scholars operating within the "second quest" paradigm, where the burden of proof is on those who assert authenticity."[7]

It's worth underscoring Arnal's comment that no serious scholars of ancient Christianity accept the historicity of *everything* in the canonical gospels. Those that do are theologians, not historians. Although, given that the Gospels each provide disparate details even on many of the most fundamental facts of their subject, it's not even *possible* for anyone to accept everything in all four gospels at face value and not contradict themselves.

But Godfrey and Arnal both expose a troubling point here: today's "Third Questers" have switched the burden of proof in a peculiar and unprecedented way. It seems that where Jesus is concerned, suddenly *the normal rules of evidence no longer apply*. It's bizarre to see the majority of a whole academic field forget that innocent until proven guilty only applies to people, not theories. Anything else is just special pleading.

David Fitzgerald

Game of Knowns
That's not the only problem. All too often, what passes for our "facts" about Jesus are just a function of our emerging knowledge of first-century Palestinian Judaism and everyday Judaean life. Historians deduce what Jesus, as a Jewish male in Palestine, "certainly would've" or "may have" or "most likely would have" done, how he would have lived, which places he would have been to in Jerusalem, or even psychological guesswork on what he would have thought.

Incredibly, this dodgy game is played even in standard reference works, as Richard Carrier has noted. Look up "Historical Jesus" in the *Dictionary of Biblical Criticism and Interpretation* (Routledge, 2007), and you will find expert Bruce Chilton weaving an elaborate and entirely new biography for Jesus, complete with in depth reports of his emotional and mental states. How does he pull off such a miraculous feat?

First, he unquestioningly accepts uncorroborated (and contradictory) gospel claims, and then proceeds from there to augment his official bio/psychological profile with a raft of gratuitous what-must-have-been assumptions dressed up as known facts. This alchemical process produces truly unique speculations, all declared to be perfectly factual, including:

- Jesus was "marginalized" in Nazareth during his youth because he was an illegitimate child.
- On childhood trips to Jerusalem Jesus emotionally experienced "an excited sense of the vastness of the Israel he was a part of."
- Jesus "ran away from his family" in a fit of religious passion.
- After becoming a "disciple" of John the Baptist, "he learned this master's *kabbalah*, the mystical practice of ascent to the divine Throne" which became "a guiding

force for the rest of his life."
- Jesus fled to Syria to avoid the clutches of Herod Antipas.
- Jesus seized the temple with a private army ("with a large crowd and in force")
- Jesus experienced a temptation "in the wilderness" near "Caesarea Philippi" at the end of his ministry in which he was tempted to raise an armed rebellion against Rome.

This last "fact" is particularly strange, as Carrier notes Chilton seems to be confusing two different gospel events. The Temptation does take place in the wilderness, but presumably near the Jordan, and at the very beginning of his ministry. It is the Transfiguration that takes place near Caesarea Philippi at the very end of Jesus' ministry but this involved no temptation – and neither episode makes any mention of raising armed rebellion against Rome.

Chilton insists "a historical picture of Jesus...involves the literary inference of what he must have taught and done to have generated that movement and its literature." But the "literary inference" he draws is not history. It's historical fiction. As Carrier says, "that this is an official entry on the topic of 'the historical Jesus' is a good example of what's wrong with Jesus studies today."[8] He adds

> "Indeed, the diversity and disagreement among *bona fide* experts on every detail of Chilton's 'reconstruction' of Jesus is broad and profound. *That* is what an entry on the "historical Jesus" should say. It's shocking to see the same arrogant presumption, and substitution of speculation for fact, among historicists as historicists claim to find in Mythicists... His entry should never have passed peer review —at least without requiring an explicit declaration that it's all tendentious speculation with which almost all scholars would substantially disagree."[9]

For what it's worth, we could play Chilton's same game with hobbits: "Since Frodo was an adult male hobbit living in the Shire in the late post-Númenórean Third Age, we can be quite certain he had furry feet, enjoyed the occasional pipeweed and lived in a cozy hobbit hole, not a nasty, dirty, wet one or a dry, bare, sandy one." This inferential process of reverse-engineering biographical data for Jesus from what we know about the social situation in Judea and the Galilee fails; not just because it begs the question in the first place, but because it also boomerangs on defenders of historicity: since the more we continue to learn about the cultural context, the less the gospels look historical at all...

Just the Facts
If they agree on nothing else, the majority of biblical scholars still put great trust in the notion that there are, at the very least, a few solid particulars we can safely pin down about the first century Christian founder. Increasingly however, other historians are calling this confidence an "assumption." What are these core facts about Jesus everyone supposedly agrees on? As an old Irish joke goes: "If you know the first thing about Irish politics... you're mistaken." One could argue the same could be said for our man from Galilee. Nonetheless, here are the most commonly heard "indisputable facts" of the life of the historical Jesus of Nazareth:[10]

E. P. Sanders, author of *The Historical Figure of Jesus* (1993) suggests this list:[11]
1. Jesus was baptized by John the Baptist.
2. Jesus was a Galilean who preached and healed.
3. Jesus called disciples and spoke of there being twelve.
4. Jesus confined his activity to Israel.
5. Jesus engaged in a controversy about the temple.
6. Jesus was crucified outside Jerusalem by the Roman authorities.

7. After his death Jesus' followers continued as an identifiable movement.
8. At least some Jews persecuted at least parts of the new movement (Gal. 1.13, 22; Phil. 3.6), and it appears that this persecution endured at least to a time near the end of Paul's career (II Cor. 11.24; Gal. 5.11; 6.12; cf. Matt. 23.34; 10.17).

To Sanders' list, Stanley Porter, author of The Criteria for Authenticity in Historical-Jesus Research: Previous Discussion and New Proposals (2000); adds four more:

9. Jesus was probably viewed as a prophet by the populace.
10. He often spoke of the kingdom of God.
11. He criticized the ruling priests as part of his Temple controversy.
12. He was crucified as 'king of the Jews' by the Romans.

There have been other lists,[12] but as Godfrey and Arnal point out, and as you probably already recognize, this list of "indisputable facts" is really nothing more than a recap of the basic plotline of the gospels.[13] And it's difficult to take the list too seriously as either "indisputable" or as "facts," since as Richard Carrier notes: a) many scholars already conclude that some of these *aren't* true facts; and b) apart from (7) and (8), (which could be true even of a mythical Jesus) none of these assertions are supported by anything whatsoever except the gospels themselves or later Christian literature based on them.[14] And even the New Testament itself lacks support. It's not unreasonable to expect many, if not all, of these "facts" should have been at least corroborated in the Epistles (at least the authentic ones); and yet bizarrely enough, they are entirely absent there.[15] Even the simple fact that Jesus *had* disciples escapes Paul (who never once even uses the term "disciple") as well as all the other New Testament writers.

In *Proving History*,[16] Carrier not only demonstrated several of these "indisputable" facts were quite doubtful indeed, but after analysis showed how the usual scholarly arguments used in defense of all of them were logically invalid (see below). In fact, of the entire list, we only have any credible evidence (both directly from the Epistles, and from the history of early Christianity in general) for points (7) and (8) – and yet neither are really about Jesus at all, and both support an entirely mythical Jesus just as well as a historical earthly one.[17]

With some work, we might be able to salvage points (6) and (10) – but only by watering them down considerably to the much less ambitious "he was crucified; most likely in Roman occupied Judea" and "he preached something controversial." Both might be loosely inferred from statements made in the Epistles, but even that would be a stretch, given the ambiguity of what they actually say,[18] as we'll see when we talk about our sources and Paul's Jesus.

Critiquing the Criteria
All these alleged facts about Jesus rest upon so-called "authenticity criteria;" a dizzying number of these have been floated in the field of Jesus studies over the years; many dozens, in fact. But for the better part of a century, there have been scholars who have called all of them into question. T. W. Manson was one of the first, over eighty years ago, joined in the 1970s by Robin Barbour and Morna Hooker, and today by Dale C. Allison Jr., Richard Carrier, Tom Holmén, Chris Keith, Anthony Le Donne, Scot McKnight, Stanley E. Porter, Rafael Rodriguez, Jack T. Sanders, Jens Schröter, Mark Strauss, Loren Stuckenbruck, Alexander J. M. Wedderburn, and others – in fact, everyone who has examined the issue[19] – all of whom have harsh criticism of the failures of these traditional methods and called for at the very least a radical overhaul, if not the end

of their use as historical tools. As Le Donne explains in *Jesus, Criteria and the Demise of Authenticity:*

> " ...almost all contemporary Jesus historians who employ the traditional authenticity criteria do so with repeated reservations and qualifications. One can hardly blame historians for establishing rules for the road or aiming towards historiographical rigor. But as the reservations about these traditional criteria become greater and as the qualifications offered by their adherents become more pronounced, it must be asked whether these traditional methods are poorly founded or perhaps should be abandoned altogether... (The authors) think it is time to rethink the traditional quest for authenticity from the ground up."

Le Donne notes the differing views on whether the criteria can be salvaged, or if it is just the conventional use that needs to be replaced with a more sophisticated historiography, or if indeed the entire criteria approach is bankrupt, and that we should not rest until, as Stanley Porter said, until "the enterprise is finally abandoned."[20] But regardless of what view they hold on whether a possible solution can be found, all acknowledge the problem at hand; and moreover, all of the contributors argue that one or more of the traditional authenticity criteria are beyond repair and should be abandoned. Their final verdict?

> "In short, we collectively argue that the crumbling foundations of historical Jesus research must be exposed and that this exposure should lead to a programmatic shift in our historiographic methods."[21]

Criteria Crunch
Carrier has distilled the dozens of proposed Jesus authenticity criteria into a short list. After putting them all through the

crucible of logic and Bayesian analysis, none withstand the scrutiny. For complete details of how each fails the reality check, see Chapter 5 of *Proving History*, but in the meantime, here is a quick thumbnail sketch of each, along with their fatal flaw(s):

Dissimilarity: (also called the criterion of discontinuity or of double dissimilarity) if an element in the gospels seems out of place to Judaism or the early church, it's probably true. *Problem:* However, we don't know a lot about the details of first century Judaism or early Christianity, and to make matters worse, we do know that both were wildly diverse during this period. So how can we know what's normal? Besides, just because someone attributed something unusual to Jesus doesn't mean he said or did it. And the very fact that an element was preserved argues against it being 'dissimilar' to the early church in the first place! (Critics generally agree that this is one of the most useless of all criteria, and yet it underlies so many of the others – not a good sign...)

Embarrassment: If it is too embarrassing to have been made up, it must be true. This is another criterion that many atheists have found convincing, but... *Problem:* Plenty; see more below.

Coherence: if it's coherent with what we have already established with other criteria, it's likely true. *Problem:* One of the more glaring problems with this one is that it's circular, but another is that material can be fabricated precisely *because* it conforms to other beliefs about Jesus, or even for the specific purpose of conforming to them! Besides, pure fiction can be just as "coherent" as pure fact. Liars tend to prefer their lies to be coherent, but even more innocent legendary development follows the same principle – even today, many apologists defend gospel stories we know are later forgeries (such as the story of the Woman caught in Adultery) by insisting that it still sounds like something Jesus *might* have said! Carrier points out the greatest folly in applying this criterion: "cohering" with a "fact" established by an invalid (or invalidly applied) criterion cannot legitimate another fact. Worse, most of our "historical Jesuses" are constructed from exactly this sort of house of cards, making the Criterion of Coherence the most insidious of them all...[22]

Multiple Attestations: if it shows up in more than one source, it's more likely true. *Problem:* This is a sound principle of the field – that is, if it shows up in more than one *independent* source, it's more likely to be true. But in the case of Jesus studies, there are few elements that are vouched for in more than one strand of tradition, and even in those few cases, establishing independence is hard to do. It's long been accepted that the first three gospels are dependent on Mark, but a growing body of evidence (see PH, p. 320) argues that even John's maverick gospel is based on Mark. What's more, there is a huge body of early Christian scriptures that didn't make the cut into our Bible (other gospels, infancy gospels of young Jesus, other acts, epistles, etc.). These are universally rejected as fabrications, despite multiple attestations. And even if there was a credible case of an element multiply attested, that only means that it originated in an earlier source – *not* that it originated as a historical fact.

Explanatory Credibility: must provide a plausible explanation for the rise of Christianity with in a first-century Jewish context. *Problem:* Claims that don't pass this test are probably false, but claims that pass it are not thereby true. So by itself this criterion is worthless. All the other exclusionary criteria also suffer from this same fatal flaw.

Contextual Plausibility: must be plausible in a Judeo-Greco-Roman context. *Problem:* Unfortunately, good storytelling also has to be plausible in context, so this doesn't help us determine what's true, only what's obviously false. Or at least, it should – the gospels don't always pass this test, either, as we'll see…

Historical Plausibility: must be a plausible historical reconstruction. *Problem:* Shares the same difficulty as Contextual Plausibility above, including the slight problem of the gospels often failing it.

Natural Plausibility: must conform with natural science, or it is probably false. *Problem:* A gospel filled with supernatural miracles doesn't fare well under this criterion, but that's not even the biggest problem: You can explain them all away with naturalistic explanations, but it doesn't change the fact that even failed miracle stories in the gospels appear to be presenting useful moral lessons about faith. So this criterion doesn't tell us anything, either.

Oral Preservability: must be capable of surviving oral transmission. *Problem:* It's the Telephone Game dilemma; any of Jesus' long-winded gospel speeches, or indeed, anything he said out of earshot of the others (such as when he prayed in the Garden of Gethsemane) are unlikely to have been memorized by his followers. Nor do we have any evidence for any institutions or mechanisms that would preserve such details. For instance, there were no early Christian schools, as there were for Jewish students who memorized the Mishnah. In fact, the opposite is true; all the pernicious discrepancies between the gospels (and Acts), not to mention all the extra-biblical Christian writings, argues that no such damage control was in place. Another problem is that if the Gospels are purely literary creations – and there are many indications that they are – then there *is* no oral tradition to preserve at all…

Crucifixion: must make sense of why Jesus was crucified. *Problem:* For starters, this begs the question in assuming that he *was* crucified, let alone that he existed. And you could just as easily try to argue, "Any theory of Attis must make sense of why he was castrated," or "Any theory of Hercules must make sense of why he was poisoned to death by centaur blood."

Fabricatory Trend: mustn't smack of legendary development, fabrication or embellishment. *Problem:* The gospels show exactly this in spades. For example, just compare Mark's earlier no-frills, fallible human Jesus with John's doubt-free SuperJesus.[23]

Least Distinctiveness: the simpler version is the more historical. *Problem:* Occam's Razor is a fine rule of thumb; and the more elaborate version of a story tends to be a later version, although sometimes more detailed stories get simplified over time. Either way, there's no guarantee that an earlier, simpler version of a story isn't still just a story to begin with.

Vividness of Narration: the more vivid, the more historical. *Problem:* So a minute ago the least distinctive version was assumed to be the more historical, and now we're supposed to think the more vividly detailed version is also more likely to be true? Hang on! Not only is vivid detail the bread and butter of storytelling and embellishment, but schools in the ancient world were specifically taught to embellish stories and speeches this way.[24] The historians we trust the most are the ones who specifically avoid embellished details and who stick to the facts, preferably with cited sources and corroborated by multiple lines of evidence.

Textual Variance: the less a text's wording changes over time, the more historical. *Problem:* The assumption here is that less variation in a text points to stability and probable preservation of the tradition. But, of course, stability of a tradition is no guarantee that the original version is historically true.

Greek Context: does it sound like something Greek-speakers would say? *Problem:* Actually, boiling it down to this definition also reveals its fatal flaw: Anything in the gospel that sounds like it may have been authentically spoken by a Greek speaker is worthless for judging if Jesus ever said anything. It could just as easily mean that it's the invention of its Greek-speaking author...or anybody else in the Greek-speaking world.

Aramaic Context: does it sound like something Aramaic speakers would say? *Problem:* New criterion, same problem as above. We know the earliest Christians spoke a Semitic-influenced Greek (a sort of ancient Spanglish), and their scripture, the Septuagint[25] (abbreviated as LXX), was also written in a Semitized Greek.[26] In addition, many early Christians were bilingual (like Paul, according to Acts 21-22). But there is absolutely no reason to believe any particular statement is historical just because it might derive from an Aramaic source.

Aramaic was spoken by millions, continually, for centuries, across a broad geographical range, far beyond just Judea. Besides, stories, revelations, quotations and anything else one likes could be made up in Aramaic (and even added into an existing story), by anyone, just as easily as any other language. So even if an Aramaic source *could* be identified and demonstrated, that still tells us nothing about its authenticity, or date or place of origin.[27]

What's more, Carrier points out that actually demonstrating an Aramaic source, as opposed to Semitic Greek, or the use of the Septuagint or a targum (an Aramaic paraphrase of the Hebrew scriptures) is a lot harder than is pretended anyway. But since even succeeding at it accomplishes nothing, there's no reason to think we can establish any historicity using that route. There is evidence, for example, that Mark relied on targumim.[28] So there are far too many ways a Semitic flavor could come into a tradition without being a sign of authenticity.

Discourse Features: Do Jesus' speeches cohere in a unique style? Are they consistent and yet different from the surrounding gospel passage? Then perhaps they preserve an earlier form of Jesus' authentic words. *Problem:* Even assuming this procedure works at all (and in this case it hasn't been shown to[29]), at best all it could do is show that the speech in question derives from a different source than the rest of the narrative, not that the source is Jesus.

Characteristic Jesus: Is it both distinctive and characteristic of Jesus? *Problem:* Like we know. This is the most recent attempt at inventing a new criterion, and as it is one huge *non sequitur*, for all the reasons we've seen so far, it is just as worthless as all the others.

Fallacies in Criteria's Clothing
Carrier also identifies other "criteria" that are really nothing more than your basic garden-variety fallacies in disguise:

Affective Criterion: Carrier is tempted to call this the Criterion of It Just Feeling True, but it already has a name: the Affective Fallacy, or judging something true because of how it affects you – how real it sounds, how moving it is, how it speaks to you, in short, its truthiness.

Criterion of Inexplicability: Just because you can't think of any other reason why a particular claim about Jesus would exist unless it was true; or assuming that because you can't find any specific evidence that a claim is false, it must be true – these do not make it true; they make it an Argument from Ignorance (and a logical fallacy).

Oral Source: Just because we can't identify or reconstruct a written source for a story or saying does not mean it must derive from an oral tradition.

Criterion of Repetition: If Jesus is depicted as frequently talking about a given topic, or performing healings, or speaking in parables, we should conclude that's what he really did. Except we shouldn't – because all this establishes is that the *author* wants to emphasize these features, not that they really happened.

Criterion of Heavy Interpretation: Anthony Le Donne has important things to say about how memory becomes distorted.[30] But his fundamental thesis is "the more significant a memory, the more interpreted it will become," and so the highly interpreted claims in the Gospels must reflect a significant memory. But as Carrier points out, myths and fables *also* become highly interpreted and multiply attested. If you say (as Le Donne does) that John the Baptist was *remembered* as a type of Elijah, there's no valid reason to dismiss the alternative possibility that John the Baptist was merely *represented* as a type of Elijah. This criterion has no valid method to differentiate between an actual memory, and a convenient literary fabrication.

Skeletons in Jesus' Closet?
One of these questionable criteria deserves a closer look; not because it is any more valid than the rest (it isn't), but because many atheists, even famous ones, still seem to find the various forms of it convincing: the **Embarrassment Criterion** (EC). An Argument from Embarrassment is based on the notion that if an author says something that embarrasses him, it must be true; because surely he wouldn't embarrass himself with a lie, would he? Ergo, since there are plenty of strange and uncomfortable passages in the Gospels, they must be historically true. Interestingly, the EC has a parallel in law: the

legal principle "statement against interest" – which has also fallen into question. The increasing trend in law now requires corroborating evidence before granting admission of statements against interest – but even when admitted as evidence, juries are instructed not to assume the testified fact is true, but to critically evaluate such testimony like any other.[31] This is a sound principle for us to follow as well.

Apart from the underlying logic, there are other problems with the EC, especially when it's being used in Jesus studies. First, there's a contradiction. The assumption is that any embarrassing material would either be suppressed or soft-pedaled in later stages of the Gospel tradition, as John P. Meier argues in *A Marginal Jew* (vol. 1, p. 168). But our surviving gospels are already in very late stages of this tradition; by the time our first gospel, Mark, appears in the 70s, Jesus had been preached across three continents for generations. Any "embarrassing" details would have been weeded out decades before Mark ever put pen to paper. The later Gospel writers that followed Mark's lead certainly had no qualms about editing out the parts of his gospel that they found embarrassing; very nearly conclusive proof that those embarrassing details never existed in the tradition at all before Mark.[32]

The only other option is to somehow prove that Mark was under different pressures than the other Gospel authors – or just more honest. Christian scholars are unlikely to concede that the other Evangelists were liars, but even that wouldn't help. Then you would be left trying to explain why Mark was compelled to tell the truth when none of the others did. Besides, *is* Mark telling the truth? Consider all the dubious material in Mark: the voice of God booming from the clouds, herds of demon-possessed swine, repeated miraculous feedings of thousands, walking on water, calming storms, cursing fig trees, appearances by Moses and Elijah, hours of supernatural darkness, etc. (see Mark 1:9-11, 5:11-16, 6:35-52, 8:1-21, 9:3-7, 11:13-20, 15:33).

We also need to be cautioned against assuming authors like Mark anticipated the audience reaction to what he wrote, or realize how embarrassing it might become down the road to later editors and evangelists. And as Bart Ehrman and other scholars such as Wayne Kannaday and C.S.C. Williams have amply demonstrated, the history of New Testament manuscripts is lousy with examples of doctored biblical passages that only became problematic for various Christian factions much later, after rival Christian factions (or 'heretics,' depending on which side you approved of) found novel new ways to interpret/exploit them.

This process at work is observable in the later Gospels. For example, it hadn't occurred to Mark that critical readers would suspect Jesus' tomb was empty because his disciples had stolen the body, but Matthew's addition of guards at Jesus' tomb (Matt. 27:62-66; 28: 11-16) shows that the objection had obviously popped up in the meantime. Had early Christians been telling the story for generations, Mark would have been obliged to fix that plot hole in his gospel. Actually, those Christian storytellers would already have fixed it for him decades ago.

Embarrassing Ignorance
Carrier calls attention to a second difficulty with applying the EC in Jesus' case: the state of our knowledge of the early church; or more accurately, the state of our ignorance. Morna Hooker explains:

> "Use of this criterion seems to assume we are dealing with two known factors (Judaism and early Christianity) and one unknown – Jesus," and adds, "it would perhaps be a fairer statement of the situation to say that we are dealing with three unknowns, and that our knowledge of the other two is quite as tenuous and indirect as our knowledge of Jesus himself."[33]

Several other bible scholars have agreed that our lack of detailed knowledge of early Christian thought makes determining what may have embarrassed them very difficult; including Richard Carrier, Stanley Porter, Gerd Theissen, and Dagmar Winter; even conservative Christian scholars John Meier and Mark Strauss concede that "what seems embarrassing to us may not have seemed so to the early church," and adds there may be reasons not obvious to us for seemingly embarrassing details in the gospels.[34]

Compounding the difficulty is the fact the early Christian movements were notoriously varied, even in Paul's time. Paul often complains about of the diversity of Christianity; particularly his rival missionaries preaching another Jesus, another gospel, another Christ (1 Cor. 1:10-13; 2 Cor. 11:4,13-15, 19-20, 22-23; Gal. 1:6-9; 2:4). The situation grows even more by the time the Gospels were written, decades later. They, too, complain about followers of rival Christs (Matt. 7:21-23; Mark 9:38; Luke 9:49). And for the next two centuries, the riotous diversity of Christianity only continued to increase unchecked. Bart Ehrman's *Lost Christianities* sheds light on the many different constantly evolving strands of Christianity in various times and places, and how nigh-unrecognizable they became to anything resembling the Christianity of today.

There are still more considerations we can discuss on this issue, and Richard Carrier does an excellent job of doing just that (for more details, see pp. 129 -134 of *Proving History*).

Embarrassment? What Embarrassment?
There's a third problem with applying the EC to Jesus: All the evidence for Jesus that survives comes to us solely via the people who controlled what was preserved and what wasn't – the Christians. So if anything was embarrassing to Christians, why is it in the text at all? Think about it; the Evangelists (and their later editors) could choose to include, omit, or alter material as they pleased. This is resoundingly apparent when

one looks at the Gospels. Matthew and Luke felt quite free to make massive rewrites of their source material, Mark's gospel. And John barely bothers to try to make his match any of theirs. If you try to argue that Matthew, Luke, and John didn't borrow from Mark (good luck!), then you are forced to admit that Mark must have then left out scads of material found in their gospels, but not in his. Either way, it shows the authors picked and chose what to include and leave out.

So it's highly unlikely that any Christian author would include anything embarrassing; which means that anything he did include was there for a deliberate reason. Mark gives no indication of being bothered by many things that clearly *did* embarrass the later Evangelists; things they correct, omit or spin doctor away in their own gospels. And the simple fact that *they* did already puts the kibosh on the Criterion of Embarrassment.

And let's face it: sometimes religious writers like to include embarrassing, even truly bizarre details. Plutarch and Plato were appalled by the incest and immorality among the gods in the Homeric epics. Romulus, Rome's mythical founder, murdered his twin. The Sumerian goddess Inanna descended to hell, was humiliated, stripped naked, killed by magic and her corpse hung up on a hook. The priests of the Attis cult imitated their savior god by castrating themselves as he did, a practice that Roman writers found shameful and disgusting. As Carrier observes:

> "We simply have no clue why these shocking stories were invented, much less became the objects of veneration and symbolic emulation. Religions frequently rally around apparently embarrassing yet entirely false myths, often in defiance of common sense. The Jews were no exception."[35]

Nor were the Christians.

Bootstrapping Belief

The last general objection to the EC is that even the scholars who employ it admit that it is insufficient on its own and insist that it must be used in conjunction with other criteria.[36] Stanley Porter recognizes that this opens the door to vicious circular arguments and calls them on it. It doesn't matter how many inconclusive arguments you pile on; you'll never reach a valid summit. As Carrier aptly puts it, not even a million logically invalid arguments can establish a conclusion – *at all*, much less "decisively."[37]

These are some of the general problems with trying to apply the Embarrassment Criterion. For a more in-depth look at all of them, as well as the problems underlying all the other criteria, see Ch. 5 of *Proving History*. But what about some of the specific gospel elements that have made scholars think real facts were peeking through between the lines?

***

For further reading:

Richard Carrier, *Proving History: Bayes's Theorem and the Quest for the Historical Jesus*, Amherst, Prometheus, 2012; and
Not the Impossible Faith: Why Christianity Didn't Need a Miracle to Succeed, Lulu Press, 2009

Neil Godfrey, "Why Todays Theologians Call Themselves Historians," in *Vridar,* April 4, 2014. Available online at: http://vridar.org/2014/04/13/why-todays-theologians-call-themselves-historians/
Neil Godfrey, "Unfair to Compare Jesus Scholars with Regular Historians" in *Vridar,* July 2, 2016. Available online at: http://vridar.org/2016/07/02/unfair-to-compare-jesus-scholars-with-regular-historians/

R. Rodríguez, "Authenticating Criteria: The Use and Misuse of a Critical Method," *Journal for the Study of the Historical Jesus* 7/2 (2009), 155-6.

For examples of how the criteria for historical Jesus studies have been criticized (even in Christian scholarly circles), see:

Chris Keith and Anthony Le Donne, eds., *Jesus, History and the Demise of Authenticity*, T & T Clark, 2012 (in particular, see Mark Goodacre's "Criticizing the Criterion of Multiple Attestation: The Historical Jesus and the Question of Sources")

---

[1] Chilton, Le Donne, Neusner, pp. 111-127

[2] It should be noted that Dale Allison, Fernando Bermejo-Rubio, Anthony Le Donne, Stanley Porter, and others have argued that this entire "Quests" paradigm is misleading and just one more facet of biblical scholarship badly in need of an overhaul: "In fact, this historiographical construct seems indeed to be only an instance of the many fanciful things one finds in the field of the study on the historical Jesus" (Bermejo-Rubio, p. 250).

[3] Arnal, *TSJ* p. 41

[4] Several sources wrongly say 1992, but see Neill & Wright, pp. 363, 379

[5] See Fernando Bermejo-Rubio for details

[6] See Neil Godfrey, "Why Todays Theologians Call Themselves Historians," in *Vridar*, April 4, 2014. Available online at: http://vridar.org/2014/04/13/why-todays-theologians-call-themselves-historians/

[7] Arnal, op. cit., p. 42

[8] Carrier, *On the Historicity of Jesus*, p. 24n10

[9] Carrier, op. cit., p. 25

[10] I am indebted to Richard Carrier's *Proving History* for the majority of the points in this analysis

[11] Cited in *Jesus and Judaism*, p. 11
[12] Such as Mark Strauss, *Four Portraits, One Jesus: An Introduction to Jesus and the Gospels* (Zondervan, 2007), p. 372
[13] Arnal, p. 42
[14] Carrier, op. cit., p. 32
[15] Ibid.
[16] pp. 121-207
[17] Carrier, ibid.
[18] Ibid.
[19] See ch. 1 of Carrier, *Proving History*
[20] Porter, *Criteria*, p. 126
[21] Keith & Le Donne, pp. 3-5
[22] Carrier, op. cit., p. 172
[23] See *Nailed*, pp. 75 - 84
[24] Ibid., p. 323, n118
[25] "Septuagint" means "seventy" (LXX in Roman numerals), a reference to the legendary 70 elders who translated it into Greek (See ch. 19 for more details).
[26] Carrier, op. cit., pp. 185-86
[27] Ibid.
[28] See Bruce Chilton's "Targum, Jesus, and the Gospels," in Levine, Allison, and Crossan, ed., *Historical Jesus in Context*, pp. 238-55.
[29] Ibid., p. 186
[30] See Le Donne, 2011 & 2009
[31] See note 9, p. 312 of Carrier, op. cit.
[32] Ibid., p. 127
[33] Hooker, "Christology and Methodology," p. 482
[34] Strauss, p. 361; Meier, *A Marginal Jew*, vol. 1, p.170
[35] Carrier, op. cit., pp. 136-7
[36] Ibid., p. 137
[37] Ibid.

Chapter Five: Embarrassing Jesus

"We have no business trying to make bad evidence into good by stripping away the very features of the story for the sake of which it was told in the first place, and then seeing if we can salvage a couple of incidental details."

– David Friedrich Strauss

Are there genuine facts about the "real Jesus" hidden in plain sight? If we read between the lines of the Gospels, will we find some uncomfortable truths waiting to be uncovered? Over the years many scholars, secular and religious alike, have thought so. Here are some of them:

Embarrassment no. 1: Born in Nazareth? Or Bethlehem?
The late great Christopher Hitchens said it best, of course: "…it can be stated with certainty, and on their own evidence, that the Gospels are most certainty not literal truth. This means that many of the 'sayings' and teachings of Jesus are hearsay upon hearsay, which helps to explain their garbled and contradictory nature."[1] But he did suspect there was a kernel of truth behind them, saying "the best argument for the highly questionable existence of Jesus"[2] was the problem of Gospel writers trying to insist that Jesus of Nazareth was really born in Bethlehem. In a 2008 debate he said:

> "Now, there is on the historicity point, only two reasons to suppose that there may have been the figure of some kind of deluded rabbi present at that time. The first is the fakery of the story. The fakery itself proves something. The prophecy says this man must be born in the house of David, of David's line, in David's town. Means he must be born in Bethlehem. Jesus of Nazareth is well known to have been born in Nazareth. In order to get him to Bethlehem a huge fabrication has to be undertaken…

None of the story of the Nativity is true in any detail, and not one of the gospels agrees with each other on this fabrication. But the fabrication itself suggests something: If they were simply going to make up the whole thing and had never been such person then why not just have him born in Bethlehem right there and leave out the Nazarene business?"[3]

Hitchens very nearly answered his own question, because the key to why Mark chose Nazareth seems to be the same reason Matthew chose Bethlehem: because he could tie it to scripture. The thing is, there wasn't just *one* Old Testament passage that believers later shaped into a prophecy about the Messiah. Jewish readers like Matthew latched onto this passage in Micah (5:2) for their best guesstimate of where the savior would be born:

"And when (King Herod) had gathered all the chief priests and scribes of the people together, he inquired of them where the Christ was to be born. So they said to him, "In Bethlehem of Judea, for thus it is written by the prophet:

'But you, Bethlehem, in the land of Judah,
Are not the least among the rulers of Judah;
For out of you shall come a Ruler
Who will shepherd My people Israel.'"
(Matthew 2:4-6)

Incidentally, there are some slight problems with this "prophecy" – if it even *is* a prophecy (and not taken from a coronation hymn for a new king or royal birth oracle, for instance). First of all, Matthew doesn't quote it quite right. It *should* read:

"But you, Bethlehem Ephrathah,

> (Though) you are little among the thousands of Judah,
> (Yet) out of you shall come forth to Me
> The One to be Ruler in Israel,
> Whose goings forth (are) from of old,
> From everlasting."

Secondly, the ruler of Israel prophesied here is a military hero who will defeat the Assyrian empire, laying waste to it with the sword, destroying their chariots, smash their citadels (Micah 5: 1-15), the usual vengeance treatment regularly promised by God's spokesmen. So it's already a bit of a stretch to try and spin doctor this passage into a prophecy of Jesus, the Prince of Peace (then again, the author of Matthew never shied away from twisting scripture like a balloon animal to suit his purposes).

In fact, Matthew also ties Jesus to Nazareth using scripture, by declaring that Joseph took his family to their new home, "a city called Nazareth, that it might be fulfilled which was spoken by the prophets, 'He shall be called a Nazarene.'" (Matt. 2:23) Who these prophets were, Matthew unfortunately doesn't tell us; and this "prophecy" isn't found in any existing Jewish scriptures we know of. But if Mathew was telling the truth (and that is not a given[4]) and there really was such a now-lost prophetic tradition,[5] it's entirely possible that fact alone was what also led Mark to make Nazareth his choice for Jesus' home over Bethlehem. But of course, that's assuming Mark even meant this to be taken as a geographic term at all...

Nazarene or Nazoraean?
Here's a little-known fact that biblical scholars have known for a long time now: despite the way many translations of the Bible read, the Gospels actually almost never refer to Jesus as "Jesus of Nazareth."[6] Mark calls him "Jesus the Nazarene," while Matthew, John and Acts always call him "Jesus the Nazoraean."[7] Both versions appear in Luke's gospel. But no Christian writer before the Gospels makes any connection at all

151

David Fitzgerald

between Jesus and Nazareth. Or Bethlehem. Or anywhere else on the map.

An additional point casts doubt that Mark ever intended to paint Nazareth as Jesus' hometown at all: in verses like Mark 2:1 and 9:33 (cf. 6:3-4) he appears to have had Capernaum in mind as Jesus' home – a town which *also* had a handy messianic prophecy attached to it (Isaiah 8:21- 9:2), as Matthew tells us in his gospel (4:12-16). So what *did* Mark mean when he called Jesus a Nazarene?

Though many bible translations often treat "Nazarene" and "Nazoraean" as interchangeable,[8] the two words are actually quite different from each other. "Nazarene" *can* work to refer to a person from the village frequently called *Nazara* in Greek, as well as *Nazareq*.[9] But "Nazoraean" means nothing of the sort. It is the name of a sect. In fact, it is one of the original names of the early Christian movement (or at least of one early faction). In Acts 24:5, Paul is accused of being a "ringleader of the sect of the Nazoreans."

And the two words and their cognates are connected in intriguing ways to *other* religious movements. The later Christian heresy-hunter Epiphanius[10] says the Nazoreans were a Jewish Christian sect, not to be confused with a pre-Christian sect he calls the Nasaraeans. J.S. Kennard has presented a plausible case that "Nazorean" was a cultic title derived from the Nazirites described in Numbers (6:1-21) and the Mishnah tractate *Nazir*.[11]

Horst Kuhli, in the *Exegetical Dictionary of the New Testament*, has suggested another etymology, deriving from *nasar*, "to guard," in the sense of "the observant" or "the faithful" (i.e., those who guard the truth, or keep secrets)[12] And sure enough, the Mandaeans, one of early Christianity's rival sects (they viewed Jesus as a Mandaean who went astray[13]), called the keepers of their secret wisdom, priests skilled in esoteric knowledge, *Naṣurai*.[14]

Scholars today still speculate on just what else the term "Nazorean" relates to, but recognize it clearly did *not* mean "from Nazareth," since the words do not share the same roots. Nor did Christians come from there;[15] besides, as Kennard points out, as a rule, religious movements don't take their name from the place their founder was from.[16]

In other Christian writings, the term seems to be neither geographical nor a religious group name. The church father Irenaeus tells us that the phrase "Jesus Nazaria" simply means "Savior of Truth." We find the identical situation in the Gospel of Phillip, which explicitly gives us this breakdown of Jesus' name:

> "Jesus" in Hebrew is "the redemption."
> "Nazara" is "the Truth."
> "The Nazarene" then, is "the Truth."[17]

His linguistics is questionable, but his interpretation is fascinating, and it's telling that we find later Christian writers who sincerely believe that the "real meaning" of "Nazarene" has nothing to do with where Jesus hailed from. And there are still more tantalizing clues: Our familiar Jesus doesn't appear in older Jewish writings such as the Mishnah, the Tosefta and the *Talmud Yerushalmi* (though other Jesuses do[18]) much later, in the early medieval Jewish satire *Sepher Toldoth Yeshu,* the Christians' Jesus is called "Yeshu ha-Notzri."

Notzri and its plural, *Notzrim,* may derive from words like *Natsar,* as perhaps "keeper of secrets,"[19] though many have proposed it could mean "those of the branch," citing Isaiah (11:1): "And there shall come forth a rod out of the stem, of Jesse, and a branch shall grow out of his roots". *Notzrim* remains the Hebrew word for Christians even today. The same word is found in Syriac; though the other Syriac word for "Christian" is *Nasrani*; in Arabic, *Naṣrānī* ... taking us back full circle…

This constellation of evocative meanings surrounding the words "Nazarene" and "Nazorean" make it hard even for Christian scholars to accept they were only ever meant to refer to Jesus' hometown. James McGrath puts it well:

> "The issue cannot be simply whether it is possible to create an unlikely but just barely possible scenario for the derivation of this term from the place name. We must also ask whether that derivation is likely and whether Matthew may not be the one trying to turn Nazorean into a geographic designation when it originally meant something else."[20]

"Nazarene" is a word chock full of rich symbolism and can mean a great many things, but using it to refer to Jesus' hometown appears to be an idea that developed *after* Mark's gospel was written and retrofitted back into place, either through a misunderstanding or a deliberate re-edit. So originally there was no "embarrassment" after all. Scholars like Catholic priest and prominent biblical scholar John P. Meier agree: if the Bethlehem vs. Nazareth issue was a problem, why didn't Mark address it? Neither Paul nor any other authors make any connection between Jesus and Nazareth before this. Why is it only *after* Mark that all the convoluted double-origin stories arise? Scholars like Susan Levin have shown that transformations like turning "Nazarene / Nazarorean" from a concept into a literary location is just one more example of a common myth-making practice, symbolic eponymy.[21] Once again, Jesus' story provides a textbook example of not history, not biography, but mythography. And there is even reason to believe that Nazareth itself may well be a result of the same process (see below).

Nazareth of Jesus?
"Can anything good come out of Nazareth?" asks a prospective disciple in the Gospel of John (1:46).
Price has shown this is an anachronism: Nazareth fell into disrepute with Jews only decades after the alleged time of Jesus – and precisely *because* it became associated with him.[22]

Before the Gospels, no one disparages Nazareth – because no one seems to have heard of it before the Gospels.

Much like Jesus himself, the archeological evidence for his putative hometown seems to be well established ... until one looks closer at it, as René Salm has done in his books *The Myth of Nazareth* and *NazarethGate*.[23]

Nazareth is never mentioned in any of the NT epistles, or any of the apocryphal gospels or Gnostic writings. Although the neighboring town of Japhia *is* well represented, both in the Old Testament (Josh. 19:12), and the Egyptian Amarna letters (14th c. BCE[24]); as well as Josephus,[25] no geographer or historian mentions Nazareth before the 4th century. That is when, along with many other holy places of the New Testament, Nazareth appears to have been "discovered" by the Emperor Constantine's mother Helena, on the same trip that gave birth to the Christian pilgrimage tourist industry.

Origen did not know whether it should be called Nazareth or Nazara; or where it was located – this is especially curious since he only lived 30 miles from Nazareth, and specifically made serious effort to travel around retracing "the footsteps of Jesus." Manuscripts of Luke show an astounding uncertainty of what Jesus' home was called: Nazara, Nazaret, Nazareth, Nazarat, Nazared, amidst other variants found in other gospels and the early Church Fathers.[26]

Salm has been frequently attacked for his lack of formal training as an archeologist,[27] and some of his claims are debatable. Nonetheless, he has been able to point out serious gaffes in the official reports – including the fact that Fr. B. Bagatti the "principal archeologist" who did the original fieldwork of the Nazareth site was not an archeologist either, but a Franciscan priest. More recent archeologist Ken Dark has never excavated anywhere in the entire area, restricting his "fieldwork" to surface surveys and "re-analysis" of earlier reports.[28]

Among the mistakes of both teams: dating the same artifact to two different periods, outright misdating artifacts to the wrong time period, spin-doctoring the dating periods to give the impression that fragments date much earlier, that the evidence for "Nazareth" appears to actually belong to Japhia, and other "serious errors of methodology, reporting and logic."[29] In fact, Salm adds, "over and over, we find that the excavators on Catholic Church property have failed to observe standard guidelines of stratigraphy, documentation, publication, and preservation."[30]

Salm further contends if Nazareth had been occupied as long as the Catholic Church maintains, it would be quite amazing for a town its size; only a handful of sites like Jerusalem and Jericho could claim such longevity. In fact, if true, that should have made Nazareth a world-class archeological site. Its neighbor Megiddo has thirty strata spanning approximately three thousand years, a treasure trove for archeologists. Nazareth, by contrast, has no man-made strata at all, despite Bagatti digging over 18 feet down to solid bedrock.[31]

After Salm issued these and still more blistering criticisms, archeologists connected with the various commercial tourist enterprises in Nazareth scrambled to issue a response; including an "addendum" three times longer than the original report! See *NazarethGate: Quack Archeology, Holy Hoaxes and the Invented Town of Jesus* for more details of the ensuing fireworks.

Embarrassment no. 2: Jesus' Female Witnesses
Hitchens' second reason to provisionally favor Jesus' historicity is one also long-favored by Christians: the idea that the gospel authors would never invent female witnesses to the empty tomb – unless it had really happened that way:

> "You can mention another thing about the resurrection. Most of the witnesses to this are women, illiterate, stupid, deluded, hysterical females, of a kind that to a Jewish Court at that time would have had about as much chance

of being listened to as they would in Islamic court today. What religion that wants its fabrication to be believed is going to say: You've got to believe it 'cause we have some illiterate hysterical girls who said they saw this?"[32]

Many apologists agree. Dr. William Lane Craig holds up elements like this as proof positive that Mark's Gospel is the real deal. Craig not only deems the discovery of the tomb by women highly probable, he declares that "given the low status of women in Jewish society and their lack of qualification to serve as legal witnesses," the most plausible explanation why women and not the male disciples were made discoverers of the empty tomb is that the women were in fact the ones who made this discovery.[33]

Like so much of what Dr. Craig argues, there are a few problems with this line of reasoning. First of all, historians like Judith Wegner have debunked the common mistaken notion that women were considered unqualified as witnesses. Their findings show the opposite was true: under Jewish law (also true of Roman law), not only was the testimony of women admitted, women held the right to bring and defend a lawsuit, and Jewish sages acknowledged both a woman's mental competence and placed reliance upon her oath and testimony.[34]

But that's all beside the point in the first place – because the women in Mark's Gospel *aren't* witnesses. As the majority of biblical scholars have long acknowledged, Mark's gospel originally ended at verse 16:8. The rest of the chapter, verses 9-20, is known as the "Marcan Appendix," because clearly Mark's genuine author did not write it. This ending doesn't appear in any of our best and earliest manuscripts of Mark, doesn't share the same vocabulary or style of the rest of the Gospel, and doesn't show up until around the same time as other forged endings to the gospel (see, for example, the *New Jerome Biblical Commentary* for more details).

This displeases many Christians, since without the forged passage Mark has no post-resurrection appearance to his followers, no Great Commission and no promises that they can exorcize devils, speak in tongues or take up deadly serpents without harm (sorry, snake handlers!). It also means that Mark's gospel originally ended at the empty tomb, like this:

> "So (the women) went out quickly and fled from the tomb, for they trembled and were amazed. And they said nothing to anyone, for they were afraid."

So the women behave exactly as you would expect from a sexist ancient Mediterranean male writer's standpoint – they panicked and ran away in terror, and *never told anyone what they had seen*. Crazy skirts! Ain't that just like a dame? Why would Mark deliberately end his gospel on such an unsatisfying note? Several reasons. First, remember that Mark's gospel was written, at the very least, four decades after the time it describes. Blaming those silly hysterical women conveniently explains why no one had ever heard the story before now, not even Paul - or any other Christian writer, apparently, since no one ever mentions this appearance to the women. And ending his gospel with a twist isn't just an unusual M. Night Shyamalanian touch of Mark's; it's his stock in trade. His gospel is filled with reversals of the reader's expectations just like this.[35] And it contains a crucial message. The women *not* delivering the good news out of fear is not just an ironic touch, but a challenge to his readers: Don't *you* be like them...

Incidentally, Craig insists there is another reason why the empty tomb story couldn't possibly be made up:

> "Furthermore, the listing of the women's names again precludes unhistorical legend at the story's core, for these persons were known in the *Urgemeinde* and so could not be associated with a false account."[36]

Yes... these women were known in the *Urgemeinde* (pompous theologian-speak for "the early church"), so no one could possibly just make up names. Unless, of course, Craig is begging the question in the first place, and this "account" wasn't even written down – or even completely made up - until generations after the time in question. Then again, if all these women and their story were so well known to the early church that they "could not be associated with a false account," then why do none of the gospels agree on their names? Or how many of them there were? Or what happened at the tomb?[37] Far from being a lock on the validity of the story, the "account," or rather, the conflicting "accounts," of the women at the tomb shows that nothing was easier to make up.

Even the names Mark provides (Mark 15:40-41;16:1) all conveniently have rich symbolism, as many scholars have noted,[38] and as we'll see ourselves in ch. 13.[39] The story of the women at the tomb is just one more artistic touch to a gospel that appears to be the entirely literary creation of the anonymous author we call Mark.

Embarrassment no. 3: Jesus' Betrayal by Judas
John Meier finds the idea that Jesus was betrayed by his close follower Judas – like his death by crucifixion – too horrific, embarrassing and too multiply-attested to have been made up by the early Christians. Meier joins Gerd Theissen and Dagmar Winter (authors of *Quest for the Plausible Jesus*) in pointing to verses where Jesus promised his disciples "when the Son of Man is seated on the throne of his glory, you who have followed me will also sit on twelve thrones, judging the twelve tribes of Israel" (Matt. 19:28, cf. Luke 22:30). As they saw it, "Early Christianity always numbered Judas Iscariot among the twelve disciples and had simply scorned and condemned him as the one who betrayed Jesus,"[40] so the fact that the early church preserved a promise that the twelve – not the eleven – disciples would rule over Israel could only mean that the saying came from Jesus himself, before Judas betrayed him.

As Carrier has shown,[41] already their first "fact" isn't true. For at least the entire duration of Paul's twenty or thirty-year ministry – that is, the entirety of "early Christianity," we never hear *any* of these claims. No one ever says that Judas Iscariot was one of "the twelve," or that he (or any of the twelve) ever betrayed Jesus or was "scorned and condemned" for it; not even in NT verses that have strong reason to mention it, such as 1 Corinthians 11:23-27, where Paul describes the Lord's Supper, adding: "Whoever, therefore, eats the bread or drinks the cup of the Lord in an unworthy manner will be answerable for the body and blood of the Lord." In fact, no one before the Gospels ever mentions Judas Iscariot – at all.

Nor does Paul mention anything about any promise from Jesus that the twelve disciples would judge over Israel when he informs believers that they will judge the world and the angels (1 Cor. 6:2-4). Later, in 1 Cor. 15:5, when Paul lists those who had visions of the risen Jesus (a list that is often cited as corroborating the gospels, though in fact it contradicts all four – not that they agree either!), he includes an appearance "to Cephas, then to the twelve." This is difficult to reconcile with the idea that one of the twelve betrayed him – or that Judas was supposed to have died immediately after Jesus...

It's also worth pointing out that in this passage, the one and only place where Paul mentions "the twelve," (assuming this passage in 1 Cor. 15 is genuine in the first place; which has been called into doubt[42]) he never identifies "the twelve" as Jesus' disciples – and that was not the only possibility; the Essenes also had a "twelve" of their own, their ruling council of twelve (*Nailed* p. 146-147). In fact, Paul never says that Jesus even *had* disciples – he never uses the word "disciple" anywhere.

Likewise, even the notion that Jesus was betrayed at all is missing. The one and only place where Paul seems to say Jesus was betrayed, he uses a word, *paradidomi*, that actually means something much more ambiguous – and arguably, one never used in the sense of "betrayal" anywhere in the New

Testament (see *Nailed* pp.134-137; and ch. 15, section 7). In addition, Meier's "multiple attestation from independent sources" breaks down immediately. His sources ("Mark, John, Paul, probably L, and probably Q,"[43]) are neither independent, nor do they give multiple attestation, since Paul never names anyone in his "Twelve" or says what their connection was to Jesus, if any, and the Gospels (which all derive from Mark in the first place) disagree with one another on the identities of the Twelve. And this is before we even begin to examine the credibility or transmission of his sources – something he never addresses.

So to try and say Judas' betrayal (let alone his very existence!) is a well-known fact in early Christianity is a non-starter. The truth is that Judas is never found anywhere, in any writing anywhere, before he makes his first appearance in the Gospel of Mark. And as we'll see later, not only does Mark appear to be the creator of the Judas story, his story makes no sense.[44]

Embarrassment no. 4: Jesus' Baptism by John
In the first volume of his series *A Marginal Jew*, Meier pleads a case for one fact of the historical Jesus: that John the Baptist mentored him. This is shown, as he put it, by the embarrassment of early Christians over "the baptism of the supposedly superior and sinless Jesus by his supposed inferior John the Baptist."[45]

Later evangelists were certainly embarrassed by the thought of their perfect Messiah being baptized by a mere mortal (so much so that Matthew plays spin doctor with it, and John does away with it altogether). But Mark was not. As Carrier notes, if Mark had been, he would have been engaged in the same damage control as the others; in fact, the spin doctoring would have occurred decades earlier, perhaps even during Jesus' alleged ministry.[46] So the EC fails already.

Meier and others employing this argument assume that Mark and the Christians before him shared their belief that

Jesus was "superior" and "sinless." But Mark and his gospel presents an "Adoptionist" theology[47] that some early Christians held: that Jesus was an ordinary man whom God declared to be his son at his baptism and, because of his obedience unto death, God raised him from the dead and exalted him to Lord. In Mark's no-frills gospel, there is no miraculous virgin birth, no star of Bethlehem, no wise men, no empire-wide taxations, no angelic announcements, nor tales of precocious young Jesus astounding the rabbis with his knowledge. These spectacular embellishments are all later Christian developments.

Instead, Mark's Jesus first arrives on the scene at his baptism. After John baptizes Jesus, thus cleansing his flesh of sin, God announces that Jesus is his son. Immediately, God's prospective new hire is put to the test in the wilderness, resisting temptation by Satan for forty days. As every Sunday school student has asked, what could the Devil tempt Jesus with? Riches? Power? Hardly, if he was God incarnate slumming on earth for a short time. The story only works if Jesus is a mere mortal like us.

Likewise, Mark's Jesus has no theological difficulties saying things like "Why do you call me good? No one is good but God alone," (Mark 10:18) because his Jesus is not co-equal with God, or part of some Trinity (a development still a century or more away from being conceived, and nearly three centuries away from being made official church dogma). Despite failures and difficulties throughout his ministry, he remains faithful to God. In a weak moment in the garden of Gethsemane, filled with a deep grief and dread, he asks God to save him from what is to come, but remains obedient, despite enduring humiliation, abuse and torturous execution. And for that, God raises Mark's Jesus from the dead, and exalts him to Lord.

So Mark had no reason to be embarrassed by the baptism scene, on the contrary, he had every reason to *invent* it; he needed his Jesus to have his sins remitted in order to set the stage for God to bring him onboard as his redeemer of humanity.[48]

Getting over the Embarrassments

After Mark wrote his gospel, Christians increasingly saw Jesus as through the lens of higher and higher Christologies. Just a few decades later, Jesus was no longer an ordinary man turned savior; now John's Jesus was equal to God himself right from the beginning of time (John 1:1-5). But once we recognize that Mark deliberately set out to depict his Jesus as a mortal man who began as human as any of us and later became divine, virtually all the other supposed "embarrassments" that have been proposed over the years go away, too. For example, Jesus' non-omniscience shows in verses like Mark 13:32, where he is ignorant of the future: "But of that day and hour no one knows, not even the angels in heaven, nor the Son, but only the Father." Mark has no qualms to present Jesus as separate from and subservient to God.

Mark's Jesus even manages to pull off an ugly sexist/racist/asshole trifecta in one instance when a Gentile woman comes to beg him to exorcize a devil from her daughter. Initially, he refuses to her face, telling her it is not right to take the bread of the children of Israel and toss it to the dogs. When she pleads further, pointing out that even the dogs under the table get to eat the children's crumbs, he relents: "For saying that, you may go—the demon has left your daughter." (Mark 7:25-27)

In fact, Jesus acts like a jerk more than once. When his disciples fail to release a boy from his life-long demon-possession (with, remarkably enough, identical symptoms as grand-mal epileptic seizures), he rolls his eyes at them, sighing, "You faithless generation, how much longer must I be among you? How much longer must I put up with you? Bring him to me." He questions the boy's father, who pleads "if you are able to do anything, have pity on us and help us." Jesus raises an eyebrow at this: "*If* you are able!" (Mark 9:14-29)

Dr. Jesus uses the same time-honored magic healing techniques as pagan miracle-workers,[49] namely, spit and magic words. Matthew and Luke weren't happy about this; they have their improved Jesus 2.0 heal without props, just by Jesus' mere command (e.g., Matt. 15:28; Luke 17:12-14). But to heal a deaf mute, Mark's fallible Jesus needs to put his fingers into the man's ears, spit, touch his tongue, and then say *Ephphatha,* "Be opened," before the miracle can happen (Mark 7: 32-35). It gets worse a chapter later, when he tries to heal a blind man in Bethsaida - but doesn't quite get it right, and has to try again.

> "(Jesus) took the blind man by the hand and led him out of the village; and when he had put saliva on his eyes and laid his hands on him, he asked him, 'Can you see anything?' And the man looked up and said, 'I can see people, but they look like trees, walking.' Then Jesus laid his hands on his eyes again; and he looked intently and his sight was restored, and he saw everything clearly." (Mark 8: 22-25)

All the elements that upset later evangelists troubled Mark not at all; in fact, as we've seen, they served his literary purposes. Here are more examples:

Jesus dies in despair and anguish on the cross; his last words: "My God, my God, why have you forsaken me?" Such a heart-breaking cry is so agonizing, surely it could only be what he really said; no one would invent a line like that. Except, of course, for the author who did: the author of the 22nd Psalm. Mark is quoting the opening line of a psalm about a faithful man who calls on the Lord and is delivered from harm.

In another example, low-blood-sugar Jesus gets hungry and spots a fig tree, and goes looking for figs. But he can find nothing but leaves, because it was not yet fig season – so he curses the tree, saying, "May no one ever eat fruit from you again." The next morning, the disciples find it withered away to its roots (Mark 11:12-14; 20).

For a perfect Son of God, Jesus is all shortcomings in this vignette; he gets cranky, he fails to find what he's looking for, he doesn't know that it's not fig season and seemingly out of spite, he puts the whammy on a poor little tree whose only crime is being just as God made it. The only way to save Jesus here is to point out the glaringly obvious: this story doesn't work – except as allegory. The fig tree represents the temple cult of Israel, which has borne no fruits, and so will be cursed by God with divine judgment. Or whatever; Christians can debate the symbolism until the cows come home, but no matter how they choose to interpret it, one thing is clear: This incident is not history, biography or reality. This is a parable.[50]

The Crucial Embarrassment
But why would Mark need to have his savior die a common criminal's death on the cross – unless that is what really happened? Meier declares that inventing such a scandalous death is the *last* thing the early church would have done:

> "Such an embarrassing event created a major obstacle to converting Jews and Gentiles alike (see, e.g., 1 Corinthians 1:23), an obstacle that the church struggled to overcome with various theological arguments. The last thing the church would have done would have been to create a monumental scandal for which it then had to invent a whole apologetic... Precisely because the undeniable fact of Jesus' execution was so shocking, precisely because it seemed to make faith in this type of messiah preposterous, the early church felt a need from the beginning to insist that Jesus' scandalous death was "according to the scriptures," that it had been proclaimed beforehand by the OT prophets, and that individual OT texts even spelled out details of Jesus' passion."[51]

As I mentioned in *Nailed*, Meier further insists[52] that the Crucifixion and Jesus' betrayal by Judas were too shocking for early believers to make up, so they can only be historical facts. But then he ironically solves his own dilemma when he notes that right from the beginning, believers (e.g. 1 Cor. 15:3-5; Matt. 27:9-10; Mark 14:21; John 13:18, 17:12; Acts 1:16, 20, and many more) repeat that all these 'events' occurred 'according to the scriptures.' Then he is quick to deny even the possibility that these Old Testament texts are being used to create a myth, insisting, 'the shocking fact calls forth the scripture texts—not vice versa.' How does he know?[53]

Meier's objections fail on multiple levels. The ancient world already had far more shocking cults. The initiates of the Attis cult flabbergasted the Romans[54] by dressing up as women, complete with bleached-blond hair and heavy make-up, and, in imitation of their lord, castrating themselves in public during their annual parade to offer their genitals to Attis' consort, the goddess Cybele.[55] And yet no one tries to argue that Attis must have been real, because who would invent a castrated drag queen god?

And the fact is, those Jewish scriptural texts *did* exist all along – and it wasn't just the early Christians who read them as prophecies of a suffering and dying messiah. We know many Jews before the first century awaited a warrior messiah to drive out their oppressors by the sword and put the kingdom of David on top of the world. But the longer their oppression continued, with no messiah to smite their foes forthcoming, the more difficult it became for other Jews to believe that a military savior was ever in the cards. Even before Christianity, some of them had already beaten Jesus to the punch – by expecting a messiah who would suffer and die to save them.

Richard Carrier has demonstrated that proof of the concept at the very least (and at best, actual confirmation) of this can be seen in the Talmud: the tractate Sanhedrin (98b and 93b) explicitly says the suffering servant in Isaiah 53 is the messiah, and will endure great suffering before dying. In the tractate Sukkah (52a-b) the Talmud presents no less than a dying-and-rising "Christ son of Joseph," even quoting Zechariah (12:10) to declare that this messiah will be "pierced" to death.[56] Carrier notes that many biblical scholars (understandably) are anxious to deny any hint of such pre-Christian rumblings. But they can't just dismiss Talmudic texts out of hand so quickly. Most will wave away the Talmudic evidence by saying it is too late (fourth to sixth century); normally not a bad argument. But consider this: although the texts are late, the theological developments they describe are unlikely to be. As Carrier points out:

> "There is no plausible way later Jews would invent interpretations of their scripture that supported and vindicated Christians. They would not invent a Christ with a father named Joseph who dies and is resurrected (as the Talmud does indeed describe). They would not proclaim Isaiah 53 to be about this messiah and admit that Isaiah had there predicted this messiah would die and be resurrected. That was the very biblical passage Christians were using to prove their case. Moreover, the presentation of this ideology in the Talmud makes no mention of Christianity and gives no evidence of being any kind of polemic or response to it. So we have evidence here of a Jewish belief that possibly predates Christian evangelizing, even if that evidence survives only in later sources."[57]

Otherwise, Carrier notes our only option is to assume it was just an incredible coincidence that Christians and Jews, completely independently of each other, both happened to latch on to Isaiah 53, decide it was really referring to the messiah (and not the nation of Israel, as it says), who would not be a military conqueror but a sacrifice for our sins, and predicted that that messiah would have a (literal or symbolic) father named Joseph, endure great suffering and die, and be resurrected.[58] A coincidence of that magnitude is too ridiculous to take seriously – but a causal connection is not: if this was a pre-Christian theological development that led to *both* the

Christian *and* the Jewish breakthroughs, it makes far more sense than trying to argue that the same idea just happened to arise twice in rival religions.[59]

But if some Christians *do* try to argue that colossally unlikely position (they've tried to push sillier ideas), they are caught in a trap: That would mean that the idea of a suffering and dying messiah was *not* a radical idea to the Jews after all.[60] They were fine with it. They made one up in the Talmud. Why couldn't they have made one up in first century Judea?

Other Pre-Christian Suffering Messiahs in Jewish Scriptures

But really, we already knew that. Well before Christianity, Jews interpreted Isaiah 53 in light of the suffering of Jewish hero-martyrs like the Maccabees, as Jarvis Williams demonstrates in *Maccabean Martyr Traditions in Paul's Theology of Atonement: Did Martyr Theology Shape Paul's Conception of Jesus's Death?* (2010). And the dying-messiah doctrine is not only found in the Talmud. Still other texts in the Jewish scriptures had already pointed the way to a suffering savior: The *Wisdom of Solomon*, an important scripture to the early Christians[61], refers to a righteous man calling himself the Son of God who is despised, killed, resurrected, and crowned as a king in heaven (2:12-22, 5:1-23). Another Pre-Christian messianic reference is the book of Daniel, which unmistakably declares that a messiah will die shortly before the end of the world, when all sins will be forgiven (Daniel 9:2, 9:24-27; cf. 12:1-13).[62]

And there are still other possibilities. We may have further evidence of that prior tradition in the Targum of Jonathan ben Uzziel, an early first century commentary on Isaiah 53, where he explicitly identifies Isaiah's suffering servant as the Christ. But this text has been multiply tampered with over the years,[63] so we can't draw any definite conclusions from it (although, again, it is unlikely rabbinical Jews would change the Targum to make Isaiah 53 messianic *after* Christians started using Isaiah 53 to make their case).[64]

The dying messiah motif shows up again, considerably more spelled out, in a seventh century Jewish apocalypse, *Sefer Zerubbabel*, which has two messiahs: a Messiah ben David, and a Messiah ben Joseph. It prophesies the Son of Joseph would come first, only to be killed by an evil tyrant named "Armilus" (a Hebraicism for Romulus, i.e., Rome, some scholars suspect). But all would not be lost, because the second messiah, the Son of David, would soon appear and resurrect him just before the end of the world.[65]

Sound familiar? Do the math: a martyred son of Joseph plus resurrection plus a triumphant, anointed son of David equals Jesus Christ. Granted, this text is late, but as Carrier asks, which is more likely: that early Christians combined two messiahs from a strand of earlier Jewish apocalyptic thought? Or that Rabbinical Jews copied the new messiah of a heretical spinoff cult, and then for some reason split that figure into two messiahs, "with otherwise all the same attributes (and then make no mention of how this responds to Christianity or why they would even do that)?"[66]

The Dead Sea Scrolls may also be talking about two messiahs, though this is less certain: a "Messiah of Aaron" who would be the "true high priest" and a "Messiah of Israel" who would be a kingly warlord figure. But it's debated whether these are actually two messiahs, what kind of messiahs they are, and whether the text says one of these messiahs "will be pierced" and killed, or whether he will pierce and kill someone else. The manuscript is too damaged to tell, so that question may be unresolvable at present.[67]

One particular Dead Sea Scroll, known as the Melchizedek Scroll (designation 11Q13 or 11QMelch), tells us about the 'messenger' of Isaiah 52-53 who is linked with a 'servant' who will die to atone for everyone's sins (a figure later Jews definitely regarded as the messiah). The scroll seems to also say this 'messenger' is the same as the messiah in Daniel 9, and the God's final victory will proceed according to the timetable in Daniel.[68]

Still, whatever one makes of the ben Uzziel Targum, *Sefer Zerubbabel* or the Melchizedek Scroll, there is simply no denying that Daniel 9:24-27 plainly predicts a messiah who will die shortly before the end of the world, when all sins will be forgiven; or that Isaiah 53 unmistakably declares that all sins will be forgiven by the death of God's suffering servant – a figure the Talmud identifies as the messiah. There is no reasonable basis to deny that some Jews expected a messiah who suffered and died long before Christianity arrived.[69]

Embarrassed to Death
For a story dripping with angels, dreams, miracles, resurrections, ascensions to heaven, historical improbabilities and outright errors, it's odd that anyone would even think it was a good idea to try to salvage any of the gospel story. And of course, if a major world religion wasn't founded on it, no one would be bothering.

Carrier notes: "Historicists will usually agree that once we trim away everything that's wrong or too speculative or inadequately demonstrated, we'll have *something* that can be reliably affirmed about the historical Jesus (even if it's literally nothing more than that he existed)."[70] As we've just seen in the past three chapters, even that may be asking too much. Part of the problem is that historians can't agree on what we are left with, once you eliminate the impossibilities. Another is that the historical criteria, the tools we've used to pick out the facts about Jesus, don't do the job, as even Christian scholars have long complained.

The upshot of all this is simply that *all* of the secular reconstructions of the 'Historical Jesus' from chapter three remain speculative. No one can claim to have cornered the market. And there is a good reason for that – our problematic primary sources for Jesus. Whatever you try to argue about what the real Jesus said and did, it all boils down to our sources.

What do *they* say?

***

For further reading:

For more clues that Mark's "Women at the Empty Tomb" scene is made up of literary tropes, and other issues pertaining to women's testimony in the ancient world:

Richard Carrier, *Not the Impossible Faith* (particularly ch. 11) Also chs. 1 & 2, 14 & 15.

---

[1] Hitchens, *God is not Great* (2007), p. 120
[2] Ibid., p. 114
[3] Debate w/Dinesh D'Souza at FreedomFest, July 10-12, 2008, Las Vegas. Available online at: http://www.youtube.com/watch?v=vMo5R5pLPBE)
[4] Matthew isn't above playing fast and loose with his source material, but in this particular case, we actually can be reasonably confident that he did know of some now-lost Jewish writing, once accepted as scripture, that claimed the messiah would be a "Nazorian." He probably would not have gotten away with saying so unless he had some proof-text to back up his claim. Then it becomes a question of why didn't Jews or early Christians preserve *that* "scripture"? See also the note below.
[5] We know that early Christian groups had different versions of our familiar biblical texts, and books that didn't survive in our bibles. So in cases like above, where Matthew claims there was – or even quotes from – "scripture" we don't recognize (e.g., see also Mark 9:12; Luke 24:46-47; John 7:38) odds are they are working off a long-lost textual

variant. See Carrier, *On the Historicity of Jesus*, pp. 91-92.
[6] Price, *The Incredible Shrinking Son of Man*, p. 53; see also McGrath, Nazorean
[7] Sometimes Nazoraean, Nazorian, or, in Greek, *Nazôraios*
[8] McGrath, Nazorean, p. 4
[9] Ibid.
[10] Epiphanius of Salamis, *Panarion* Book I, Tome II, Section 29. Epiphanius adds: "all Christians alike were called Nazoraeans. They also came to be called 'Jessaeans' for a short while." The name "Jessaeans" comes from Jesse, the father of King David, and certainly refers to Isaiah 11:1: "a rod out of the stem of Jesse, and a branch (*netzer*) shall grow out of his roots." As Frank Zindler points out in *The Jesus the Jews Never Knew*, "the title *Yeshua' Netzer* — "The Savior, The Branch"— became "Jesus the Nazarene." (p. 431)
[11] Kennard, "Nazorean and Nazareth," pp. 79-81
[12] *Exegetical Dictionary of the New Testament*, p.456
[13] McGrath, Notsrim
[14] McGrath, Nazorean, p. 4
[15] Proving History, pp. 142-45
[16] Kennard, "Nazorean and Nazareth" JBL 66 (1947) 79
[17] Irenaeus, *Against All Heresies*, 1.21.3
[18] See *Nailed* p. 41 and Frank Zindler's *The Jesus the Jews Never Knew* (2003)
[19] Carrier, *Proving History*, p.315, n49
[20] McGrath, op. cit.
[21] Levin, pp. 197-207
[22] Price, *The Incredible Shrinking Son of Man*, p. 193
[23] René Salm, *The Myth of Nazareth: The Invented Town of Jesus* 2008, and *NazarethGate: Quack Archeology, Holy Hoaxes and the Invented Town of Jesus,* Cranford, NJ: 2015
[24] For details, see "Amarna Letters" in the *Ancient History Encyclopedia*; available online at:

http://www.ancient.eu/Amarna_Letters/
²⁵ Josephus, *Life*, 45; *Jewish War*, vol. II, 20.6
²⁶ Frank Zindler; cited in Salm, 2015, p. xviii
²⁷ I find some of Salm's points stronger than others, but I particularly appreciate Salm's response here from the paper he delivered to the *Society for Biblical Literature*: "Not being an archaeologist myself, I am often asked: 'How can you date evidence, Mr. Salm?' or: 'How can you presume to correct professional archaeologists?' or: 'How can you have any opinion on these matters?' However, there is a misunderstanding inherent in these questions, for I have never dated anything at all. I have simply identified the relevant archaeological experts and quoted *their* published datings: Hans-Peter Kuhnen on kokhim tombs, Varda Sussman on bow-spouted oil lamps, Roland Deines on Jewish stone vessels, Amos Kloner on circular blocking stones, and so on. The case regarding Nazareth does not rest on my opinion at all. Anyone who disagrees with *The Myth of Nazareth is* not disagreeing with me but is taking issue with the leading archaeological experts in the world." While I remain provisionally agnostic on the Nazareth question, I agree 100% with his paper's conclusion: "Nazareth archaeology presents a persistent pattern of error, internal contradiction, and outright fraud." The entire paper is available online at: http://nazarethmyth.info/SBL_2012_Salm_%28Nazareth%29.pdf
²⁸ Salm, 2015, pp. 25, 72
²⁹ Ibid., p. 72
³⁰ Salm, *The Archeology of Nazareth: A History of Pious Fraud?* Paper presented to SBL, November 17, 2012 (See note above for link)
³¹ Ibid., pp. 34-35
³² Debate w/Dinesh D'Souza – see note 3 above
³³ Dr. William Lane Craig, "The Historicity of the Empty

Tomb of Jesus." Available online at: http://www.leaderu.com/offices/billcraig/docs/tomb2.html - text83)

34 Wegner, pp. 119 -127
35 See, e.g., Mark 3:31-24; 4:30-32; 7:15; 8:35; 9:35; 10:29-30, 31, 44; 12:1-11; there are many other examples.
36 Craig, op. cit.
37 cf. Matthew 28:1, Mark 16:1, Luke 24:1 & 10, John 20:1
38 Carrier, NtIF pp. 314-15
39 See "The Name Game" in ch. 13.
40 Theissen and Winter, *Quest*, p. 175
41 Carrier, *Proving History*, pp.151-155
42 See Price, "Apocryphal Apparitions: 1 Corinthians 15:3-11 as a Post-Pauline Interpolation" in *The Empty Tomb*, pp. 69-104
43 Meier, John P., "The Circle of the Twelve: Did it Exist During Jesus' Public Ministry?" p. 663
44 See "Payment in Blood," in ch. 8 and "Kiss of Death," in ch. 9.
45 Meier, *A Marginal Jew*, vol. 1, pp. 168-69
46 Carrier, op. cit. p.145
47 Along with the community or communities that embraced Mark's gospel, the Ebionites ("The Poor") and the Theodotians are other early sects who appear to be Adoptionist Christians; see Helms, pp. 32-34
48 Carrier, ibid, p. 146
49 For examples, see: Celsus, *De Medicina* V, 28, 18B; Galen, *On the Natural Faculties*, III, VII, 163; Pliny, *Nat. Hist.* 28. 7; cf. 28. 4, 22; Theocritus, *Idyll*, VI, 39. Rabbinical sources also advise healing with spit (BB 126b; Shab. 14.14d; 18; Sotah. 16d, 37).
50 For still more examples, see Myth no. 6 in *Nailed*
51 Meier, "The Circle of the Twelve," pp. 665-66
52 Ibid.
53 From *Nailed*, p. 157

[54] Vermaseren, p.115
[55] Ferguson, pp. 264-269
[56] Carrier, *On the Historicity of Jesus* p. 73
[57] Ibid.
[58] Ibid.
[59] Ibid.
[60] Rabbinical Jews could be just as comfortable with the idea as Christians were; see "The Last Desperate Objection" in Carrier, *On the Historicity of Jesus*; pp. 610-616
[61] See ch. 13 for more on the *Wisdom of Solomon*.
[62] Carrier, op. cit., pp. 78-87
[63] Chilton, 1982, p. 94
[64] Carrier, op. cit., 73-75
[65] Ibid.; see also Reeves, pp. 40-66
[66] Ibid.
[67] See note in Carrier, op. cit., p.75n34 for more discussion.
[68] See note in ibid., p.76n36 for more discussion.
[69] Ibid., p. 77
[70] Ibid., p. 50

Part Two: The Sources for Jesus

Chapter Six:
The Source of our Problems (and the Problems of our Source)

"Every story must be considered as suspicious which depends in any degree upon religion."

-Francis Bacon

In chapter four, we saw what biblical historians – even devout Christian biblical historians – have been steadily complaining about for nearly a century: that all the tools we have been using to determine what's authentic in our various Jesus traditions simply don't work. Instead, they've only made a much worse mess of what precious little we thought we could know for certain about Jesus. The closer we look, the less we find any indisputable core facts of Jesus.

In chapter three, we saw that one major problem with the secular consensus on Jesus is that there *is* no consensus: what we have is a menagerie of Jesuses, many of them perfectly plausible, many of them quite convincing – until you read the next one. Increasingly, historians (like Hector Avalos, John Dominic Crossan, Richard Carrier, Robert Price, and more) are complaining that as a field, Jesus studies has become impossible to take seriously. And it's not just secular historians – even devoutly religious Jesus historicists are complaining that the historical Jesus is a theory in crisis. Phillip Davies is one of those biblical historians who complains the problem is not limited to the Historical Jesus question:

> "Can biblical scholars persuade others that they conduct a legitimate academic discipline? Until they do, can they convince anyone that they have something to offer to the

intellectual life of the modern world? Indeed, I think many of us have to convince ourselves first!"[1]

How *do* we know what we know about Jesus? Whether a historian is arguing that the real Jesus was just a failed apocalyptic prophet, a revolutionary zealot, or some combination of any of the other dozens of possibilities that have been floated over the years, how can we know which, if any, are close to the truth? Not to crucify a dead horse, but we have to keep in mind that if there *is* an answer to the question of who the real Jesus was, it can only be found in our sources for Jesus. And therein lies the problem.

Sources for Jesus
Our pool of information on Jesus come down to three groups of sources: 1) The Gospels, 2) the rest of the New Testament, and 3) texts from outside the Bible; both from Christian writings that didn't make the cut to become scripture, and writings from non-Christian outsiders. But as we'll see, all of these sources come with reasons to not to take them too seriously – or even accept them at all. And we must keep in mind that whether Jesus really existed or not, whether Christianity is true or not, all these problems remain; suggesting that at the very least, perhaps a healthy agnosticism would be a good starting point to any discussion of Christianity's origins.

First Problem: The Black Hole
The first problem is with the initial blackout period of early Christian scripture. As Bart Ehrman and numerous other historians have long made very clear, we don't have the originals of any book of the New Testament. What we have are copies of copies of copies of copies… This situation is stranger than it might seem at first glance. We do have other surviving texts from the first century, and even far older writings. Yet we have no surviving Christian texts from the first hundred years of Christianity, and only tiny scraps for another half century,

possibly even a full century more.² And yet, it was the Christians who were in charge of preserving the writings of the ancient world. This is why the western world lost so much of Greek philosophy and science (well over 95% was lost), and why the only remaining ancient criticisms of Christianity can only be found in quotes from the apologetic manuals of the Church Fathers who tried to rebut them.³

It's not until the late second/early third century⁴ that we begin to get the complete texts of some of the individual books of the New Testament, and not until the early-to-mid fourth

---

The First New Testaments & their Differences

Codex Vaticanus (c. 325–350) contains:

1) The Septuagint. Some of Genesis, Psalms and 2 Kings have been damaged or lost, and

1-4 Maccabees and the Prayer of Manasseh is missing.

2) A partial New Testament. *Vaticanus* lacks 1 & 2 Timothy, Titus, Philemon, and Revelation; and its Epistle to the Hebrews is cut off at verse 9:14.

Codex Siniaticus (c. 330–360) contains:

1) The Septuagint, a Greek translation of the Jewish scriptures. The Septuagint in *Siniaticus* has about half of the Old Testament (most of the books from Genesis to 1 Chronicles are missing and presumed lost) and some of the Apocrypha (2 Esdras, Tobit, Judith, 1 & 4 Maccabees, Wisdom and Sirach).

2) the New Testament (in different order than our NT)

3) two early Christian texts not found in modern Bibles: The Shepherd of Hermas and the Epistle of Barnabas

There are also many differences between their copies of the NT and ours. Notably absent from both are the Marcan Appendix (i.e., the end of our gospel of Mark, verses 16: 9-20) and the Story of the Woman Caught in Adultery (John 7:53 – 8:11). Each is missing several other passages and phrases; and each has additional verses than ours, some found nowhere else.

Sources:

Bruce M. Metzger (2001). *A Textual Commentary on the Greek New Testament*. Stuttgart: Deutsche Bibelgesellschaft. United Bible Societies. pp. 179, 187–189

Aland, Kurt; Barbara Aland (1995). *The Text of the New Testament: An Introduction to the Critical Editions and to the Theory and Practice of Modern Textual Criticism*, trans. Erroll F. Rhodes. Grand Rapids, Michigan: William B. Eerdmans Publishing Company. p. 109.

century that we have our first two complete New Testaments, the *Codex Vaticanus* and the *Codex Siniaticus*. And even that is a bit misleading; since both codices have different books from each other – and for that matter, from our own bibles (see below). They have books we don't have. We have books they don't have. And of course, even today the major branches of Christendom (Catholic, Orthodox and Protestant) still differ in their canons. Contrary to popular belief, the Council of Nicea in 325 CE never settled the matter of which books would make it into the New Testament canon; it was a much messier (and bloodier) process that went on for centuries; in fact, one could argue that it has *never* been settled…

Some try to claim this is not a problem. Bruce Metzger, a respected giant in New Testament studies, famously said that even if we lost all our manuscripts of the New Testament, we could still recreate its contents from the quotations in the sermons and letters of the early church fathers.[5] But this bold claim is immediately refuted – by none other than Metzger himself, who giveth and then taketh away, quickly backpedaling with this caution: "On the other hand, however, before the textual critic can use the patristic evidence with confidence, he must determine whether the true text of the ecclesiastical writer has been transmitted."[6] He goes on to describe several of the difficulties involved with this, and then discusses these early church fathers who are meant to provide our failsafe backup of the New Testament. One glaring problem immediately arises: his list of "early" church fathers (including a few heretics, too) are a little late: none of the Church Fathers he cites are from the first century of Christianity, and only three are even from the second century; the vast majority are from the third, fourth, and even the fifth and sixth centuries![7]

This is not to imply that no early Christian scripture was written until the end of the second century. The problem is that only tiny scraps remain from any Christian writing (both canonical and non-canonical) for the first 150 - 200+ years of the fledgling religion. Anyone who tries to assure you (and apologists do, constantly) that we can fully trust that our existing New Testaments are 99.9999% reliable and faithful to their divinely inspired originals; and that any possible niggling devil in the details is far too small and innocuous to worry about (and certainly no one's salvation depends on it!) is only fooling themselves. This blackout period means short of a time machine, we have no way to know, and never will have a way to know, how closely our oldest intact New Testament manuscripts matched up to the originals. In fact, we have no way of even *recognizing* if any manuscript *was* the original – even if it survived and we had it in our hands... Which brings up our second problem.

Second Problem: Scribal Alterations – Unintentional Errors and Deliberate Tampering
Perhaps if we could magically be assured somehow that the texts had been preserved faithfully, maybe that century or two of total blackout wouldn't be a problem. Apologists certainly seem willing to overlook the difficulty and give their New Testament texts the benefit of a doubt. The only trouble is, *which* text should they trust? – because they can't trust them all. To begin with, none of them agree with one another. No two complete New Testament documents match, and between our copies there are differences in not hundreds, not thousands, but in hundreds of thousands of places.[8] This isn't necessarily a problem when the differences are from simple scribal errors.

Professional (or at least professionally trained, since monks weren't paid) Christian scribes didn't emerge as a class until the fourth and fifth centuries.[9] For the centuries before that, most copyists were amateurs; the more or less literate members of local churches who were more or less willing to do the job more or less competently.[10] Mistakes were made, all the time. Even when the work had become the purview of full time monks, it was still long, grueling, painstaking work in an age long before the benefits of electrical lighting or prescription eyewear. Copyists varied in their ability for a number of reasons. As Bart Ehrman has noted,[11] sometimes scribes grew inattentive, or hungry, or sleepy, or just couldn't be bothered to give it their best effort. But even competent, trained and alert scribes made their share of mistakes, too. There were other factors that contributed to scribal error. For example, the lack of punctuation marks and spacing in ancient times caused problems for copyists and still make it tricky to interpret some verses today.[12] But errors aren't necessarily our biggest difficulty. For the most part, typos, grammatical flubs and other minor scribal fails are easy to catch (though not always), and this is indeed the case in the vast majority of textual differences. However, it's the exceptions that are interesting.

Deliberate Changes
These are the many cases where changes in texts occurred deliberately. Ironically, another reason for differences in our surviving texts is *harmonization*, the process of trying to make the scriptures conform to one another. Attempts to iron out disagreements between the gospels occur with far greater frequency than other kinds of scribal modifications,[13] and we should bear in mind it's anyone's guess how much harmonization had already occurred by the time any of our surviving texts were written. The same can be said for the other kinds of deliberate changes we have detected in our existing manuscripts.

Scribes often felt the need to make *corrections* to the mistakes of earlier versions of scripture. Mark, our first gospel, starts off on a bad note by declaring, "As it is written in Isaiah the prophet..." (Mark 1:2) and then giving a mashup of Malachi 3:1 and Isaiah 40:3. Later copyists recognized the problem, and fixed it to "As it is written *in the prophets*..." a reading still found in the King James Version.

A similar mistake can be found in the Gospel of Matthew. When verse 27:9 claims to be quoting a prophecy of Jeremiah ("Then was fulfilled that which was spoken by Jeremy the prophet, saying, And they took the thirty pieces of silver, the price of him that was valued, whom they of the children of Israel did value"), Matthew's actually citing a non-prophecy from the story of Zechariah ("I told them, 'If you think it best, give me my pay; but if not, keep it.' So they paid me thirty pieces of silver." Zech. 11:12).

John 19:14 has Jesus being crucified on the "sixth hour" (i.e., noon). A few scribes changed this to the "third hour" (i.e., 9 a.m.) to match Mark 15:25.[14] But since John has Jesus crucified on a completely different day than the other gospels,[15] this doesn't solve the problem. The church father Origen altered John 1:28 ("These things were done in Bethany beyond Jordan, where John was baptizing.") to avoid what he thought was a geographic mistake changing the town from "Bethany" to "Bethabara" – and modern bible versions are still split on which town it should be.[16]

Some scribes couldn't resist the temptation of gratuitous insertions to bring *adornments* to their texts, adding words and phrases when the original language didn't sound exalted enough, or just seemed to be lacking something. For instance, where Matthew 9:13 had Jesus say, "for I am not come to call the righteous, but sinners," more than a few scribes felt the need to add "to repentance."[17]

What could a scribe do when he found himself in the unhappy predicament of having two variants of the exact same passage? If he picked one over the other, he ran the risk of accidentally preserving the wrong version and omitting the genuine reading. So most of them tried to escape their quandary by incorporating *both* into the new copy – creating what is known as a *conflation of readings.*[18]

There are many examples of *elaboration* of minor characters in the New Testament. Some lesser anonymous figure might get a name or other biographical info from a helpful later scribe; unfortunately, we often wind up with a surplus of different names for the same character. For instance, the two robbers crucified along with Jesus: in various Old Latin manuscripts, the one on his right has been named Zoatham, Joathas, and more; the one on his left, Camma, Maggatras, Capnatas, and more.[19]

Similarly, the texts have undergone *expansions*, the most famous/infamous being the multiple endings tacked on to Mark, which originally ended at 16:8 (see ch. 12). And there are still other kinds of random alterations that occur, sometimes for less obvious reasons.[20]

There is also the matter of accidental scribal *interpolations*; where margin notes become mistaken for missing text and become inserted into the document. For example, in Epiphanius' 4th century treatise *The Weights and Measures*, an accidental scribal interpolation occurs on practically every other page of the text. In one case from that same text, evidence suggests about five accidental interpolations took place *in the very same passage*, which in the end amounted to creating an entire new paragraph, with none of the five scribes involved having any idea.[21] Bruce Metzger gives still more examples of all these types of alterations in his *The Text of the New Testament; Its Transmission, Corruption and Restoration* (1992).

Curiouser and Curiouser
If you are already feeling a bit like Alice in Wonderland, I'm afraid our situation only grows more complicated still. Hang on...

All our New Testament books are modern reconstructions. It's yet another skeleton in Christianity's closet that all our myriad bible translations today are based not on any actual manuscript, but on a hypothetical and artificial reconstructed composite text.[22] At countless places in that text, choices had to be made as to which variant wording was the original reading. And for every single one of them, devout Christian scholars with the necessary expertise in textual criticism and the relevant ancient languages have come to opposite conclusions on just what that original reading was.[23] Some of them are in fact undecidable; we may very well never be able to tease out which reading is the right one. Assuming we ever could decide that we finally have the actual correct version of the original text, there remains the equally unanswerable question of what the correct *interpretation* of those words should be, but I won't open *that* can of worms...

That there are significant differences among our texts is troubling enough; but it's the differences *in meaning* that are worrisome; particularly when one manuscript says one thing – and another copy of the exact same manuscript says the opposite. Another factor makes the matter still worse: often these disagreements aren't just from honest mistakes, but in many cases, are deliberate.

Even a casual reading of the New Testament shows abundant evidence that the early church was constantly raging with countless debates, even over issues (including: circumcision, keeping kosher, whether salvation was by grace or by works, taking supper with unbelievers, and many more) that Jesus had supposedly already settled long ago. But even if the gospels and epistles never mentioned these fights that were tearing the early church apart, we could still trace them simply by looking at the places where scribes altered the texts of scripture to make it say what they *wished* it had said – or as they probably saw it, merely "correcting" what surely had to have been a mistake in their copy...

Unthinkable? Not at all. In fact, all of our surviving texts provide indisputable evidence that competing factions of early Christians were engaged in aggressive scribal push-me-pull-you, altering scripture in opposite directions, for centuries. How many of *these* sorts of changes should we be concerned about? Bart Ehrman surveys our texts to find dozens of them, and cautions us that we have almost certainly not uncovered them all, and may never recognize the full extent of the problem.[24]

His *The Orthodox Corruption of Scripture* demonstrates that even before anyone ever thought to create a New Testament, the theological dogfight was already raging: Adoptionist factions like the Ebionites and the Theodotians believed Jesus was an ordinary human being who became exalted after his death; their rivals made changes to verses that emphasized his human nature (such as Matt. 24:36, where they removed "nor the son" from "But about that day and hour no one knows, neither the angels of heaven, nor the Son, but only the Father.").

Scribes who followed Christians with Docetist leanings, like Clement and Origen, de-emphasized his humanity. To thwart them, verses in Paul's letters, such as Romans 1:3, that said Jesus was "made from" or "came from" the seed of David was changed to read that Jesus was "born from" the seed of David; and Gal. 4:4, which said Jesus was "made from" a woman, was changed to read that Jesus was "born" of a woman.

Other factions believed that Jesus Christ was actually two persons; that God had sent a divine emissary of the Godhead into Jesus to empower him for his mission – a spiritual Christ who jumped ship just before the crucifixion and returned to heaven, leaving the hapless human Jesus to die.

And still other factions like the Patripassianists ("Suffering Father"-ists) believed that Christ was no less than God the Father himself made flesh. The faction that eventually would become the Roman Catholics had their own dogmas to defend against all of these, and still more, rivals. And all of them altered the documents in their hands to better reflect what they thought the correct reading should be.

Or perhaps, to simply reflect their own prejudices. For instance, many scholars have accused the Bible of having a tendency to denigrate women. But several early scribes apparently thought their scriptures didn't go far enough to put the womenfolk in their place. In fact, often they preferred to eliminate any mention of them altogether. Prisca and Aquila are a married couple in the book of Acts. Some scribes reversed their names so that Aquila came first, but odder still, other scribes removed the name of Aquila's wife Prisca; with some even going so far as to remove her entirely from the story, changing all references of "them" to "him."[25]

Were Christian women too sinful to even *appear* in the Bible? In several instances, scribes certainly went to a lot of trouble to rewrite women out of Christian history. Colossians 4:15 originally read: "Give my greetings to the brothers in Laodicea, and to Nympha and the church in her house." But look up that verse in your King James Version (and others), and a sex change occurs; now it gives greetings to "Nymphas," and the church in *his* house. Incidentally, the common female name Nympha appears frequently in Latin inscriptions and Greek literature.[26] The name "Nymphas" on the other hand, seldom occurs.[27]

Likewise, in Romans 16:7 Paul salutes a man and woman, Andronicus and Junia, both prominent apostles. The idea that a female might be "foremost of the apostles"[28] rankled some Christians, who changed the female apostle Junia to a male apostle, "Junias." Apparently the idea still doesn't sit well with some translators, since even today several modern versions prefer to keep the alteration, despite that there is no evidence in the ancient world for any man named "Junias." What does *your* bible say?

Bishop Eusebius of Caesarea, quoting a writer of an earlier generation, shows the outrage rival Christians had for each other's handiwork (in this case, an orthodox scribe railing against the Theodotians for "boldly perverting" scriptures):

> "...they fearlessly lay their hands upon the holy Scriptures, saying that they have corrected them. And that I do not say this against them without foundation, whoever wishes may learn; for should any one collect and compare

their copies one with another, he would find them greatly at variance among themselves. For the copies of Asclepiodotus will be found to differ from those of Theodotus. Copies of many you may find in abundance, altered, by the eagerness of their disciples to insert each one his own corrections, as they call them, i.e., their corruptions.

"For one may compare those which were prepared before by them, with those which they afterwards perverted for their own objects, and you will find them widely differing. But what a stretch of audacity this aberration indicates, it is hardly probable themselves can be ignorant. For either they do not believe that the holy Scriptures were uttered by the holy Spirit, and they are thus infidels, or they deem themselves wiser than the holy Spirit, and what alternative is there but to pronounce them dæmoniacs?

"For neither can they deny that they have been guilty of the daring act, when the copies were written with their own hand, nor did they receive such Scriptures from those by whom they were instructed in the elements of the faith; nor can they show copies from which they were transcribed."[29]

See chapter 7 of *Nailed* (esp. pp. 108-123) for more examples of other early Christians complaining about their own scribes altering scriptures and other Christian writings (and simultaneously denying to pagan critics that the problem existed).

(above) Page from the *Codex Vaticanus* [30]

The marginal note to the left of the middle column is from a supervisor scolding a scribe for making a change to the text at Hebrews 1:3: "Fool and knave! Leave the old reading alone, don't change it!"[31]

David Fitzgerald

Third Problem: Forgery
At a debate with Richard Carrier a few years ago,[32] amateur Internet apologist J.P. Holding insisted that we have no reason to suspect such scribal misconduct was occurring during the blackout period (despite the undeniable textual evidence of widespread alterations occurring at every stage *after* the blackout, for hundreds of years afterwards). During the Q & A I told him if he wanted proof, he need look no further than his own scriptures: The Bible ends with a warning to just such would-be scribal vandals (Rev. 22:18-19). And 2 Thessalonians 3:17 declares that Paul's handwritten signature is a distinguishing mark in all his genuine letters - ironically, a letter virtually all scholars recognize is a forgery! Holding couldn't grasp that insisting 2 Thessalonians is genuine impales apologists like him on the horns of a dilemma: If this *was* authentic, then Paul himself is warning against letters being forged in his name... and that all the other New Testament letters in his name that don't have this "distinguishing mark" are forgeries! So either way, it is inescapable – Christians were forging scripture in his name. And not just in his name.

"Arguably the most distinctive feature of the early Christian literature is the degree to which it was forged." Bart Ehrman opens his massive survey of pious fraud in early Christianity, *Forgery and Counterforgery* (2013) with this observation, later adding that the literary landscape of the first several Christian centuries is littered with falsely attributed and forged writings. Even outside the Bible, Christian forgeries of every kind abound all the way into the Middle Ages.[33] Over the course of 628 pages, Ehrman provides fifty examples of canonical and non-canonical forgeries in early Christianity, as well as examining the phenomena of forgery in the ancient world in general, and in Judaism before Christianity.

In the process, he explodes the oft-repeated and self-serving (not to mention ridiculous) Christian myth that falsely writing under the name of a famous apostle was not considered fraud, but was simply a sign of respect, or an acceptable way for the early Church to show a document's theological value and legitimacy. Of course, as we've already seen, the truth is that the ancient world despised literary frauds as much as we do, and roundly condemned them as "lies," "bastards" and "counterfeits."[34] The early Church denounced the practice just as loudly and vociferously – even when they were engaged in blatant literary deceit behind the scenes.

We don't have to suppose any Machiavellian plot behind all their widespread alteration. Even if the motives of the scribes were pure as the driven snow, it was all too easy for changes to accumulate, even quite unintentionally; most especially before they were canonized, but even long after one would think their contents were already well-established and inviolate. As Carrier notes, it doesn't require a conspiracy theory, but the fact of all this tampering is so indisputable, there is more than enough evidence to support you if you were to choose to propose one:

> Any such community will organically produce the same effect as a conspiracy, without ever having to conspire to do anything. They do not require any top-down instructions or orders to follow, nor any collusion. If each independently did what made sense to him, each on his own initiative, the effect on the evidence that survives for us now will have been the same. For example, no one "colluded" to forge an ending to Mark. It was not an order issued from the Pope or some cabal of archbishops. Someone just did it.[35]

All we need to account for all this is for Christians to do what they've always done, or indeed, what any other religion would do. Only two factors were needed, and we know the early church met both criteria swimmingly. As long as 1) they believed they already knew "what would Jesus do?" and 2) had no qualms against doctoring, forging, or even outright destroying, inconvenient evidence (or at the very least, just fail to mention or preserve it), any other religious community would exhibit the same amount of tampering as we see in early Christianity.

This is not an idle hypothesis, but well established fact.[36] And the scribes in question would still sleep easy at night, secure that they had done the right thing in "correcting" their texts of the scriptures. Consequently, as we'll see shortly, the New Testament sags under the weight of forgeries; the forged books outnumber the genuine ones over 3 to 1, and even those few authentic books contain signs of later tampering and editing.

A Troubled History

All these three issues dovetail into a perfect storm of uncertainty for Christian origins. We don't have to speculate that Christians tampered with scripture, or made errors in its transmission, or outright forged scripture; we know very well that they did, from the abundant textual evidence of every single surviving early New Testament document. And we know that we have no way to trace the original version of any book in the New Testament.

> "Unlike most other questions in history, the evidence for Jesus is among the most compromised bodies of evidence in the whole of ancient history," says Carrier. "That some text has been forged, or interpolated, or altered by Christians even outside the canon is a caveat I encounter in scholarly analysis of document after document, to the point that it becomes frustrating, and would be alarming in any other field. And yet, it's so common to this field that it is now simply taken for granted and thus often shrugged off."[37]

Carrier illustrates the depth of the problem with a brilliant, albeit wicked, thought experiment based on our provenance for the Gospel of John:

"This problem can be illustrated with a mock analogy. Imagine in your golden years you are accused of murdering a child many decades ago and put on trial for it. The prosecution claims you murdered a little girl in the middle of a public wedding in front of thousands of guests. But as evidence all they present is a religious tract written by "John" which lays out a narrative in which the wedding guests watch you kill her.

Who is this John? The prosecution confesses they don't know. *When did he write this narrative?* Again, unknown. Probably thirty or forty years after the crime, maybe even sixty. *Who told John this story?* Again, no one knows. He doesn't say. *So why should this even be admissible as evidence?* Because the narrative is filled with accurate historical details and reads like an eyewitness account. *Is it an eyewitness account?* Well, no, John is repeating a story told to him.

Told to him by an eyewitness? Well...we really have no way of knowing how many people the story passed through before it came to John and he wrote it down.

Although he does claim an eyewitness told him some of the details. *Who is that witness?* He doesn't say.

I see. So how can we even believe the story is in any way true if it comes from unknown sources through an unknown number of intermediaries? Because there is no way the eyewitnesses to the crime, all those people at the wedding, would have allowed John to lie or make anything up, even after thirty to sixty years, so there is no way the account can be fabricated.

If that isn't obviously an absurd argument to you, then you didn't understand what has just been said and you need to read that paragraph again until you do. Because seen in this more neutral context, that last argument *is monumentally absurd.*"[38]

David Fitzgerald

The Sources We *Don't* Have
More absurdity abounds. Despite spending considerable portions of his pro-historicist book *Did Jesus Exist?* pointing out how problematic the evidence is for every aspect of Jesus' life,[39] Bart Ehrman still manages somehow to insist there is enough evidence to make it "almost certain" that "at the very least one must say that he existed."[40] But when virtually everything about a subject's life is in question, why would it be unreasonable to question his existence as well?

Like other biblical scholars, Ehrman asserts that the gospel authors were interested in writing history, and had sources to rely on.[41] He doesn't even feel the need to defend this position with any argument; it's simply an assumption taken for granted. What are these sources lying behind the gospels?

Jesus Historians have postulated many: the hypothetical source "Q," "M" (or "proto-Matthew"), "L" (or "proto-Luke"), oral traditions, Aramaic sources, and more... There's just one catch. Ehrman and company don't know if these hypothetical sources ever even *existed* – let alone that they agree with what they argue. Besides accusing mythicists of this same tactic (though I know of no serious mythicists who do), Ehrman reprimands his fellow scholars for appealing to imaginary sources – but then turns around and commits the exact same offense himself![42]

If appealing to non-existent sources sounds completely unscholarly and deserving of ridicule, Raphael Lataster agrees with you, dubbing this bizarro-methodology *Ehrman's law*: if your preferred theory is not well aligned to existing evidence, simply invent as much non-existent evidence as needed and furthermore, proclaim the unquestionable reliability of your imagined sources.[43]

Even (in)famous Christian apologists like William Lane Craig, Richard Swinbourne and others have happily embraced this non-method and cite never-never sources to prop up their arguments for the resurrection and other wildly implausible events from the life of the Jesus of Faith.[44] But it's especially disturbing to see atheist New Testament scholars like the late Maurice Casey pulling the same cheap trick.[45]

Lataster points out we should be concerned if the case for Jesus' historicity is so flimsy that even its most prestigious and respected proponents need to create the sources they would like to have, while simultaneously ignoring the sources that they actually have.[46]

So, bearing all these issues in mind, let's look at those sources we actually do have...

***

For further reading:

For common examples of New Testament forgeries and interpolations, see the relevant sections of: *Nailed* (pp. 110-113)

Bart Ehrman, *Forgery and Counterforgery* (2013), *Jesus, Interrupted* (2009) and *Misquoting Jesus* (2005) *The Orthodox Corruption of Scripture* (1993)
Paul Tobin, *The Rejection of Pascal's Wager: A Skeptic's Guide to the Bible and the Historical Jesus* (2006).
Hector Avalos, *The End of Biblical Studies*, 2007
Wayne Kannaday, *Apologetic Discourse and the Scribal Tradition: Evidence of the Influence of Apologetic Interests on the Text of the Canonical Gospels* (Atlanta, GA: Society of Biblical Literature 2004)
C. S. C. Williams, *Alterations to the Text of the Synoptic Gospels and Acts* (Oxford, UK: Basil Blackwell, 1951)
On the whole problem of detecting interpolations in the Epistles:
Winsome Munro, "Interpolation in the Epistles: Weighing Probability," *New Testament Studies* 36 (1990): 431-43
W.O. Walker, Jr., "The Burden of Proof in Identifying Interpolations in Pauline Letters," *New Testament Studies*

33 (1987): 610-18 and "Text-Critical Evidence for Interpolation in the Letters of Paul," *Catholic Biblical Quarterly* 50 (1988): 622-31

Harmonizing Bible verses is still going strong today. Paul Davidson has collected a lovingly researched list of deliberate mistranslations in the modern NIV (New International Version, evangelical Christianity's favorite translation). Available online at: http://isthatinthebible.wordpress.com/articles-and-resources/deliberate-mistranslation-in-the-new-international-version-niv/

---

[1] "Do We Need Biblical Scholars?" *The Bible and Interpretation*, June 2005
[2] There are several collections of these early NT fragments (e.g. see Comfort & Barrett) and most if not all can now be seen online under their papyrus number, e.g., see the Wikipedia page "List of New Testament Papyri" available at: https://en.wikipedia.org/wiki/List_of_New_Testament_papyri
[3] For examples of these ancient critics (Porphyry, Celsus, Julian, et al.) see Carrier, *On the Historicity of Jesus*, pp. 301-2
[4] Our dating methods are not precise enough to be more specific. The earliest complete text of any epistle is from 200 C.E. +/-30 years. No complete gospel text is even that old.
[5] Metzger, *Text of the NT* (1992), p. 86
[6] Ibid., pp. 86-87
[7] Ibid., pp. 88-89
[8] Ehrman, *Misquoting Jesus*, pp. 207-85
[9] Ibid., p. 55
[10] Ibid.

[11] Ibid.
[12] e.g., see Metzger, *A Textual Commentary on the Greek New Testament* (2001), pp. 195-96; 520-23
[13] Ehrman, *Orth. Corr. of Script.*, p. 46, n124
[14] Metzger 1992, p. 199
[15] See "Meanwhile, in a Parallel Universe…" in ch. 10.
[16] Ibid.
[17] Ibid., pp. 198-99
[18] Ibid., p. 200
[19] Ibid., p. 205
[20] Ibid., pp. 203 - 206
[21] Private correspondence with Richard Carrier.
[22] Avalos, *End of Biblical Studies*, p. 88
[23] Ehrman, op. cit., p. 208
[24] Ibid., pp. 32; 46, n124
[25] Harnack, pp. 2-13
[26] See Bonnie Thurston's entry on 'Nympha' in *Eerdmans*, p. 977
[27] Entry for 'Nympha Nymphas' in *Hastings' Dictionary of the NT*
[28] Ehrman, MJ, p. 185
[29] (Eusebius, *Ecc. Hist.* Book 5, ch. 28 (pp. 215-6) Christian Frederick Cruse, trans., Grand Rapids, MI: Baker Book House, 1989
[30] Page from Codex Vaticanus B (Bibl. Vat., Vat. gr. 1209; Gregory-Aland no. B or 03).
[31] Metzger, op. cit., pp. 195-96; also Ehrman, op cit. p. 56
[32] "The Text of the New Testament: Do We Have What They Had?" Debate between Richard Carrier and J.P. Holding, at Amador Christian Center in Plymouth, California on April 9, 2011. (for video, see Richard Carrier, "Debates & Interviews," Richard Carrier Blogs [24 February 2012] at http://freethoughtblogs.com/carrier/archives/389; for the accompanying slideshow: http://www.richardcarrier.info/NTReliabilitySlideshow.pdf)

[33] Ehrman, *Forgery and Counter Forgery*, p. 149
[34] Ibid., pp. 29-32
[35] Carrier, *On the Historicity of Jesus*, p. 276
[36] For a sample of supporting evidence, see ibid, pp. 214-222
[37] Ibid., pp. 276-77
[38] Ibid., pp. 251-252
[39] e.g., Ehrman, *Did Jesus Exist*, pp. 70-71,73, 82, 97, 179, 268-69, and more.
[40] Ibid., p. 93
[41] e.g., see ibid., pp. 72-74
[42] Lataster, *Jesus Did Not Exist*, p. 56
[43] Ibid., e.g. pp. 48, 56, 88 and especially p. 59.
[44] See ibid., p. 60
[45] Ibid., p. 60n108
[46] Ibid., p. 53. For a full treatment, see "Madness: The Gospels and the Folly of the Hypothetical Source," in Lataster, *Jesus Did Not Exist*, pp. 41-64

Chapter Seven:
The Gospel Truth

"At the center of every myth there is another, that of the people who created it."

– Nuruddin Farah

What are the Gospels?

What *is* a gospel? Like almost every other aspect of Biblical Studies, the genre of the Gospels is still a matter of fierce debate. Unsurprisingly, most Christian scholars prefer that they be classed as ancient biography, but the matter isn't quite so tidy as that. The more forthright of them, such as Charles H. Talbert, will admit that by "ancient biography," they really mean a genre that at best combines biography and mythology[1] and agree with E. P. Sanders that the gospels "were written with the intention of glorifying Jesus and are not strictly biographical in nature."[2] Besides, even having completely mythical subjects didn't prevent ancient writers from crafting detailed biographies of figures like Romulus and Hercules.

The evangelists themselves most likely didn't call their works "gospels." In the first century, a "gospel" was a message proclaimed, heard and believed,[3] such as Jesus "preaching the gospel of the kingdom of God" (Mark 1:14) or Paul's gospel of Jesus, which he claims he received by divine visions (Gal. 2:2) and searching the scriptures (Romans 1:2, 1 Corinthians 15:3-4). For early Christians like Paul, there couldn't be four gospels, only one. All others were false (cf. Gal. 1:6-9).

Our four familiar gospels (not to be confused with the many other gospels that didn't make the cut[4]) are entitled "The Gospel According to" Matthew, Mark, Luke and John, respectively. This is already somewhat unusual. As Matthew Ferguson notes, ancient authors did not always name themselves within their texts. But when they didn't, there are other types of evidence to support their authorship. Often our surviving manuscript traditions have a name and title affixed to a text. An attribution like this may still be doubted for any number of reasons, but it is important that at least there *is* a clear attribution. Here we already have a problem with the authors of the Gospels.[5]

The manuscript traditions for our gospels do not have any such clear attribution declaring Matthew, Mark, Luke, or John as their authors. Instead, they use the Greek preposition κατά, meaning "according to" or "handed down from." For example, *Matthew* is titled εὐαγγέλιον κατὰ Μαθθαίον, "The Gospel *according* to Matthew." These titles aren't naming an author. They indicate the source of their information is no single person, but traditions that have been "handed down" to the early church. This is problematic. It means that right from the beginning, the earliest title traditions for our gospels distance themselves from any explicit claim of authorship.[6] In the case of other ancient writers, Ferguson points out we don't see this kind of ambiguity. For example, none of our surviving works of Tacitus say that the *Histories* or *Annals* were written "according to Tacitus" or "handed down from Tacitus." Instead, we have clear attribution to Tacitus in one case, and only vague and ambivalent attributions in the titles of the Gospels.[7]

Incidentally, for the last 150 years, mainstream scholarship has found authorial traditions for ancient writers like Tacitus or Plutarch are reliable. On the other hand, the vast majority of mainstream scholars doubt the traditional authors of the Gospels. Why? Because the traditions identifying Tacitus pass multiple *independent* criteria, and the best explanation for how Tacitus could satisfy these lines of inquiry is because he is genuinely the author of the text (see Matthew Fergusson's online essay "Why Scholars Doubt the Traditional Authors of the Gospels," for details). In contrast, the Gospels' traditional authors can't withstand the same questions, and the best

Jesus: Mything in Action

explanation for why they fail is that these later attributions genuinely don't fit the data.[8]

We should note that even those dubious traditional author names were assigned much later; all four of our gospel "sources" were originally anonymous sources. The first recorded naming of the authors is not until Irenaeus of Lyons, writing around the year 180. Once he names them, the identities of our four Evangelists become widespread throughout Christendom. Before that, there are only references to "memoirs of the apostles" by Justin Martyr in the mid-second century and before then, a few scattered and unsourced "quotes" from early church fathers like Clement of Rome that don't quite hold up as quotes.[9]

Even Christian scholars such as Raymond Brown admit that the titles were not added until the latter half of the 2nd century, a time when Christianity was embroiled in one vicious canonical dispute after another. During this war for scriptural dominance, competing factions began to invent apostolic authors as a means to bestow authority and official canonical status on their favored scriptures.[10]

This evangelical name-game was a change in strategy. Originally, the evangelists didn't want to put their names on to their writings. They wanted them to be anonymous for the same reason as many of the authors of the Old Testament books. Bernard M. Levinson explains in *Deuteronomy and the Hermeneutics of Legal Innovation*, in a culture governed by ancient authoritative texts like that of the early Hebrews, how is any legal innovation or religious evolution possible? The solution is to disclaim authorship and to deny originality. Religious writers with something new to say wouldn't voice their opinions in their own scribal voice in order to revise older traditions. Instead, they would defer to the voice of authoritative antiquity[11] and create an ostensibly timeless document; one they could hold up and say, "It is written..."[12]

So who *did* write them? In actuality, nowhere do the four gospels ever claim to be the work of eyewitnesses, nor do they read like first-hand accounts; quite the opposite, in fact (see below)[13]. Who really wrote them, and when and where, are all unknowns, though there are a few clues to some of these questions.

Who wrote them?
The gospels paint the twelve disciples largely as simple, illiterate, Aramaic-speaking fishermen and commoners. What about the gospel writers? Christian tradition identifies them as:

Matthew – one of the disciples. He also appears to be a conflation of two characters, "Matthew" (Matt. 9:9) and "Levi" (Mark 2:14, Luke 5:27), into one: "Mathew Levi, the tax collector." Virtually all critical scholars, Christian and secular alike, find the evidence that the real author was *not* a disciple conclusive,[14] as we'll see for ourselves shortly. The evidence also strongly suggests that "Matthew Levi" was not a tax collector, either.[15]

Mark – John Mark, said by second century church father Papias to be the apostle Peter's interpreter. The name may come from Paul, who mentions a Mark as one of his fellow missionaries (Philemon 1:24). *That* Mark appears again in the much later books of Acts and Colossians, again connected to Paul. The only book to link anyone named Mark (in this case, a Roman Christian) with Peter is 1 Peter (5:13), but as that book is a much later forgery,[16] so it's of questionable value. Likewise, there's no reason to trust Papias' claims that Mark worked alongside Peter. Mark is a Gentile, advocating Paul's brand of Gentile-friendly Christianity against Peter's style of Torah-observant Christianity. He would have been Peter's opponent, not his representative.[17] Mark's relatively unpolished Greek[18] made some scholars suspect he had a limited education, but his sophisticated literary composition and knowledge of classic and Jewish source material shows that he was employing his folksy style quite deliberately.[19]

Luke – The same verse in Philemon (1:24) that mentions a Mark also mentions a Luke, another colleague of Paul's. Colossians, a later epistle written in Paul's name, but not by him,[20] refers to "Luke, the beloved physician." Later traditions reached back to these sources to say that they referred to the author of the third gospel, Luke – a Syrian from Antioch, a physician and traveling companion of Paul. Still later traditions in the 8th century would say he was also a painter who gave us several venerated portraits of the Virgin Mary. We have no reason to put much trust in any of these claims.

Whoever wrote Luke's Gospel, a broad consensus agrees he is also the author of the New Testament book of Acts. There are four scattered places in Acts (16:10-17; 20:5-15; 21:1-18; 27:1-28:16) where the narration curiously shifts from third person to first person, called the "we" passages. Many have pointed to them as proof that Acts is based on a genuine source; some have used them to try to argue a companion of Paul really did write it, but few scholars agree. The conclusion doesn't follow;[21] and besides, nowhere in Acts (or Luke) does the author claim to be a companion of Paul. If the author really had such star power available, he wouldn't have missed the chance to broadcast the fact and boost his gospel's approval rating (and he probably wouldn't disagree with Paul's theology, either[22])

John – By tradition, "John" is John, son of Zebedee, one of the disciples. But that name only came about by pious guesswork in the mid-second century, and even so the real authorship was the subject of much debate in the second and third centuries.[23] The gospel itself mentions a mysterious unnamed "Beloved Disciple" who continues to show up all the other disciples, even everyone's favorite Disciple No. 1, Peter (e.g., 13: 23-25, 19:26-27, 20:1-10, 21:7). In one of the endings tacked on to the fourth gospel (John 21:24), a later editor identifies "the disciple Jesus loved" as its author.[24] However, this "beloved disciple" doesn't exist in any of the earlier gospels. What's more, he has been gratuitously inserted into their rebooted plotlines: for example, in Luke, Peter runs to go see the empty tomb (24:12). In John, both Peter and the beloved disciple run to the tomb – and the beloved disciple conspicuously outruns Peter there (20:3-4).

Who is this mystery disciple? A good argument can be made that we *do* know who this was meant to be – and it wasn't John. As many scholars have argued, starting with Floyd Filson over half a century ago,[25] only one character in the fourth Gospel is described (repeatedly; as "the one whom Jesus loved" (John 11:3, 5, 36). The day after this character is introduced (and described as Jesus' beloved), he is reclining with Jesus at supper (12:1-2, 12:9-11). One final and most compelling clue comes at the end of the gospel (21:21-24), when we learn a rumor has arisen that this Beloved Disciple would never die. Why would anyone think that? Because Jesus had already resurrected him from the dead (11:1- 44). There's only one character who fits the bill: Lazarus, the brother of Mary and Martha.

James Charlesworth tried to argue against this,[26] pushing for Thomas as his best bet for the mystery disciple. But his reasons aren't impressive. Case in point, his seventh "argument" (p. 290) is that since the Beloved Disciple outran Peter to the tomb, it couldn't possibly be Lazarus – because, after all, he had just been resurrected from the dead a few days before. Because of course if you know the first thing about your basic miraculous resurrections, you need some time to shake it off...

Incidentally, Lazarus is a pivotal character in John's story; his spectacular resurrection is the reason for Jesus' arrest and execution (11:45-53;12:9-11). But despite that, bizarrely enough, Lazarus doesn't even *appear* in the other gospels – except as the name of a fictional beggar in a parable told by Luke's Jesus (16:19-31).

Whoever the real author was, he tells us outright in verse 19:35 that he is not an eyewitness (nor an apostle, apparently, according to verses 20:30-31). For reasons like these and others, this whole idea of a beloved disciple seems to be a convenient fabrication. In contrast to Matthew, the author of John seems very anti-Semitic; his hostility isn't confined to the Scribes and priests, but "The Jews" as if they were all one collective blob of evil. Nonetheless, he's very well versed in Jewish Scriptures.

According to the church heresy-hunter Epiphanius of Salamis, at least one early heretical Christian group, nicknamed the "Alogi," (a pun meaning both "without *logos*" and "without logic") rejected the gospel of John because they believed that the heretic Cerinthus was its real author.[27] Gaius/Caius, a 3rd century presbyter of Rome, and Dionysius patriarch of Alexandria, seemed to have believed the same.[28] If true (not to make any claim that it is), he, Paul and John of Patmos (if that *was* his real name) would be the only New Testament authors whose names we actually know.

Who Were They Really?
So who were the evangelists really? We may never know their names, but the real Evangelists (as well as all their later redactors and editors) were well-educated, highly literate Greek-speaking theologians, familiar with both pagan classics and Jewish scriptures. They were not conducting interviews, investigating the facts, or recording history. They were each constructing a singular religious document, not giving their own independent take on a biography of Jesus. It's important to realize that, whether Jesus was a real figure or not, none of the gospel authors could have known him, or even anyone who claimed to know him. Since we have no other names to use, for simplicity's sake we'll keep calling the anonymous authors by the names traditionally assigned to them, but keep in mind that this is just a handy fiction.

David Fitzgerald

When Were They Written?
It's highly unlikely that any contemporary of Jesus would have still been alive by the time any of the Gospels were written. And indeed, none of the authors claimed to be disciples, or even acquaintances of Jesus, or even eyewitnesses, or even his contemporaries. Quite the opposite, in fact; as we're about to see, all were written long after the time they portray. What's more, just like the rest of the New Testament, all were edited and re-edited by others in an ongoing process over centuries.

The opening to Luke (1:1-3) explicitly declares that it is the product of a later Christian generation, at a time when many others have been writing competing gospels. One of the added endings of John (21:24) reveals that the editing of that gospel was the work of later Christians as well. If the author of Matthew was even trying to pose as a contemporary with Jesus, he gives the game away at several points, with lines like "this saying is commonly reported among the Jews *until this day,*" (Matt. 28:15), "Wherefore that field was called the field of blood, *unto this day,*" (27:8) and "And from the days of John the Baptist *until now...*" (11:12 – even though just a few verses before, John the Baptist was still alive and communicating with Jesus!).

When was Mark written?
Most scholars agree that Mark, our oldest Gospel, was written shortly after the destruction of the Jerusalem Temple in the year 70, during the Jewish War with Rome of 66-70 CE[29] Randel Helms argues convincingly that we can fine-tune this even further. Based on Mark's use of the prophecy in Daniel 12, Helms suggests[30] the gospel was written between 71-73, and that Mark fully expected the world was about to end in the year 74.[31] Though some evangelical scholars still try to argue for an earlier date, they can only do so by ignoring a great deal of evidence.[32]

To be fair, we really have no solid evidence that Mark was written any earlier than the year 100, apart from the fact that

Mark seems to have the Jewish War strongly in mind.[33] Matthew appears before Mark in the lineup of our bibles because several early church fathers like Augustine believed Mark was an epitome (that is, a summary) of Matthew.[34] Still, for over a century, the prevailing opinion of biblical scholars has been that Mark was the first gospel.

How do we know it was first? One key indication is what historians call the Synoptic Problem, although it is really only a problem for those that wish all four of our gospels were independent accounts of Jesus. Matthew, Mark and Luke are called the *Synoptic* Gospels, from the Greek συνοπτικός, *synoptikos* ("seen together"), because their extensive structural and verbal agreements are far too similar (often verbatim) to be coincidental, let alone what one could expect if they were all relying on oral tradition.

How similar? Fully half of Mark's text is reproduced in Luke; in Matthew, a whopping 90%. Of the 661 verses in Mark's Gospel, Luke's Gospel uses about 360 and Matthew's Gospel uses about 607.[35] The parallels are so widespread and apparent that the majority opinion among biblical authorities has been in strong agreement ever since the discovery of this striking (and incestuous) literary relationship. And the most widely accepted solution to the synoptic problem continues to be Markan Priority, that is, that Matthew and Luke both used Mark as their main source, and made changes, corrections and alterations as they saw fit. But is there another, even older source document behind Mark?

Q is for Questionable

Scholars have also long proposed a hypothetical second source used by Luke and Matthew in common, referred to as "Q" (from *quelle,* the German for "source"). Combined with Markan Priority, this theory is known as the "two-source" or "two-document" hypothesis. Some have also proposed additional (and equally hypothetical) "M" and "L" sources for Matthew and Luke. But while Markan Priority remains the dominant solution to the Synoptic problem, increasingly this other half of the "two-source" (or "four-source") theory, the "Q" hypothesis, has been called into question. In 1955, Austin Farrer argued in *On Dispensing With Q* that the material shared by Matthew and Luke can be easily explained without the need to imagine any theoretical additional source if Luke was simply using *both* Mark and Matthew. Other scholars, including Michael Goulder and Mark Goodacre, have since picked up the Farrar hypothesis.

Whenever we hear anything asserted about what "Q" said, or its textual layers, structure, nature, or any of the other aspects of Q endlessly debated by biblical scholars, we need to bear one crucial fact in mind: *Q doesn't exist – and may very well never have.* It is a purely hypothetical document. And as multiple scholars have demonstrated, there are serious methodological flaws in the defenses made on behalf of Q's contents - and its very existence...[36] Richard Carrier and a growing number of others, including Mark Goodacre and Austin Farrer, John Drury, Michael Goulder, Nicholas Perrin, Barbara Shellard, and more, argue that it appears far more likely that what we call "Q" is nothing more than additions made to Mark by Matthew, which were then redacted into Luke. Carrier adds: "I see no merit in assuming otherwise without very good evidence, and the evidence presented even by staunch advocates of Q cannot honestly be described as even 'good.' Whereas the evidence for Luke using Matthew *is* very good." (see below)

Recently Dennis R. MacDonald has proposed another possible alternative to Q, which he calls the Q+ or the *Logoi* hypothesis. MacDonald draws on the writings of the second-century church father Papias of Hierapolis, who knew of (what he thought was) two Greek translations of Matthew's Gospel. MacDonald suggests that the texts Papias actually had were Matthew's Gospel and an early now-lost gospel called the *Logoi of Jesus* ("the Words of Jesus"), which Papias mistook for an abridged version of Matthew.

MacDonald's reconstruction of the *Logoi of Jesus* remains (highly) speculative, but is interesting: it would appear to be a reworked version of the Old Testament book of Deuteronomy, with Jesus standing in for Moses. The title itself evokes the opening line of Deuteronomy: "These are the *logoi* that Moses spoke..." There was no gathering of "oral tradition" arranged into speeches. Instead, MacDonald says "it was a strategic rewriting of Deuteronomy with a coherent and compelling structure and plot. To be sure, it is not a narrative such as one finds in the Synoptics, but it is a narrative nonetheless."[37] If MacDonald is right, then we can immediately jettison the idea that the gospels are based on a historical Jesus, whether one existed or not.

But even if Q+/*Logoi* turns out to be just as illusionary as Q already appears to be, the Synoptic problem remains – and the most realistic (arguably, the only) solution is that both Matthew's and Luke's gospels are beefed-up and reworked versions of Mark's original gospel. One of the several indications of this is called **intercalation**, a literary device Mark likes to employ. Basically, it means that he would break away from the action in one scene to cut to another, and then return to the first. Not that there's anything wrong with sandwiching one scene with another; it's just one of the stylistic choices he uses for dramatic effect. But when Matthew and Luke make the same identical cuts as Mark does, *in the same places*, it's a dead giveaway that they are cut-and-pasting from his story. And they do, repeatedly – for instance, John Dominic Crossan lists a half dozen (and possibly more) unmistakable instances just of copycat intercalations.[38]

Another giveaway that Matthew and Luke are reworking Mark is in their order of stories and events. Matthew and Luke's sequence of events only agree with each other when they also agree with Mark. Historians used to suppose they all agreed simply because this was just the actual order of events historically – but if that was the case, what about all the places where the gospels disagreed on when events occurred (or even, if they *did* occur at all)? This presumption didn't survive long after William Wrede showed that Mark's sequence of events was actually only the writer's own invention – an artificial timeline he constructed for purely theological, not historical, reasons, with little if any relationship to any actual ministry of Jesus.[39] Yet another reason is the way Matthew and Luke alter Mark's apocalyptic message to downplay the notion that the world would be ending any second now (Matt. 24:14; 36-44, 50; 25:1-13; Luke 12:39-40; 17:22-37)

When was Matthew written?

Most secular biblical scholars date Matthew's gospel between 80 – 110 CE, for several reasons: Matthew is clearly based on Mark, itself written in the early 70s, so there had to be time for it to both a) become respected and b) be in need of a tune-up. As B.H. Streeter puts it, Matthew is simply Mark 2.0: "Matthew is a fresh edition of Mark, revised, rearranged, and enriched with new material."[40] Remember, for the evangelists, there would be only one gospel, not a quartet. Matthew was just improving the only gospel he knew.

Scholars agree that Matthew has the Jewish war with Rome and the destruction of the Temple in sight in verses like Matt. 22:7. But unlike Mark, Matthew doesn't seem to be overwhelmed by the catastrophe; it seems to be further away in time and space. Instead, Matthew appears to be intensely concerned with troubling new developments in Judaism in the generation *after* the war, possibly including Christians being targeted by the "*Birkath ha-Minim*" ("Curse against Heretics") that began with the post-war rabbinic court at Jamnia in the 80s.[41] The Gospel of Matthew is repeatedly echoed in the book of Revelation, a book we know was written in the 90s – but the correlation could be going in the opposite direction, if Matthew is actually echoing Revelation instead.[42] Still, Matthew may have been used in two sets of early second-century Christian writings: a church manual called the *Didakhê*, and the letters attributed to Ignatius, dated to c. 107-110 CE which might give us an upper limit on the window for Matthew's composition. Apart from that, most objective scholars would agree any date in the 80s or 90s is feasible.

When was Luke written?

Christians love to describe Luke as an excellent historian whose uncanny accuracy has been vindicated again and again. He is not, and it has not. As a historian, even by ancient standards, he leaves much to be desired.[43] He opens his gospel with a lie: telling us because so many people are writing gospels lately, he has closely investigated the eyewitness accounts handed down to his generation and he feels he should write one too:

> "Since many have undertaken to set down an orderly account of the events that have been fulfilled among us, just as they were handed on to us by those who from the beginning were eyewitnesses and servants of the word, I too decided, after investigating everything carefully from the very first, to write an orderly account for you, most excellent Theophilus (meaning "Lover of God" – if this name *isn't* made up, it certainly couldn't have been more apt!), so that you may know the truth…" (Luke 1:1-4)

But Luke has not "investigated everything carefully." The Synoptic Problem shows that, like Matthew, he has taken the basic material for his story from Mark. And the simplest solution to the Q question is Mark Goodacre's modification of the Farrar Hypothesis: that "Q" is nothing more than the places in the text where he is borrowing from Matthew as well.

As several Josephan specialists have pointed out,[44] Luke has also plagiarized details and window dressing from the Jewish historian Flavius Josephus' *Antiquities of the Jews*, a book written c. 93 CE (and for numerous demonstrations of this fact, see "Luke and Josephus" in Chapter 14). Scholars who try to argue that Luke was written earlier in the first century either ignore this or are unaware of it, hanging their case on reasons that are inconclusive at best, such as: since Luke-Acts doesn't mention Paul's death, they must have been written prior to then.

But Luke had any number of reasons for not bringing up the subject: wanting to end his story on an optimistic note and not a gloomy one, is just one possibility – for another; Paul probably didn't die in Rome in the first place.[45] Whatever Luke's reasons for omitting Paul's death, there's no question he knew well that Paul was dead decades before he put pen to paper. Because his borrowings from Josephus' *Antiquities* means a date before the mid-90s is flatly impossible. Besides, Luke has Paul give a farewell speech at his departure from Ephesus that makes it clear Paul knows he shall never return (see Acts 20:25, 38). It's an obvious death speech.

Many experts have argued that Luke and Acts were written sometime around 110-120 CE and perhaps as late as c. 130 (when Acts may have been used by Polycarp),[46] though there is evidence that both continued to undergo further editing over the years. It's also curious that Papias (Bishop of Hierapolis c. 140-150) an early collector of traditions about the Apostles, doesn't seem to know of either Luke or Acts[47] (or John, for that matter). Even today there remain two different versions of Luke-Acts – only one of which became canonized (ours is the shorter version), despite both being equally ancient, and the fact that scholars cannot agree which is the original...[48]

Building on recent scholarship, Joseph B. Tyson has honed in even closer on a possible date for Luke and Acts in his book, *Marcion and Luke-Acts: A Defining Struggle* (2006). He proposes that the writing of both Acts and Luke were prompted by the threat of a rival Christian movement. Around the years 120-125 CE, Marcion, a wealthy founder of a new theological school in Rome, began to proclaim a new version of the gospel,[49] kicking off a brand new religious movement and creating a popular rival to mainstream Christianity – not that our familiar brand of Christianity *was* quite the unchallenged mainstream yet. Tyson believes that Luke and Acts were crafted in response to the Marcionite threat.[50] If he's correct, that gives us an approximate date between 120-130 CE

When was John written?
As almost every biblical historian agrees, John was the last of our four gospels written. Some scholars insist that he is a fourth independent source for Mark's Jesus story, but this wishful thinking doesn't hold up for John any more than it does for Matthew or Luke. Frequent protests and the odd dissenting opinion notwithstanding, there is simply no evidence to support that claim. Instead, Johannine experts point to abundant evidence that John was familiar with all three earlier Gospels, and used them as his sources, freely rewriting them in his own words, and not particularly troubled over how well his story aligned with theirs.[51] For example, L. Michael White in *From Jesus to Christianity* notes that even when John is completely diverging from the Synoptics, his changes still seem to show full awareness of the earlier gospels; he appears to be irreconcilably altering their stories quite intentionally – such as radically changing Jesus' personality, his travels, his entire career, his teaching methods, the motive for why Jesus was killed, even the day on which Jesus dies (p. 309).

A growing consensus among Johannine specialists is that John was specifically written in response to Luke. They also agree our version is not the original version – it has been redacted and re-edited, repeatedly, by a variety of other authors. But we don't know anything about those later editors.[52]

Our earliest surviving New Testament text (or so we thought), Rylands Library Papyrus P52, comes from a page of John's gospel. Christians have long insisted that it dates to c. 125, and thus John's gospel must have been written considerably before then. But not so fast: first, the dating is actually given as a *range* roughly centered on the mid 2nd century; 125 is simply the *lowest* end of the proposed window.

David Fitzgerald

So based solely on this criterion, P52 could just as plausibly be dated towards the end of the second century. But it isn't even that simple.

Noted paleographers Pasquale Orsini and Willy Clarysse have recently chastised biblical scholars for embracing insupportably early dates for their manuscripts, including P52.[53] They remind us there are *no* first century New Testament papyri, and the few that can be assigned to the second century (P52 and two other tiny fragments, P90 and P104), are probably all from the *later* half of the 2nd century – or even the early third century; almost a century later than apologists wish.

As *Vridar's* Neil Godfrey notes: "One gets the impression that if a later date for P52 is thought to be a 'new' date, it is so only for biblical scholars. It looks like few paleographers have ever been persuaded by the hopes of many of their New Testament peers." [54]

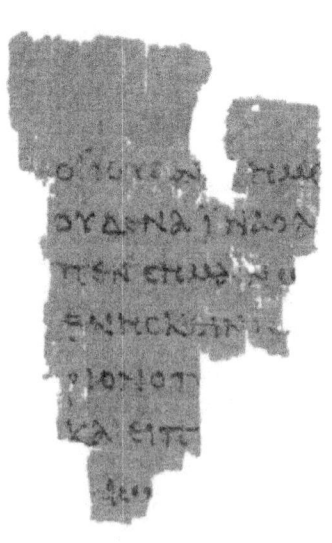 

Jesus: Mything in Action

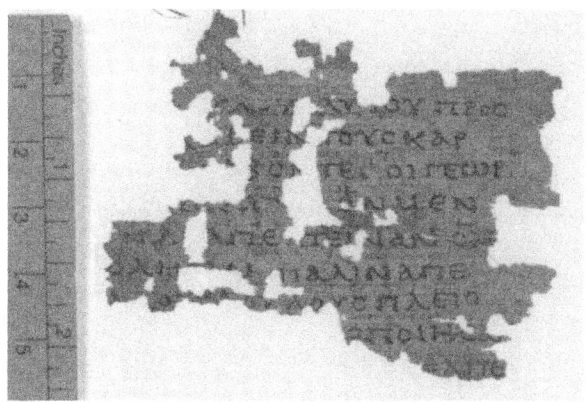

Previous page, left: front of P52 (previously thought to be the oldest NT fragment); Contains partial text of John 18:31-33 (front) and 37-38 (back).
Previous page, right: front of P90, contains text of John 18:36-19:1 and 19:1-7.
Above: P104, contains text of Matt. 21:34-37 and traces of verses 43 and 45. The fragment does not include verse 44 (one reason why scholars think the verse is not genuine).

Second, even that wide range is based solely on one criterion: judging from the script style – and we have no way to accurately determine when a particular style was in use. In the case of P52, this tiny fragment, slightly smaller than a credit card, containing partial verses of 18:31–33, 37–38 but no complete sentences, we have other late second-century NT texts that compare with it stylistically, but no associated archeological clues or dated textual references to help us pinpoint its actual date any further that that.[55]

John's gospel was a favorite in heretical circles (in fact, the first commentary on John was written by a heretic, Heracleon), a fact that caused much doubt and debate over it in the third and fourth centuries.[56] The other earliest surviving citations of it fall sometime in the final half of the second century.[57] So what *do* we know for certain? All this means

John could have been written as late as the mid – late second century (though some have argued it came even later,[58] and as early as the 120s (provided that Luke was written as early as c.115)[59].

Where were the Gospels written?
If answering the question "when were the Gospels written?" seemed fraught with uncertain guesswork, asking where they were written is even more so.

Judging from his geographical errors and mistakes about basic Judaism (e.g., see *Nailed*, p. 72 and Helm's *Gospel Fictions*, p. 103[60]), Mark was neither from Palestine nor a Jew, and writing for a gentile Christian audience who were just as unfamiliar as he was. He feels compelled to explain Jewish customs and refers to Jews in the third person (e.g., 7:3-4). Ernest Best points out that Greek-speaking diaspora Jews would know at least a little Aramaic, but Mark doesn't expect his readers to recognize even common Aramaic words and phrases (5:41; 7:34; 10:46; 14:36; 15:34 – 3:17 and 15:22 may be other examples).[61]

He *does* expect his audience to be familiar with Latin terms; he uses Roman military terminology and occasionally explains a Greek word by referring to a Latin term that he transliterates (12:42; 15:16).[62] Because Mark was supposed to have gotten his facts from Peter, tradition assumed that Mark wrote in Rome. But early Christian writings from Rome contain no evidence that they were familiar with Mark.[63] We have only guesses as to where in the Roman world Mark was actually written.

Matthew corrects Mark's mistakes, showing that he at least is more familiar with Judaism. There have been many suggested locales for Matthew's Jewish-Christian community, from Palestine to Syria to Egypt to the Transjordan, with the majority leaning towards Antioch.[64] The city had a large Jewish population, probably the largest in Syria, and other early Christian writings from Antioch such as the letters of

Ignatius and the *Didakhê*[65] show some connections with Matthew's gospel, and there are still other reasons making Antioch a good guess.

Luke repeats Mark's mistakes about Palestinian geography and Judaism; but on the other hand, seems quite familiar with sites in and around Rome, like the Appii forum, and the Three Taverns, which he casually mentions without any explanation (Acts 28:15). Where John was written is anyone's guess, unless Cerinthus of Ephesus really *was* the author... (he probably wasn't).

The Evolution of the Gospels
Again, all of our allegedly biographical info for Jesus comes from the four gospels. But in turn, all four stem from the first, what we call Mark's Gospel. We do not have four independent eyewitness accounts, or even four independent historical reports. What we have is a single religious document, written at least a generation after the time it portrays, by an anonymous author far away from the setting of the story for purely theological purposes.

That original story was taken, rewritten, beefed up and freely expanded upon in different and mutually incompatible ways by later redactors who show no signs that they were interested in keeping details consistent with any other gospel, but who show every sign that they felt theirs was the one true gospel (e.g., cf. Luke 1:1-4, John 21:24).

In every new gospel, Jesus becomes more impressive, more perfect, more divine; his career and miracles grow more spectacular and earth-shaking; his human frailties, weaknesses and mistakes get stripped away further. The humble, fallible but supremely faithful mortal Jesus who passes through all the trials and tribulations to be raised from the dead and exalted to the status of Lord in Mark's story becomes increasingly improved in Matthew and Luke; and by the time John's story is written, Jesus has become a cosmic deity from the very creation of the universe who strides around Judea fearlessly declaring to all that he is God almighty made flesh.

All four of these stories (and the many others like them) were subsequently re-edited further still by other editors. Then, the copies of the copies of the copies were heavily tampered with, repeatedly, by opposing factions of scribes for generations and generations before our oldest complete surviving texts finally appear, sometime between one and a half to two centuries later

But what *about* that original story? Is there a kernel of historical truth underlying it?

***

For further reading:

For an excellent survey of the evidence of Mark's intended audience:

Ernest Best, "Mark's Readers: A Profile," (in Van Segbroeck, et al., *The Four Gospels 1992*)

For the updated dating for P52 and some interesting comment on its misuse by apologists:

"'New' Date for that St John's Fragment, Rylands Library Papyrus P52," *Vridar*, 03-08-2013, available online at: http://vridar.org/2013/03/08/new-date-for-that-st-johns-fragment-rylands-library-papyrus-p52/

Brent Nongbri, "The Use and Abuse of P52: Papyrological Pitfalls in the Dating of the Fourth Gospel." *Harvard Theological Review* 98:1 (2005) 23–48

---

[1] Talbert, p. 42
[2] Sanders, 1995, p. 3

[3] Christopher M. Tuckett, "Jesus and the Gospels," in the *NIB NT Survey*, p. 17

[4] See Bart Ehrman's *Lost Scriptures* for plentiful examples.

[5] Matthew Fergusson, "Why Scholars Doubt the Traditional Authors of the Gospels," available online at: https://adversusapologetica.wordpress.com/2013/12/17/why-scholars-doubt-the-traditional-authors-of-the-gospels/

[6] Ibid.

[7] Ibid.

[8] Ibid.

[9] Whenever Clement "quotes" Jesus himself, he's actually either simply quoting the OT, or making something up (or at least, his "quote" isn't coming from the Gospels). See Ch. 18.

[10] Brown, *An Intro. to the NT*, pgs. 158; 208; 267

[11] Levinson, p.34

[12] I'm indebted to Neil Godfrey for this point. See his "An Explanation for the Gospels Being Anonymous," available online at: http://vridar.org/2009/12/05/an-explanation-for-the-gospels-being-anonymous/

[13] Some object that the gospels *do* read like eyewitness accounts, pointing out (rightly) that a common convention in ancient histories was for narrators to refer to themselves in the third person. However, even in these cases, the narratives are still told *from the point of view of the historian.* For instance, throughout the *War of the Jews*, Josephus describes many incidents which occurred to him, including some which clearly *only* he could have known (e.g., Book III, ch. 8, where he tells a highly dubious story in which he and a companion are the only survivors of a mass suicide). By contrast "Matthew," once introduced (in 9:9; his name is listed in 10:3), doesn't even appear in his own gospel. All the other problems with this attribution aside, he would be the only evangelist who could realistically be a companion of Jesus – and yet his gospel

depends on "Mark," a non-eyewitness.

[14] *NIB NTS*, p. 48

[15] See Matthew Ferguson, "Matthew the τελώνης ("Toll Collector") and the Authorship of the First Gospel," Κέλσος, April 15, 2014, available online at: https://adversusapologetica.wordpress.com/2014/04/15/matthew-the-%cf%84%ce%b5%ce%bb%cf%8e%ce%bd%ce%b7%cf%82-toll-collector-and-the-authorship-of-the-first-gospel/

[16] According to many scholars; e.g., see Peter H. Davids, "First Letter of Peter," *Eerdmans Dict. Of the Bible*, p. 1037; also see *Nailed* and the forthcoming *Complete Heretic's Guide to the New Testament*

[17] See *On the Historicity of Jesus*, p. 266, 458

[18] *NIB NTS*, p. 49

[19] For abundant examples, see *On the Historicity of Jesus*, pp. 402 - 456

[20] Again, according to many scholars; e.g., see Andre T. Lincoln, "The Letter to the Colossians," in the *NIB NT Survey*, p. 254

[21] See Robbins, pp. 215-242

[22] *NIB NTS*, p.77

[23] Gail R. O'Day, "The Gospel of John," in the *NIB NT Survey*, p. 101

[24] And actually, it isn't even that cut and dry. The editors who wrote John 21:24 say: "This ("the Beloved Disciple") is the disciple who is testifying to these things and has written them, and we know that his testimony is true," a very odd way to say he is the author. It could also be claiming that he wrote some other book that they used as their source for this gospel.

[25] Filson, p. 84

[26] Charlesworth, *Beloved Disciple*, pp. 185-92

[27] (Epiphanius, *Panarion*, LI) Irenaeus, *Against Heresies*, III.2.9).

[28] Eusebius, *Hist. Eccl.* 3.28; 7.25
[29] See Pheme Perkins, "The Gospel of Mark," in *The NIB NT Survey*, p. 67
[30] Helms (1997), p. 8
[31] For more details see ch. 23, (esp. note 19)
[32] See Carrier, *On the Historicity of Jesus*, n24, p. 265-266
[33] Ibid.
[34] Perkins, pp. 55-57
[35] Carr
[36] See the list of scholars provided in Carrier, *On the Historicity of Jesus*, pp.269-70, n33
[37] MacDonald, p. 512
[38] See Crossan, *The Birth of Christianity*, p. 106; with the list and details repeated in Smith, Ben C., "Intercalations in the Synoptic Tradition," in *TextExcavation*, 2008. Available online at:
http://www.textexcavation.com/intercalations.html
[39] Koester, pp. 44–6
[40] Streeter, p. 159
[41] M. Eugene Boring, "The Gospel of Matthew," in *NIB NTS*, pp. 44-48
[42] Carrier, op. cit., p. 267
[43] For a survey of Luke's methods as a historian compared to his contemporaries, see Carrier, *Not the Imposiible Faith*, pp. 173-87.
[44] See *Nailed*, p. 67-69, 79; also Richard Carrier, "Luke and Josephus" (2000), available online at:
http://infidels.org/library/modern/richard_carrier/lukeandjosephus.html,
and Mason, "Josephus and Luke-Acts," in *Josephus and the New Testament*, pp. 185–229. Richard Carrier's *On the Historicity of Jesus* also cites numerous other references: p. 267, n26
[45] See "Clement of Rome," in ch. 18.
[46] For example, see Carrier, *Not the Impossible Faith*, pp. 174-

76; MacDonald, *Two Shipwrecked Gospels*, pp. 43-67); Richard Pervo, *Dating Acts* and *Acts: A Commentary*; Price, *Pre-Nicene New Testament*, pp. 481-99; Joseph Tyson, "Why Dates Matter: The Case of the Acts of the Apostles" in Scott, ed., *Finding the Historical Jesus: Rules of Evidence*, pp. 59-70; and David Trobisch, "Who Published the Christian Bible?" *CSER Review* 2.1 (2007): 29-30

[47] Price, *The Pre-Nicene New Testament: Fifty-Four Formative Texts*, p. 493

[48] Robert Price provides a translation of the longer version in *The Pre-Nicene New Testament*, pp. 563-634. For more on the matter of Luke-Acts, see also: Thomas Brodie, "Re-Opening the Quest for Proto-Luke: The Systematic Use of Judges 6-12 in Luke 16:1-18:8," *Journal of Higher Criticism* 2, no. 1 (Spring 1995): 68-101; W. A. Strange, *The Problem of the Text of Acts* (New York: Cambridge University Press, 1992); and Richard Pervo, *Acts: A Commentary,* Minneapolis, MN: Fortress Press, 2009

[49] See "The Other One True Christianity," in ch. 25.

[50] Adding to the difficulty of dating these texts, Tyson thinks an early version of Luke was pre-Marcionite but our version was an edited/augmented version of that earlier one.

[51] Carrier, *On the Historicity of Jesus,* p. 487-488. For the consensus of experts on John, see the additional bibliography in MacDonald, *Two Shipwrecked Gospels*, p. 48, n11, and the analysis in Crossan, *Power of Parable*, pp. 218-42

[52] See Carrier, op. cit, p. 268-269; n31 & n32, where Carrier has provided a wealth of further documentation on Johannine specialists including: White, *From Jesus to Christianity*, pp. 305-14; Mark Strauss, *Four Portraits, One Jesus: An Introduction to Jesus and the Gospels* (Grand Rapids, MI: Zondervan, 2007), pp. 334-35;

Herman Waetjen, *The Gospel of the Beloved Disciple: A Work in Two Editions* (New York: T & T Clark, 2005); C. K. Barrett, *The Gospel according to St. John*, 2d ed. (Philadelphia: Westminster Press, 1978; pp. 15–26) F.L. Cribbs, "St. Luke and the Johannine Tradition," *Journal of Biblical Literature* 90 (1971): 422-50, expanded in "A Study of the Contacts That Exist between St. Luke and St. John," in George MacRae, ed., *Society of Biblical Literature 1973 Seminar Papers* (Cambridge, Massachusetts: Society of Biblical Literature, 1973), vol. 2, pp. 1-93) C. H. Dodd, *Historical Tradition in the Fourth Gospel* (Cambridge: Cambridge University Press, 1963); P. Parker, "Luke and the Fourth Evangelist," *New Testament Studies* 9 (1963): 317-36) John Bailey, *The Traditions Common to the Gospels of Luke and John* (Leiden: E.J. Brill, 1963); and Raymond Brown, *An Introduction to the Gospel of John*, rev. ed. (New York: Doubleday, 2003) and *The Gospel according to John* (Garden City, NY: Doubleday, 1966-1970), and many more.

[53] Clarysse is the founder of the extremely valuable LDAB, the Leuven Database of Ancient Books, which provides data on all published/edited manuscripts from the ancient world

[54] "'New' Date for that St John's Fragment, Rylands Library Papyrus P52," *Vridar*, 03-08-2013, available online at: http://vridar.org/2013/03/08/new-date-for-that-st-johns-fragment-rylands-library-papyrus-p52/

[55] See Brent Nongbri's article "The Use and Abuse of P52: Papyrological Pitfalls in the Dating of the Fourth Gospel." *Harvard Theological Review* 98:1 (2005) 23–48

[56] White, p. 305

[57] O'Day, in *NIB NTS*, p. 105

[58] Carrier, op. cit., p. 269

[59] Or it could be as early as 100, if Luke was written in the mid-90s (though that is the *earliest* possible date for Luke,

not the most probable).

[60] Some scholars suggest that Mark's geographical gaffe in 7:31 may be a clunky attempt to bring the gentile region into the story. "Tyre and Sidon" were often linked together in people's minds, as can be seen in the OT: e.g., Joel 3:4, Ezra 3:7, Zech. 9:2, Jer. 25:22, 27:3, 47:4, and throughout Isaiah 23 and Ezekiel 28.

[61] Best, Ernest, "Mark's Readers: A Profile," in Van Segbroeck, et al., *The Four Gospels*, 1992

[62] Ibid.

[63] Perkins, in *NIB NTS* p. 66

[64] Boring, in *NIB NTS* p. 48

[65] Ibid.; also H. van de Sandt (ed.), *Matthew and the Didache*, Assen: Royal van Gorcum; Philadelphia: Fortress Press, 2005

Chapter Eight: Jesus Gets a Life

"My point, once again, is not that those ancient people told literal stories and we are now smart enough to take them symbolically, but that they told them symbolically and we are now dumb enough to take them literally."
- John Dominic Crossan

Jesus as Jenga

Does Jesus make his mark – or does Mark make his Jesus? Ever since biblical history has existed as a modern field of study, Jesus scholars of both Christian and secular persuasion have taken apart the gospels to seek out nuggets of historical truth at the core. They have separated out the various elements, judging this difficulty or that as just a legendary add-on, or a simple scribal error, or as theological symbolism. But as we've already seen (see ch. 3), there is no consensus on which parts are the genuine historical ones, or on what remains after you've removed all the elements too problematic to accept, like playing a crucifix-shaped game of Jenga...

And was Mark – the original basis that all later gospels were built upon – even meant to be taken literally in the first place? Mark tells us what he is doing right from the outset: he is writing a gospel, not a history or a biography (Mark 1:1). Numerous historians across the theological spectrum, both historicists and mythicists alike, have confirmed this; including Thomas Brodie, Calum Carmichael, Richard Carrier, John Dominic Crossan, Tom Dykstra, Arnold Ehrhardt, Randel Helms, Ernst Käsemann, Dennis MacDonald, Jennifer Maclean, Norman Perrin, Robert M. Price, Paul Nadim Tarazi, Thomas Thompson and many others. All have detailed the ways that Mark's entire Gospel is a treasure trove of symbolic, rather than historical, meaning, with parts created by borrowing from the Old Testament, the Homeric epics, and the letters of Paul. From start to finish, this is allegory, not history. Mark wasn't writing a biography of Jesus any more than C.S. Lewis was writing a biography of Aslan.

Mark as Myth

For examples of this wealth of symbolism, let's spend the next portion of this book taking a walk through that first gospel (with a few side trips into the others). We'll cover many of them, but these are by no means all the examples. As we do, watch out for a recurring trend: how many times, again and again, any given passage in question makes no sense historically or logically – until you recognize it as a religious allegory, just as we see in the teachings of other ancient Mediterranean religions like Mithraism or the Eleusinian Mysteries. Just as we are instructed by early Christian Church Fathers like Theophilus of Antioch, Macarius Magnes,[1] or Irenaeus of Lyons, who declares, "the prophets have very often expressed themselves in parables and allegories, and not according to the mere sound of the words."[2] Or Origen of Alexandria, who advises us: "Scripture contains many contradictions, and many statements which are not literally true, but must be read spiritually and mystically..."[3]

The Gospel of Jesus Christ, the Son of God

As noted earlier, Mark's gospel doesn't claim to be written by anyone named Mark, or claim to be an eyewitness account, or claim to be a history at all – and it's not even entitled "The Gospel According to Mark." Its real title is right there in the first verse:

"*The Gospel of Jesus Christ, the Son of God*" (1:1) In our earlier manuscripts, Mark opens his gospel with, "As it is written in Isaiah the prophet..." but then misquotes a mashup of the prophet Malachi (3:1) and Isaiah (40:3). Later scribes caught this and changed the verse to read, "As it is written in the prophets..." instead.

Mark starts by portraying John the Baptist as a newly reborn Elijah, describing him (Mark 1:6) as "dressed in a rough coat of camel's hair, with a leather belt [*zōnēn dermatinnēn*] round his waist [*peri tēn osphyn autou*]." Notably, this is the same vocabulary used to describe Elijah in the Septuagint translation of 2 Kings 1:8: "girt with a leathern girdle [*zōnēn dermatinnēn*] about his loins [*tēn osphyn autou*]." Elijah had gone straight to heaven in a whirlwind (riding a chariot of fire driven by horses of fire; 2 Kings 2:11) without dying, and many Jews were waiting for the Lord to send him back before the end of the world, since Malachi had prophesied Elijah would return first (Mal. 4:5-6). And Mark didn't just base John on Elijah; as we'll see, (in addition to many other sources) he used stories about Elijah – and *his* own spinoff character, Elisha – for constructing many of his stories about Jesus.[4]

To Baptize or not to Baptize?

Unlike the later gospels, there is no virgin birth, no nativity story, no connection to Bethlehem, or any tales of young Jesus in Mark; he first arrives on the scene as a grown man from Nazareth of Galilee. No sooner does Jesus appear (1:9-12) than he is baptized by John in the Jordan River. This causes the heavens to open, the Holy Spirit to descend upon him like a dove, and a voice from heaven to declare, "You are my Son, the Beloved; with you I am well pleased," echoing the coronation hymn in Psalm 2:7: "You are my son, today I have begotten you."

Except, that is, in John's Gospel. The authors of later gospels will be uncomfortable with this scenario (see Embarrassment no. 4 in ch. 5). Why does *Jesus* need to be baptized? Matthew has John the Baptist protest that Jesus should be baptizing him before Jesus talks him into it (3:14-15). But when John the Baptist says he's not fit to baptize Jesus, John the Evangelist agrees. Unlike Mark's original fallible Jesus, John's Jesus comes so perfect and sin-free right out of the box, he removes the baptism altogether (1:27-34).

But he does like the idea of the Holy Spirit descending like a dove, and an announcement from the voice of God; so instead he has John the Baptist proclaim that he saw the Holy Spirit descend on Jesus (adding, "and it remained on him.") and heard God vouch for this stranger, Jesus:

> "I saw the Spirit descending from heaven like a dove, and it remained on him. I myself did not know him, but the one who sent me to baptize with water said to me, 'He on whom you see the Spirit descend and remain is the one who baptizes with the Holy Spirit.' And I myself have seen and have testified that this is the Son of God."
> (John 1:32-34)

The Ministry Begins
But again, in Mark's original story, Jesus is so far a mere mortal. Having thus been promoted to God's son, the next step is to see if he is up to the task; so appropriately enough, he is sent off to be tested. The Holy Spirit immediately drives him out into the wilderness for forty days, communing with the wild animals and tempted by Satan, cared for by angels (1:12-13). Though John feels no need for his Jesus to go through a probationary period and dumps the whole idea altogether, Matthew (4:1-11) and Luke (4:1-13) embellish this storyline. Both add temptations from Satan that make no sense from the modern Christian standpoint: how do you tempt the incarnation of God almighty with merely all the kingdoms on earth?

Jesus acquires disciples in an appropriately miraculous way: he simply spots them at work in their fishing boats, makes his pitch and they immediately drop their nets and follow him (1:18, 20; likewise Levi in 2:14). Could there be a more perfect metaphor for the example Mark wants all prospective Christians to follow? Jesus spends the rest of the first few chapters casting out demons, performing miraculous healings, confounding the scribes and Pharisees, and becoming incredibly famous everywhere, even though he constantly and sternly tells everyone not to say a word (1:34,43-45; 3:12)

One of Jesus' early miracles is the healing of a man with a withered hand. Again, in a trend we'll see repeated throughout this gospel, the miracle echoes an Old Testament book: here, 1

Kings. There, an unnamed holy man opposes King Jeroboam. But when the king "stretched forth his hand" (*exeteinen... tēn cheir autou*) to command the arrest of the prophet, "his hand withered" (*exēranthē hē cheir autou*). After the king repents, the holy man appeals to the Lord "and the king's hand was restored." (1 Kings 13:4-6. Mark's retelling uses the same language. Jesus commands the man to stretch out his withered hand. The victim "stretched forth his hand, and his hand was restored..." (Mark 3:5)

The Mystery of the Kingdom of God
In chapter four, he begins teaching the multitudes by telling parables, but his disciples don't understand. Afterwards, in private, Mark has Jesus say something remarkably revealing – in fact, it's nothing less than downright astonishing:

> When he was alone, those who were around him along with the twelve asked him about the parables. And he said to them, "To you has been given the mystery[5] of the kingdom of God, but for those outside, everything comes in parables; in order that they may indeed look, but not perceive, and may indeed listen, but not understand; so that they may not turn again (from their sins) and be forgiven." And he said to them, "Do you not understand this parable? Then how will you understand all the parables?" (4:10-13)

As usual for Mark, he is taking these lines of dialogue not from anything historical, but from a twist on scriptural passages; Isaiah 6:9-10 in this case:

> And he said, "Go and say to this people: 'Keep listening, but do not comprehend; keep looking, but do not understand." Make the mind of this people dull, and stop their ears, and shut their eyes, so that they may not look

with their eyes, and listen with their ears, and comprehend with their minds, and turn and be healed.'"

What a strange passage Mark chose for inspiration. Look at what he is telling us. He has his Jesus deliver his message through parables, *not* to facilitate his audience's understanding, à la Aesop, so they can turn from their sins and be saved – but for the exact opposite reason: to *deliberately disguise it so that they cannot.* This makes absolutely no sense for the kind of Jesus that has always been preached to us, a savior who came to redeem all of us if we just ask – but it makes perfect sense if he is presenting his Jesus as a mystery faith deity (as we'll see in ch. 21). Mark appears to be making this abundantly clear – he is literally giving us the key to the mystery of the Kingdom of God, and warning the reader, if you do not understand this, you will not understand any of the rest of his gospel…[6]

An Imperfect Storm
Even in ancient times, pagan critics noted story problems with the gospels (e.g., see *Nailed*, p. 105). For example, for a career set in land-locked Galilee, it's a bit odd that Jesus and his disciples manage to have several maritime journeys, let alone such hazardous ones. In the 3rd century, Porphyry of Tyre (the same critic who recognized the OT book of Daniel was a later forgery) pointed out that the so-called "Sea of Galilee" was actually "the Lake of Genneseret" (as Luke 5:1 identifies it), nothing more than a small river-fed freshwater lake, easily crossed in two hours by any small boat, and not big enough to be beset by the massive storms depicted in the Gospels. Which makes incidents like Mark 4:37-40 doubly unbelievable:

> "A heavy squall came up, and the waves broke over the boat, until it was all but swamped. Now he was in the stern asleep on the cushion; and they roused him and said, "Master, we are perishing! Do you not care?" He awoke up, rebuked the wind, and said to the sea, "Hush! Be still!"

The wind dropped and there was a dead calm. He said to them, "Why are you such cowards? Have you no faith even now?" And they were awestruck and said to one another, "Who can this be? Even the wind and the sea obey him?"[7]

Besides Jesus commanding the elements, there is actually another miracle here: a violent windstorm is sending waves crashing over the sides of a small open fishing boat, filling it with water so badly that it was in danger of sinking at any moment – and yet Jesus, lying on a cushion in the stern, is able to sleep like a baby until the drenched and terrified disciples awaken him.

Just two chapters later (6:45-51) Jesus has another improbable nautical adventure when he inexplicably sends the disciples away in the boat while he remains behind to pray. By nightfall, he can see they are still only halfway across (presumably with his miraculous sight), struggling against another windstorm. For some reason, he leaves them toiling at the oars (actually, the Greek isn't "toiling," but βασανιζόμενους, *vasanizomenous;* literally, "tormented") until 3 a.m. ("the fourth watch"), when he deigns to saunter over to them, walking across the very storm-tossed sea itself. Somewhat perversely, the gospel goes out of its way to say that Jesus *meant* to keep walking past them – until they spot him and are once again terrified, thinking the water-striding apparition they see is some evil ghost coming after them:

> "When he saw that they were straining at the oars against an adverse wind, he came towards them early in the morning, walking on the sea. He intended to pass them by. But when they saw him walking on the sea, they thought it was a ghost and cried out; for they all saw him and were terrified. But immediately he spoke to them and said, "Take heart, it is I; do not be afraid." Then he got into the

boat with them and the wind ceased. And they were utterly astounded…"

(Mark 6:49-51)

On a side note: as a complete heretic discussing issues like these, at times I nearly forget there are still over 2 billion people who read stories like these and take them seriously as eyewitness historical reporting. So it's kind of adorable to read a classic Christian reference like the *Pulpit Commentaries* offering these reasons why Jesus left his hapless disciples rowing for their lives in a storm all night, or why he first meant to blow right past them:

"It may be asked why our Lord suffered them to be tempest-tossed so long; and the answer is:

1. It was a trial of their faith, so as to urge them to seek more earnestly the help of God.
2. It was a lesson to accustom them to endure hardness (sic).
3. It made the stilling of so tedious and dangerous a storm all the more grateful and welcome to them at last."

Following these three not-exactly reassuring reassurances comes the real reason. The commentary goes on to discuss all the fine spiritual meaning of the story, telling us that the Lord allows his followers to be tried by dangers to teach patience, perseverance and faith; the "fourth watch" is the age when the Church will be buffeted by the spirit of antichrist and by the storms of the world; and his reception into the ship and the consequent calm prefigures the eternal peace of the Church after his second coming. This is exactly the response we see from the 3rd century Church Father Macarius Magnes responding to the pagan critic Porphyry of Tyre's criticism of the storm-calming story in Mark 4:37-40:[8] though little if any of either story makes sense in reality, every single element in both works brilliantly as allegory.

Randel Helms' *Gospel Fictions* (Prometheus, 1988) discusses in detail not only the allegorical nature of passages like these, but also the Old Testament stories they are emulating; in this case, finding links to Job 9:8, Jonah 1:13-15, Psalm 106 and others. Incidentally, here as in so many other places, Matthew feels free to expand on the story, adding further allegory to his version by having Peter walk on the water too – until his fear and doubt nearly sinks him (Matt. 14:28-33).

It's no coincidence that Peter is the one Matthew picked. The disciples begin as a unified Greek chorus to Jesus. But as Mark's gospel goes on, Peter increasingly becomes the spokesperson for them (Mark 10:28-30; 11:12-14; 20-22). In the later gospels, this trend continues.[9]

The Problems of the Passion of the Christ

Jesus' execution is perhaps the only event of his life that nearly all biblical scholars seem to feel confident actually occurred. And yet, when we look at the details of the passion story, his triumphant entry into Jerusalem, ridding the temple of the moneylenders, his arrest, trial, execution and resurrection, and even in small, seemingly incidental mundane details, we find the same situation as we do for his miracle stories: the story is filled with historical difficulties that make it difficult, if not impossible, to accept at face value, but make perfect sense as allegories crafted from Old Testament passages. The difficulties accumulate further as each new gospel makes additions, subtractions and alterations to Mark's story. But allegory is a consistent presence inundating all four gospels. In fact, it runs through all the non-canonical Christian gospels and acts as well.

Chapters 11-16, over a quarter of Mark's gospel, are dedicated to the final week of his life and his passion story. But as Randel Helms and others have demonstrated, the episodes of that passion story have been structured by a series of Old Testament verses, from such books as Zechariah, Isaiah, Jonah and the Psalms; carefully constructed typological fiction, happenings "according to the Scriptures."[10]

Mark begins his passion story with Jesus' arrival at the Mount of Olives, east of Jerusalem. We know from Josephus[11] that many Jews of the time interpreted Zechariah 14:4 ("On that day his feet will stand on the Mount of Olives...") to mean that the coming of the messiah would commence there. First Jesus sends two disciples ahead into Bethany, where he says they will find a colt that has never been ridden. He adds, if anyone asks why they are untying the colt, to tell them the Lord needs it and they'll have no problem making off with it. Naturally, all this comes to pass without a hitch (11:2-7) and Jesus rides the never-ridden, unbroken, untrained colt just fine into Jerusalem, where he is greeted by many who spread the garments and palm branches before him and acclaim him with cries of adoration and praise (11:8-10). Why all the improbable bother just to obtain an unridden colt? That plot point is dictated by the verse in Zechariah:

> "Rejoice greatly, O daughter Zion! Shout aloud, O daughter Jerusalem! Lo, your king comes to you; triumphant and victorious is he, humble and riding on a donkey, on a colt, the foal of a donkey." (Zech. 9:9)

Matthew goes even further in his version. He is so literal-minded that when he retells the story, he goes back to the source material and decides that when Zechariah said the king would come riding on "a donkey, on a colt, the foal of a donkey," the prophet wasn't being poetic. To Matthew, that meant *two* riding animals: a donkey *and* a colt, the foal of a donkey. So his Jesus instructs the disciples to go look for a donkey and her foal, and (without explaining how this is possible without looking like a rodeo act) has Jesus mount and ride *both* (Matt. 21:2-7).

The joyful crowd that welcomes Jesus into Jerusalem get their lines from Hebrew scripture as well: "Blessed is he who comes in the name of the Lord!" (Mark 11:9) and "Hosanna in the highest!" (Mark 11:10) are direct quotes from the Septuagint (Psalms 117:25 LXX and 148:1 LXX), as are their shouts of "Hosanna!" (Ps. 117:25 LXX).

As we've already seen (see ch. 5), crabby Jesus taking divine revenge on a poor fig tree for having no figs out of season scarcely makes sense even for a mere mortal Jesus, let alone for a perfect son of God (Mark 11:12-14, 20-21). But once again, as allegory, in this case for the rejection of the temple sacrifice system, it finally makes perfect sense, as R.G. Hamerton-Kelly has shown.[12] Mark even broke up the story of the cursed fig tree and wrapped both parts around another highly symbolic, highly improbable event: the casting out of the moneychangers from the temple. This sandwiching of two scenes is called intercalation, a literary device he uses often. Mark's use of it here is for emphasis, a one-two punch to the temple and its convoluted system of sacrifices, which Jesus is about to make obsolete.

Apocalypse Now
Skipping ahead past some parables to chapter 13, brings us back to the Mount of Olives again, where Jesus sits a few of his disciples down, overlooking the temple, to warn them of the impending doom about to befall them. This scary pep talk is known as the "Olivet Discourse," or more appropriately, the "Little Apocalypse." In theology-speak, eschatology is the study of the end of the world, and the Gospel's single biggest chunk of it comes straight from this dialogue.

False messiahs, wars and rumors of wars, earthquakes, famines – these are just the beginning of the birth pangs, Jesus tells them. You will be handed over to councils and be beaten in synagogues. Brother will betray brother to death, and a father his child, and children their parents. You will be hated by all. But those who endure to the end will be saved.

There's more. He adds cryptically, when they see the "desolating sacrilege" set up where it ought not to be, then those in Judea must flee to the mountains; don't stop to take anything or turn back to grab your coat. Woe to those who are pregnant and to those nursing their infants in those days! Pray that it may not be in winter, for there will be suffering "such as has not been from the beginning of the creation that God created until now, no, and never will be." And if anyone says to you, 'Look! Here is the Messiah!' or 'Look! There he is!' – don't believe it. False messiahs and false prophets will appear and do signs and omens, to lead you astray.

Finally, after suffering all that, the sun and the moon will be darkened, and the stars will fall from heaven, and 'the powers in the heavens will be shaken.' Then they will see 'the Son of Man coming in clouds' with great power and glory. Then he will send out the angels, and gather his elect from the four winds, from the ends of the earth to the ends of heaven.

Theologians have been trying to make sense of this eschatological smorgasbord ever since, with much debate and little agreement. Certain clues in this monologue, like the aside in verse 14 that says "let the reader understand" caused 19th century French biblical scholar Timothée Colani to argue that the entire discourse originally came from an earlier document; perhaps an apocalyptic leaflet. Eusebius says (*Ecclesiastical History* 3.5) there was just such a pamphlet in circulation at the time of the First Jewish–Roman War, a "revelation" which alerted the Jerusalem Christians to flee the doomed city before the Roman siege clamped down in February of 70 CE[13] Perhaps the author of Mark wrote it as well. In any case, whoever wrote the discourse, they employed the same sources for it as Mark did for rest of his gospel. As numerous scholars, such as John Bowman, Dale Miller, Patricia Miller, Robert M. Price and others[14] have noted, though this speech supposedly comes straight from Jesus, it's actually a medley of Old Testament verses:

- Mark 13:8 ("nation will rise against nation, and kingdom against kingdom") comes from Isaiah 19:2 and/or 2 Chron. 15:6
- Mark 13:12 (family members betray each other) comes from Micah 7:6
- Mark 13:14 ("the desolating sacrilege," "flee to the mountains") comes from Daniel 9:27, 11:31, 12:11 & Gen. 19:17
- Mark 13:19 (suffering such as has never been) comes from Daniel 12:1
- Mark 13:22 (false prophets lead the people astray) comes from Deut. 13:1-2
- Mark 13:24 (sun and moon darkened) comes from Isaiah 13:10
- Mark 13:25 (stars fall from heaven) comes from Isaiah 34:4
  Mark 13:26 ("the Son of Man coming in clouds'") comes from Daniel 7:13
- Mark 13:27 (gather his elect from the four winds, and from the ends of heaven) comes from Zech. 2:6 & Deut. 30:4

In the next chapter, the Passover is only two days away, and the Jewish leaders are brainstorming ways to get their hands on Jesus and kill him. Back in Bethany, Jesus is at the house of Simon the Leper, where an unnamed woman anoints him at dinner with a vial of very expensive spikenard perfume (14:3-9). Incidentally, in later gospels, all these details will vary considerably: In John (12:1-3), this becomes the house of Lazarus, Jesus is there six days before Passover, and his sister Mary does the anointing. In Luke (7:36-38), he never hangs out in Bethany at all, and the anointing takes place much earlier in his ministry, at the house of a Pharisee in the city of Nain, by a local woman "who was a sinner," who heard Jesus was dining there. But in all cases, they are inspired by Song of Solomon

1:12: "While the king sitteth at his table, my spikenard sendeth forth the smell thereof."

Payment in Blood
A few verses later (14:10-11), Judas Iscariot decides out of the blue to betray Jesus; his first action in the entire gospel. In Mark, no motive is given for his betrayal. He approaches the chief priests to betray him, apropos of nothing. Upon hearing this, the delighted priests offer him an unspecified amount of money.

Matthew expands on this basic story and has them pay him 30 pieces of silver (26:15). This is an odd amount to be tempting someone with; *Argurion*, the word Matthew uses here, simply means "a silver," and could refer to any silver coin. A common first century silver coin was the Greek drachma, a basic unit of currency also nearly equivalent to a Roman silver denarius, or a quarter of a silver shekel. According to *Smith's Bible Dictionary*, drachmas were originally worth a handful of arrows. In Athens, Judas' 30 pieces of silver could buy him 3 goats or 30 liters of olive oil, but he'd still need another 20 drachmas to buy a cow.

In *Decline and Fall of the Roman Empire*, Edward Gibbon noted that butcher's meat cost 2 denarii/lb. Athenian Potters, acropolis workers, and mud carriers earned 1 drachma a day. In Jesus' day, a Roman legionnaire under Augustus Caesar would earn slightly more than this, a little over a denarius a day. "A silver" could just as easily mean a coin as small as a quarter-drachma, or as large as a shekel, but it seems whatever coin we're talking about, Judas basically had sold Jesus out for the same amount he would have made after a month of sweeping the acropolis or hauling mud.

All this is moot, since this odd amount doesn't come from reality, it comes from scripture: Zechariah 11:12-13 ("So they paid me thirty pieces of silver").[15] This is the same verse that Matthew explicitly quotes when he tells us what happened to

Jesus: Mything in Action

Judas and what the priests did with the blood money afterwards – even though he mistakenly attributes it to Jeremiah:

> "When Judas, his betrayer, saw that Jesus was condemned, he repented and brought back the thirty pieces of silver to the chief priests and the elders. He said, "I have sinned by betraying innocent blood." But they said, "What is that to us? See to it yourself." Throwing down the pieces of silver in the temple, he departed; and **he went and hanged himself**. But the chief priests, taking the pieces of silver, said, "It is not lawful to put them into the treasury, since they are blood money." After conferring together, **they used them to buy the potter's field as a place to bury foreigners. For this reason that field has been called the Field of Blood to this day.** Then was fulfilled what had been spoken through the prophet Jeremiah, *"And they took the thirty pieces of silver, the price of the one on whom a price had been set, on whom some of the people of Israel had set a price, and they gave them for the potter's field, as the Lord commanded me."*
> (Matt. 27: 3-10, emphasis added)

Oddly, none of the other gospels mention any of this. In the rest, once Judas kisses and tells, he exits the stage and vanishes. Luke, however, does briefly revisit Judas in Acts, and also brings up Jewish scripture (Psalms 69:25 & 109:8) for support. Does Luke's version conflict with Matthew's? Only on virtually every point:

> "Friends, **the scripture had to be fulfilled**, which the Holy Spirit through David foretold concerning Judas, who became a guide for those who arrested Jesus— for he was numbered among us and was allotted his share in this ministry." Now **this man acquired a field** with the reward of his wickedness; and **falling headlong, he burst open in the middle and all his bowels gushed out.** This became known to all the residents of Jerusalem, **so that the field**

> was called in their language *Hakeldama*, that is, Field of Blood. For it is written in the book of Psalms, *Let his homestead become desolate, and let there be no one to live in it*; and *Let another take his position of overseer.*" (Acts 1:16-20)

The obligatory dubious Christian response to this dilemma is to propose that when Judas hung himself, it was somehow overlooking the edge of some cliff, and further, that later the rope snapped, so that his body fell headlong and popped like a water balloon at the bottom. The remaining contradictions, harder to harmonize, are simply ignored.

The Death of Judas, Take Three
And if two conflicting stories weren't enough already, 2nd century bishop Papias gives a *third* account of Judas' death. Apparently Judas lasted much longer – and had it worse than we realize:

> "Judas was a terrible, walking example of ungodliness in this world, his flesh so bloated that he was not able to pass through a place where a wagon passes easily, not even his bloated head by itself. For his eyelids, they say, were so swollen that he could not see the light at all, and his eyes could not be seen, even by a doctor using an optical instrument, so far had they sunk below the outer surface. ...When he relieved himself there passed through it pus and worms from every part of his body, much to his shame. After much agony and punishment, they say, he finally died in his own place, and because of the stench the area is deserted and uninhabitable even now; in fact, to this day no one can pass that place unless they hold their nose, so great was the discharge from his body and so far did it spread over the ground."[16]

This then is the testimony of Papias, who supposedly knew the apostle John personally and vouched for the Gospels of Mark and Matthew (all problematic claims[17]) But if he knew Matthew had said Judas ran out of the Temple and hanged himself, then how could he give us this David Lynchian nightmare? It's shocking to realize a man whose word is held up as evidence for the Gospels says with a straight face that Judas suffered a long, painful existence as a mutant freak with a head swollen wider than a wagon before finally dying like a bloated piñata of pus and worms.

We could spend a lot of time discussing other problematic issues surrounding Judas. Like so many other characters in the Gospels, his name works remarkably apt as symbolism. Though modern translations give his name as "Judas," in actuality, his name in all NT documents is Judah (*Ioudas*); basically, "Jew."[18]

His motive for the betrayal is unconvincing regardless of which gospel you choose to believe. Choices range from none at all in Mark (14:10), petty theft in Matthew (see above), Satanic possession in Luke (22:3), or both in John (12:5-6; 13:2, 27); and none of the Evangelists think to explain how *they* know what Judas was thinking, or what occurred in secret meetings between him and the Priests, or how they are able to pinpoint the exact moment when Satan enters his heart, etc....

Devil in the Details
Speak of the Devil, Robert Price has pointed out an interesting paradox: in Mark and Matthew, Satan's goal is to tempt Jesus into *avoiding* the cross. When Jesus teaches that he must undergo great suffering, be rejected by the authorities and killed, and rise again three days later, Peter pulls him aside to talk him out of it. Jesus gets angry and tells him to back off: "Get behind me, Satan!" (Mark 8:31-33; Matt. 16:21-23) For Mark and Matthew, Judas isn't Satan's pawn; he betrays Jesus for his own motives (or none, apparently).[19]

This is the complete opposite of Luke and John, where crucifying Jesus is all Satan's evil plan, and he hijacks Judas to make it happen. Notably, neither Luke nor John ever have Peter try to talk Jesus out of his fate, not even when Jesus gives the same speech in Luke 9:22. John even has his Jesus call Judas "a devil" (6:70-71).[20] And this isn't the end of the kerfuffle. Earlier Christians like Paul muddle the situation even worse by declaring that Satan and his minions had no idea who they had on the cross; "for had they known it, they would not have crucified the Lord of glory" (1 Cor. 2:7-8; see ch. 15). This in turn was reversed by the Church fathers who later argued that the reason there were so many similarities between Christianity and earlier pagan religions was that Satan had seen it coming all along. Obviously, he had read the Old Testament prophecies and gone to work inspiring counterfeit Christianities in advance of the real thing.[21] Which is it already?

Still, it seems the real sin of Judas is not treachery, petty theft or demon possession, but all the plot holes he causes. What did they need Judas for, again? It's not like Jesus was hard to locate: the Gospels claim he had just entered Jerusalem as a hero to the entire city ("all the city was moved" Matt. 21:8-10). He was completely in the public eye, teaching in the Temple daily, traveling freely; he even had just driven out the moneychangers from the Temple (unless you ask John - according to him that happened at the start of Jesus' career, three years earlier). Why wasn't he arrested on the spot for that alone?

Nor was he holing up in some remote hideout. Luke says every night he went to the Mount of Olives (Luke 21:37), and the place Judas supposedly tracked him down was where Jesus often went with his disciples (John 18:2). According to the Jerusalem-based scholar Haim Cohn, "He could be followed there with no difficulty, without the aid of any informer....the Mount of Olives rises not far from the city wall to the northeast, with all of its possible avenues easily overlooked from the battlements; and however flourishing and fertile the "gardens" on the mount may then have been, the distances are not such that a person entering them could not at once be detected."[22] Cohn adds not even the Romans would have required a guide to find their way around the mount; and the Jewish temple police would have regarded an offer to guide them there as an insult to their intelligence.[23]

Peter (according to John) attacks the posse with a sword and even cuts off a man's ear; why isn't *he* arrested? (Mark 14:47; John 18:10) In fact, if Jesus' teachings were so dangerous, why didn't *all* the disciples get rounded up as well? The evangelists all give different versions of the story of Judas Iscariot, and yet his "betrayal" makes no sense in any of them. But we're getting ahead of ourselves.

The Last Supper
Back to our story. For Passover, Jesus has the disciples pull the same impromptu trick they used to boost his ride into Jerusalem: he foresees the room they will need, and sends two ahead to look for a man carrying a jar of water.[24] He says wherever he goes, enter and tell the homeowner that the Master asks, "Where is my guestroom where I may eat the Passover with my disciples?" (Mark 14:14)

Richard Carrier reveals there is a symbolic double meaning hidden in that choice of words. The Greek word translated here as "guestroom" is *kataluma;* from the verb *kataluô,* which means dissolve, disintegrate, destroy, kill. The noun form just happened to take on the meaning of any place, like an inn or lodge where someone "breaks up" a journey. Mark uses the verb *kataluô* in three places (13:2, 14:58, 15:29); each time referring to the destruction of the temple, which we know Mark used as a metaphor for Jesus' body – just as Paul used the same verb and body/building metaphor in 2 Corinthians 5:1-2.[25] So Mark is having Jesus make a pun here; saying, in effect, that he will be destroyed (broken up) in that room at Passover, just as the Passover lamb would be.[26]

As you can well imagine, they score the room without difficulty. But at dinner that night (14:18-21), Mark has Jesus drop a bombshell – one of the twelve is going to betray him. He adds, "Woe to that one by whom the Son of Man is betrayed!" echoing the cry in Zechariah 11:17, "Woe to the worthless shepherd, who deserts the flock!" The traitor, Judas Iscariot, is clearly patterned here on the Worthless Shepherd in Zechariah 11, who sells his flock to be killed as meat; he cares more for the money than for them. He has "no pity," saying he will not feed them anymore, "any that are to die, let them die..." (Zech. 11:5, 9)

After the dust from that news settles, Jesus inaugurates a new ritual, the breaking and eating of bread, to represent his broken body; and the drinking of wine, to represent his blood, which is shed for many (14:22-25). This last supper would be called the Lord's Supper, or the Eucharist, from *eucharistia* ("thanksgiving"). Remarkably, we have no fewer than six different canonical versions of the Eucharist liturgy,[27] including two variants of Luke (Codex Bezae, "the Western Text," has a longer version than other manuscripts). Each makes subtle changes to the wording of the liturgy, but all echo our oldest version: the "new testament" Paul gives us in 1 Cor. 11:23-26, which itself springs from the original covenant of blood instituted by Moses in Exodus 24:8.

Paul unveils this new ritual to believers and claimed that Jesus revealed it to him direct from heaven – which makes no sense, if there had been disciples of Jesus who had been passing on the tradition all along before Paul's vision. What's more, Christianity is not the only – or the first – religion to celebrate a "Lord's Supper" (as we'll see in ch. 15).

The Lost Supper

It's strange that John *doesn't* have his Jesus establish the Eucharist at his last supper – or ever. Instead, he has Jesus say something somewhat along the same lines in a much earlier sermon at a Capernaum synagogue (6:48-59); yet another event the other Gospels missed. There, John's Jesus describes himself as the Living Bread, and outrages his Jewish audience by insisting they eat his flesh and drink his blood (6:51-58).

John also gives us a unique account of the last supper, found nowhere else. It starts with Jesus stripping: "He rose from supper, and laid aside his garments; and took a towel, and girded himself. After that he poured water into a basin, and began to wash the disciples' feet, and to wipe them with the towel with which he was girded." (John 13:4-5) Afterwards, he gets dressed and asks his disciples, "Do you know what I have done to you?" (13:12). He explains "I have set you an example, that you also should do as I have done to you." (13:15) Odd that so many Christians today have chosen to ignore this example from their towel-clad Lord…

Despite having no Eucharist, Jesus does have a lot to say in John's last supper – an awful lot. After spending virtually all of chapters 13 & 14 talking to his freshly -washed disciples, he concludes, "Rise, let us be on our way" (14:31) – and then continues talking for another three chapters. John's gospel shows many instances like this, where later editors have felt free to insert more material.

Here's another: in John 2:11, Jesus performs his first miracle, the first of his "Seven Signs," changing water into wine at the wedding in Cana. (By the way, if you suspect such an alcoholic miracle is more appropriate for some pagan fertility god, you're absolutely right. John has his Jesus imitating an annual miracle performed by the priests of Dionysus at Sidon and Eleia and other cult centers long before it showed up in the Bible.[28]) Of course, none of the other Gospel writers know anything about this miracle, either, or these "Seven Signs." Verse 2:23 then says Jesus performed many more miracles at the Passover feast later. But then long after that, Jesus heals a nobleman's son, which we are told is his *second* miracle (4:54)! Oops – someone has been padding the books…

If all that seems a bit strange, it's *very* strange that John's last supper isn't even on the same day as the other gospels. In fact, none of the events of the Passion – his triumphant entry, the cleansing of the temple, last supper, trial(s), his death – occur on the same day as that of the other gospels, as we'll see before long…

Gethsemane

After dinner, they sing a hymn (14:26). This is the *Hallel*, the traditional Passover hymns, taken from the Psalms. Parts of Psalms 113 & 114 are sung before the meal, and 115-118 sung afterwards. The after-dinner hymn taken from Psalm 116 contains these lines, particularly apt for the situation:

> I kept my faith, even when I said, "I am greatly afflicted;"
> I said in my consternation, "Everyone is a liar."
> What shall I return to the Lord for all his bounty to me?
> I will lift up the cup of salvation and call on the name of the Lord,
> I will pay my vows to the Lord in the presence of all his people.
> Precious in the sight of the Lord is the death of his faithful ones.

They return once more to the symbolic messianic launching pad, the Mount of Olives. There, Jesus tells them they will all desert him, " for it is written, *I will strike the shepherd, and the sheep will be scattered*," citing the Old Testament book of Zechariah (13:7). As we've already seen, Zechariah is one of the sources for much of the unfolding finale of Mark.[29] He adds (14:27-28), "But after I am raised up, I will go before you to Galilee." Peter famously denies he'll deny Jesus, who tells him he'll be a three-strike denier before the cock crows twice (14: 29-31). They continue on to the

Garden of Gethsemane. Here an agonized Jesus leaves behind his disciples, taking only three with him further, Peter, James and John (14:33). Then he charges them to keep watch; he must leave them behind as well. "I am deeply grieved, even to death; remain here, and keep awake." He continues on, alone and in agony, until he can go no further and collapses to the ground, and last of all, leaves behind even his very own self. He prays to God to deliver him from the suffering to come, but not without adding the ultimate expression of obedience: "yet, not what I want, but what you want." (14:35-36)

It's a moving story, and personally I find it even more so when you think of it not through the lens of today's Christians, but as Mark actually portrays Jesus: just a regular man of fallible flesh and blood like us, before God adopted him to be his son after his death. When we do that, the fear and temptation become real and tangible, something we lose if we impose our modern evangelical view on Jesus: an incarnation of omnipotent God who is just slumming on earth before returning to heaven after a really bad weekend.[30]

But moving or not, when all's said and done, it *is* a story, not history. This one is patterned on the story of Elijah fleeing Jezebel in the Greek Septuagint version of 1 Kings 19 (III Kings 19 in the LXX). In both stories, the prophet (Elijah/Jesus) knows that the authorities (the King and Queen/the chief priests) are coming to arrest and kill them. In both, the prophet leaves behind his (servant/disciples) and goes on alone to pray. He seeks solace (under a juniper tree/in a garden of olive trees) where he prays for deliverance, saying "Take (my soul/this cup from me)."

Luke's version follows the pattern even closer than Mark; by having an angel (help him go "in strength"/strengthen him). There are other probable biblical models as well. Both Jesus (Mark 14:34) and the reluctant prophet Jonah found themselves "deeply grieved" (Jonah 4:1, LXX) and pray in their despair. Jesus cries out, "My soul is deeply grieved, even unto death." (14:34), echoing Jonah's prayer, "I am greatly grieved, even unto death." (Jonah 4:9, LXX)[31] And both characters have three dark days ahead of them; Jonah in the belly of a great fish (Jonah 1:17), and Jesus in the grave.

Incidentally, no matter which Gospel version you read, with scenes like these it's obvious we're in the realm of fiction; since according to the story, any potential eyewitnesses to Jesus' prayerful monologue were asleep. This is good to keep in mind throughout the Gospels when we're told other things that only an omniscient narrator could know; i.e., angelic visitations in dreams to Joseph, secret meetings of Jesus' enemies, Mary's innermost thoughts, Satan entering Judas' heart, Pilate's examination of Jesus, Herod's examination of Jesus, the trial before the Sanhedrin, etc.

Or, as we're about to see, what happens when they come to arrest Jesus.

***

For further reading:

Robert M. Price gives a thorough demonstration of even more elements from OT scripture (dozens more, in fact) that the Gospels and Acts used to construct their stories in his essay "New Testament Narrative as Old Testament Midrash," in *The Christ-Myth Theory and its Problems*, pp. 59-263 (American Atheist Press, 2011).

In addition to Price's examples above, see the relevant sections in:

Thomas Brodie, *Beyond the Quest for the Historical Jesus: A Memoir of a Discovery* (2012)
Randel Helms, *Gospel Fictions* (1988)
Dennis R. MacDonald, *The Homeric Epics and the Gospel of Mark* (2000)

Thomas Thompson's *The Messiah Myth: The Near Eastern Roots of Jesus and David* (2005)

---

[1] Theophilus of Antioch: *Letter to Autolycus*; see Doherty, *JP*, pp. 277-78. Macarius Magnes: *Apocriticus* 3.6; see *Nailed*, pp. 105-6.
[2] Irenaeus, *Against All Heresies* 2.22.1
[3] Origen, *Commentary on John*, vol. 10, ch. 4
[4] For more detailed analysis of how Mark employs the Elijah-Elisha narratives as source material for constructing stories about Jesus throughout his Gospel, see Helms, *Gospel Fictions*, pp. 65-67; as well as Adam Winn, *Mark and the Elijah-Elisha Narrative: Considering the Practice of Greco-Roman Imitation in the Search for Markan Source Material* (Eugene, Oregon: Pickwick Publications, 2010).
[5] Some mss. have "secret."
[6] Jesus in the *Gospel of Thomas* also makes a similar reference to his teachings: "I tell my mysteries to those worthy of my mysteries" (Saying 62).
[7] Translation: Helms, pp. 77-78
[8] In *Apocriticus* 3.6. See *Nailed*, p. 106 for more details
[9] See Robert M. Price's *The Incredible Shrinking Son of Man*, pp. 198-199
[10] Helms, GF, p. 102
[11] e.g., *The Jewish War* 2.13.5; *Antiquities* 20.8.6
[12] R.G. Hamerton-Kelly, "Sacred Violence and the Messiah: The Markan Passion Narrative as a Redefinition of Messianology," in James Charlesworth, ed., *The Messiah: Developments in Earliest Judaism and Christianity* (Minneapolis: Fortress, 1992), pp. 461-93 (esp. pp. 467-71). I am grateful to Richard Carrier for this and several of the other citations in this chapter.
[13] Price, *The Incredible Shrinking Son of Man* p. 277
[14] Bowman, pp. 241-42; Miller and Miller, pp. 300-301; Price,

op. cit., p. 277
15 See also Exodus 21:32, which sets the price of a slave at 30 shekels; "the price of the one on whom a price had been set."
16 *Exposition of the Sayings of the Lord* as quoted in Apollinaris of Laodicaea, *The Apostolic Fathers*, p. 323-324, 1989, Baker Book House, Grand Rapids, Michigan. See also Carrier, *On the Historicity of Jesus*, p. 325 n67.
17 See "Papias of Hierapolis" in ch. 18.
18 Carrier, *Proving History*, 317-18
19 Price, op. cit., pp. 306-307
20 Ibid.
21 See "The Devil's Christs," in *Nailed*, p. 166
22 Cohn, p. 81
23 Ibid.
24 Incidentally, both these missions are based on 1 Samuel 9:5-14; where Saul enters a city looking for his donkeys and meets women carrying jars of water. See Price, *The Incredible Shrinking Son of Man*, p. 297.
25 See Carrier: *Proving History*, p. 190 and *On the Historicity of Jesus*, p. 424n74.
26 Ibid.
27 The other five are: Mark 14:22-25, Matt. 26:26-29, Luke 22:12-20, Luke (Codex Bezae) 22:15-19a, John 6:48-57ff; see Price, op. cit., p. 298.
28 Price, op. cit., p.159
29 For example: see: Henk Jan de Jonge, "The Cleansing of the Temple in Mark 11:15 and Zechariah 14:21," in Christopher Tuckett, ed., *The Book of Zechariah and Its Influence* (Burlington, VT: Ashgate, 2003), pp. 87-100, Mark Black, "The Messianic Use of Zechariah 9-14 in Matthew, Mark and the Pre-Markan Tradition," in Patrick Gray and Gail R. O'Day, ed., *Scripture and Traditions: Essays on Early Judaism and Christianity in Honor of Carl R. Holladay* (Boston: Brill, 2008), pp. 97-114; and

Craig Evans, "Zechariah in the Markan Passion Narrative," in Thomas R. Hatina, ed., *Biblical Interpretation in early Christian Gospels. Vol. 1, The Gospel of Mark* (New York: T & T Clark, 2006), pp. 64-80.

[30] I'm reminded of comedian David Cross' stand-up bit depicting Jesus hollering at the Romans to hurry up and crucify him already so he could get the hell out of hot, stinking first-century Judea and back up to heaven.

[31] Helms, GF, pp.109-110

Chapter Nine: The Kiss of Death

"If anything is historically true in the Bible, it is there not because it is historically true but for different reasons."

– Northrop Frye

The Kiss of Death

Three times Jesus returns from his anguished prayers, each time only to find his disciples asleep, unable to keep watch and pray, as he asked them – another clear spiritual lesson for the reader. And then it is too late. The hour has come; the Son of Man is betrayed into the hands of sinners (14:41).

We know what happens next. Judas arrives, with an armed entourage of goons courtesy of the Jewish temple leadership, and betrays Jesus with a kiss. That is, except in John's gospel; he refuses to have his manly Jesus get kissed on by Judas and simply removes that from his version. The other Evangelists have no problem with the kiss-off; after all, there were already good precedents for treacherous kisses in the Bible. "The kisses of an enemy are perfidious," Proverbs 27:6 warns us. Then there's the story in 2 Samuel 20:9-10, where David's kinsman and ex-army commander Joab greeted Amasa, (also David's kinsman, and his soon-to-be ex-army commander) saying, "I hope you are well, my brother." He then grasped his beard with one hand to kiss him; with the other hand stabbing him in the belly with a sword. Amasa died immediately with "his entrails poured out" upon the ground – the identical Greek wording used when Judas dies in Acts 1:18.

As more than one scholar has remarked, the whole arrest scene seems a bit contrived, and as we've already seen, totally unnecessary. Even Jesus seems to think so:

"Have you come out with swords and clubs to arrest me as though I were a bandit? Day after day I was with you in the temple teaching, and you did not arrest me. But let the scriptures be fulfilled." (Mark 14:48-49)

Again, scripture is the basis of yet another feature of the storyline. At this, all the disciples flee, just as Jesus predicted (again citing scripture!). But then something quite unpredicted, and quite bizarre, happens.

The Streaker in the Garden
Next comes an eyebrow-raising event that rarely gets mentioned in sermons:

> "A certain young man was following him, wearing nothing but a linen cloth.
> They caught hold of him, but he left the linen cloth and ran off naked."
>
> (Mark 14:51-2)

What was a scantily clad youth doing hanging around Jesus and the disciples, you may well ask? Another fitting question: why the hell haven't we heard about *him* before this? Intriguing and potentially titillating possibilities spring easily to mind, especially for godless perverts like myself (and do see the forthcoming *CHG to Sex & Violence in the Bible* for more prurient details on this whole near-naked boy business). It certainly seemed to embarrass the other evangelists; none of them included Jesus' young naked friend in their gospels. Though this incident may at first glance look like a perfect fit for the criteria of embarrassment, the truth is there is a perfectly respectable explanation behind this invention by Mark – and it is yet another literary one.

Even before Mark, equating the body with a garment was an ancient cliché,[1] and a popular metaphor with early Christians, including Paul (see 1 Cor. 15:53-54; 2 Cor. 5:1-4).[2] Plato said that at death, souls leave their bodies and ascend to judgment naked (*Gorgias* 523). Empedocles said primordial souls became clothed "in the unfamiliar tunic of flesh" (Empedocles frag. 126). According to Philo of Alexandria, the "garments of skins" that God gave to Adam and Eve after their fall (Gen. 3:21) were their physical bodies, and that the soul that pursues God has "disrobed itself of the body...and fled far away."[3]

The reason the mysterious unnamed youth appears here for the very first time is because he is the metaphorical representation of Jesus losing his life. How do we know? Mark makes this very clear at the end of his gospel – when he brings the young man back. As we'll see before too long...

Disorder in the Court
Mark 14: 53-65 takes us into Jesus' dramatic trial before the Jewish council, the Sanhedrin. By the story's own logic, the disciples have all scattered (Mark 14:50), so there would have been no witnesses to report the details of this secret trial – and therefore, once again, we know every version of this would-be trial transcript is fiction for starters. But even if that weren't the case, we would still know the story is 100% made up from the howling historical inaccuracies alone, as modern Jewish scholars have pointed out for over two centuries.[4] As I wrote in *Nailed*,

> Jewish legal authority Haim Cohn (Attorney-General of Israel and later Justice of the Israeli Supreme Court) scrutinized the different biblical accounts of Jesus' trial with a fine-toothed comb in *The Trial and Death of Jesus*, and his verdict is harsh: even where the Gospels do agree with each other, on point after point he finds that the Gospel writers get their facts wrong, sometimes ridiculously so.
>
> The trial is incompatible with multiple well-established provisions of ancient Jewish law; in fact the violations of Jewish law in Jesus' trial dog-pile on each other so fast it's hard to keep up. (*Nailed*, p. 93)

For some (not all) of the examples: Jesus was unlawfully arrested and unlawfully interrogated.[5] No person could be tried on a criminal charge on festival days or the eve of a festival (*M Sanhedrin* IV 1). No person could be convicted on his own testimony

(*T Shevu'ot* III 8). A person could only be convicted of a capital offense upon the testimony of two lawfully qualified eyewitnesses;[6] had the eyewitnesses' testimony failed to agree (per Mark 14: 56), Jesus' case would have been dismissed. Trials for capital crimes had to be conducted over the course of two days (*M Sanhedrin* IV 1, V 5). They could not be conducted on or even interrupted by a Sabbath or holy day. Nor could they be conducted at night; trials had to commence and be completed during the daytime (*M Sanhedrin* IV 1). Nor could they be conducted in secret. Nor could the ancient Jewish equivalent of the Supreme Court ever hold a trial outside the temple precincts (*B Avodah Zarah* 8b; *Sanhedrin* 41b; *B Shabbat* 15a, *et al.*), let alone in a private house, let alone in *the judge's own house*. Nor would the high priest act as interrogator; not because there is a rule against it, but for the simple fact that in Jewish courts there were no prosecutors in criminal trials at all.[7]

And again, all this was during Passover; as Cohn notes (and as anyone who was actually familiar with Jewish culture would have known), "every single member of the Sanhedrin, not least the high priest in person, must have been busy and preoccupied with the somewhat cumbersome and complicated preparations for the feast, or with its celebration, whether in his home, or in the temple, or both. That the Sanhedrin should have been called that particular night to a meeting in the high priest's residence, and should eventually have spent long hours there until well into the next morning, requires very cogent and convincing explanation to be credible."[8]

We should also point out that the gospels don't even agree about when this trial occurred. Mark (14:55-64) and Matthew

(26:59-66) claim it was at night; Luke (22:66-71) crams it into his already overcrowded morning (see Ch. 10); and John (18:13-14) has no trial before the Sanhedrin at all, only an interrogation before Annas and Caiaphas.

In reality, Jesus would not have been arrested on the eve of a festival. But even if the authorities were so inexplicably anxious to immediately lock him up that they went ahead and arrested him during Passover, he would have simply been held over in jail until Sunday, and could only have been convicted on Monday at the earliest. Executions were not performed on holy days.[9]

All these objections and more have been pointed out before. Richard Carrier sums up the verdict on Jesus' trial: "Mark's (trial account) has no historical credibility... as history, this narrative makes zero sense. But as symbolic myth, every oddity is explained, and indeed, expected."[10] So it should come as no surprise that in *Gospel Fictions*, Randel Helms[11] has demonstrated that Mark has constructed his trial account from Old Testament Septuagint (LXX) passages:

"The chief priests and the whole council sought [*ezētoun*] testimony against Jesus in order to kill him; but they found none." [*ouch heuriskon*] (Mark 14:55)

Daniel 6:4 LXX – "Then the governors and the satraps sought [*ezētoun*] to find [*heurein*] occasion against Daniel in connection with the kingdom. But they found against him [*ouch heuron*] no occasion."

"For many gave false testimony against him, and their testimony did not agree. Some having stood up [*anastantes*] gave false testimony [*epseudomarturoun*] against him..." (Mark 14:56-57)

Psalms 34:11/35:11 LXX – "Unjust witnesses standing up [*anastantes martures adikoi*]; asked [*epērōtōn*] me..."

"Then the high priest, standing up [*anastas*] in the midst, asked [*epērōtēse*] Jesus…"(Mark 14:60)

Psalms 26:12/27:12 LXX – "Unjust witnesses [*martures adikoi*] have stood up [*anastantes martures adikoi*] against me, and injustice has lied [*epseusato*] within herself…" (from Helms, *Gospel Fictions*, pp. 118 - 20)

Silence!
Not all the scriptural inspirations worked as well as others. The Suffering Servant passage in Isaiah (52:13-15, 53:1-12) became popular with the early Christians looking for signs of their messiah in the ancient Hebrew scriptures. Mark was no exception; one of the verses he wanted to include when he was putting together his story was Isaiah 53:7, "He did not open his mouth," which in Mark becomes "But he was silent and did not answer." (14:61) However, Mark had more for Jesus to say. This dilemma caused problems for all four Evangelists, who wanted to have their silence and speak it too. So Jesus' silence turns out very short-lived; in fact, the very next verse he opens his mouth again. And then all hell breaks loose.

> Then the high priest stood up before them and asked Jesus,
> "Have you no answer? What is it that they testify against you?"
> But he was silent and did not answer. Again the high priest asked him,
> "Are you the Messiah, the Son of the Blessed One?"
> Jesus said, "I am; and you will see the Son of Man seated at the right hand of the Power, and coming with the clouds of heaven."

Of course, "I am" is not just answering the question, it's name-dropping God himself (Gen. 2:4; Ex. 3:14; Deut. 32:39);

just as John has Jesus do in his gospel: "Truly I tell you, before Abraham was, I am" (8:58). And the Son of Man coming with the clouds is referring to the prophecy of the coming of the Son of Man as cosmic judge in Daniel 7:13-14, and of sitting at the right hand of the Lord, from Psalms (110:1).

Blasphemy? What Blasphemy?
Mark makes this declaration the tipping point. Once the high priest hears it, it's all over for Jesus:

> Then the high priest tore his clothes and said,
> 'Why do we still need witnesses? You have heard his blasphemy!
> What is your decision?' All of them condemned him as deserving death.

However, Mark has made several major mistakes in this passage, and the biggest one is: Jesus has not committed any blasphemy. Christian theologians have presumed that Jesus' reply "I am" was the sacrilege in question. But as it turns out, Haim Cohn has shown this is spectacularly wrong. The words "I am" (*Ani Hu* in Hebrew) are not the same as pronouncing the holy and ineffable name of God, i.e., the Tetragrammaton, YHWH, or as it becomes transliterated in English, Yahweh or Jehovah. Indeed, Cohn adds that anyone familiar with the rudiments of Hebrew knows that the words *Ani Hu* come up hundreds of times in everyday speech, and there is no more crime attached to saying them singly or jointly than there is in speaking aloud any of the many other words or phrases that God uses to describe himself in the scriptures.[12]

Nor was it blasphemy for Jesus to declare that he was the Messiah, or the Son of Man, that he would be seated at the right hand of God, or be coming with the clouds of heaven. Cohn adds, "Not only was there nothing criminal in his words, there was nothing in his pretensions or pretentiousness that could, in reason, shock or scandalize his hearers."[13] First century Judea was rife with wanna-be saviors making similar messianic claims. Hearing one more Jesus-come-lately spouting the same overblown spiel might have made them roll their eyes, but wouldn't have had anyone clapping their hands over their ears.

Mark makes other errors in this scene. Though he was wrong about what constituted blasphemy, he knew just enough about Judaism to know that the high priest would rip his garments if he heard the name of God, Yahweh, spoken aloud. In fact, he was legally required to do so – and not just him. By law, *everyone* in the court would have been tearing their clothing at the sound as well.[14] And then Jesus would have been promptly taken out and stoned to death, as Mosaic law required (Sanhedrin 7: 4-5). Then again, why should we worry about legal niceties by this point? Virtually every facet of this entire "trial" has completely flunked the reality check, right from the start.

In addition to just being wrong about bitter political rivals the Pharisees and Sadducees being in cahoots with one another (see *Nailed*, p. 94), Mark makes another mistake. Forgetting that he made the condemnation unanimous, a little later in the chapter he introduces Joseph of Arimathea as both a follower of Jesus and "a respected member of the council." Later, Luke will compound the problem by adding a cameo appearance of the beloved rabbi Gamaliel to Peter's trial in Acts – which means Gamaliel should have been present and prominent at Jesus' trial as well. It doesn't help Luke's credibility that there is no Jewish record of either trial at all, much less that the famous rabbi was on the scene for either.[15]

You're out of order! This whole court's out of order! On top of all these basic fails of Judaean Judaism 101, Mark's overwrought legal drama turns into a grotesque black comedy: Jewish law forbade anyone from striking the prisoner (B Sanhedrin 58b, 45a) and yet, the gospels all have not only that, but more: "some began to spit on him, to blindfold him, and to strike him, saying to him, 'Prophesy!' The guards also took him over and beat him." (Mark 14:65) What Mark depicts here isn't just a kangaroo court; it's a ridiculous circus of blatant errors, basic misunderstandings and the ugliest brand of crude stereotypes.

Which is more implausible: that such a ridiculous farce could have ever occurred in the first place? Or that if it had, contemporary historians took note of less lurid scandals like that of Carabas or Jesus ben-Ananias (as we'll soon see next chapter) but missed this one? No need to worry too long about the question, since (hopefully unsurprisingly by now) the details of this trial scene with its wholly unbelievable collapse into madness... are also taken completely from Hebrew scriptures. None of these abuses could realistically have occurred in a trial before the Sanhedrin – but every one appears in the Septuagint translation of Isaiah 50:6, as Randel Helms again demonstrates:

> "I gave my back to scourges, and my cheeks to blows
> (in Greek, *hrapismata*, the same word used in Mark 14:65, *hrapismasin*, to describe Jesus being struck);
> and I turned not away my face from the shame of spitting."

Mark cuts away from this dramatic moment to another intense scene: Peter's triple denial (14:66-72). In Mark's original (details change in later gospels), Peter is lurking outside the High Priest's courtyard, warming himself by the fire. A servant girl ID's him as one of Jesus' accomplices, and just as Jesus predicted earlier, Peter denies it, insisting he doesn't know what she's talking about. He skulks away and the cock crows; she continues to tell the crowd that he is one of them, and he denies it a second time. Now the bystanders are catching on, and can tell by his accent that he is a Galilean country boy. At this he curses and swears he doesn't even know the guy – just as the cock crows again. Incidentally,

Luke's version turns ups the drama by putting Peter in the very same hall as the trial, and then having Jesus turning and looking at Peter at this very moment (22:55, 61). But in Mark's version, he is outside by the gateway, and suddenly remembers Jesus' prediction: 'Before the cock crows twice, you will deny me three times,' and breaks down in tears. Just as per Mark's theological (and story-telling) needs, even Jesus' no. 1 disciple has failed and abandoned him. He is completely alone.

Before Pilate
After such an already improbably-grueling night, a second trial awaits: "As soon as it was morning, the chief priests held a consultation with the elders and scribes and the whole council." (15:1) This is yet another unrealistic feature of the story that Christian apologists have long tried to explain away. One evangelical guess-in-fact's-clothing purported that the Sanhedrin would always, and had to, pronounce sentence at dawn. Cohn rejects such hollow pronouncements as nothing more than "another of those unfounded and rather absurd theories invented for the purpose of proving the historicity of some otherwise inexplicable Gospel report."[16]

The verse continues: "They bound Jesus, led him away, and handed him over to Pilate" (15:1). But why on earth did the Jews need to pile on yet *another* trial? If this story was occurring in real life, and Jesus really had committed blasphemy, they would have simply marched him out and dispatched him by stoning, as per Jewish law. But that won't suit Mark's theological needs. He wants his savior to die shedding his blood, raised up on a cross. So he takes still more poetic license, and introduces a new character.

Things don't go any better for Jesus or historical accuracy when Mark has the proceedings handed off to the local Roman governor, Pilate (15:1-15). All four gospels follow Mark in presenting a curious portrayal of Pontius Pilate; a sensitive and indecisive man, so amazed by this mysterious Jewish preacher and so fretful about what to do with him that he defers to the

Jesus: Mything in Action

crowds outside his palace to determine the man's fate. If such a concerned, gentle spirit seems like an unrealistic choice for an imperial provincial governor of a restless occupied foreign country... you're absolutely correct.

As we know from several different contemporary historical accounts, the real Pilate was the absolute opposite of the gospels' fictional Pilate in virtually every way imaginable: an arrogant, offensive, cruel despot who cared nothing for the native population and certainly never lost sleep worrying whether or not to execute anyone; in fact, his reputation for ruthlessness and savagery terrified political observers.

Philo of Alexandria said he was "at all times a man of most ferocious passions" who feared being impeached "in respect of his corruption, and his acts of insolence, and his rapine, and his habit of insulting people, and his cruelty, and his continual murders of people untried and uncondemned, and his never ending, and gratuitous, and most grievous inhumanity."[17] He was responsible for repeatedly carrying out horrific massacres on crowds of innocent Jews and Samaritans, before he finally was indeed removed by Rome for killing too many.

Later, Matthew would find Mark's depiction of Pilate unrealistic; or was responding to critics who did. He adds a subplot (Matt. 27:19) to explain why Pilate was uncharacteristically merciful in Jesus' case, using his favorite plot device: divine messages delivered via dreams. Pilate's wife suffers a nightmare and sends a warning to her husband to "have nothing to do with that innocent man." Apparently Matthew found angelic dream messengers more believable than Mark's picture of Pilate. We have to ignore all these difficulties (see "Pilate Light" in Ch. 6 of *Nailed* for details of still more historical blunders about Pilate and the trial) to get through Mark's fictitious account – and more are to come...

Mark doesn't say how he knows the details of Pilate's interrogation; of course, the real answer is because he invented them. When Pilate asks, "Are you the King of the Jews?" Jesus cryptically replies, "You say so." At this the chief priests chime in and lob a variety of accusations at him. Pilate is baffled by Jesus' silence. "Have you no answer? See how many charges they bring against you." But Jesus says no more, amazing the governor (15:2-5). And then Mark's historical accuracy, already stretched painfully thin, snaps and flies out the window completely.

Pardon?
Mark tells us (15:6) that Pilate had a custom for his beloved subjects: "at the festival he used to release a prisoner for them, anyone for whom they asked." On cue, a crowd appears outside his palace, demanding he release his customary prisoner. Accommodating as always, Pilate quickly obliges. Recognizing that the chief priests are jealous of Jesus, he asks if the crowd wants him to release this "King of the Jews." Although he is the current ruler of occupied Judea, admirably, Pilate harbors no ill will towards the man Jerusalem has just hailed as their new king and messiah just a few chapters earlier (11:8-10).

But the public has a short memory. The chief priests (who just 12 hours before were so afraid of the wrath of Jesus' adoring multitudes that they desperately resort to an illegal secret night trial to prevent a city-wide uproar) spring into action. They stir up the crowd to demand the release, *not* of their beloved new messiah Jesus, but instead, Barabbas, a notorious murderer and anti-Roman rebel. Not an obvious choice.

Pilate is surprised at this unexpected turn of events. He asks, "Then what do you wish me to do with the man you call the King of the Jews?" The crowd shouts back, "Release him too, of course! We just unanimously hailed him as our blessed and long-awaited king foretold to us by the prophets! Hosanna in the highest!" Or, at least… that's what an impartial observer could be forgiven for expecting them to say, considering how effusively the entire city welcomed their messiah just the other day. Instead, the fickle multitudes aren't just over Jesus – now they want him to die horribly. So they roar, "Crucify him!"

Poor Pilate is just as baffled as we are, asking them, "Why, what evil has he done?" They shout back even louder for Jesus' blood; howling *"Crucify him!"* Not wanting to hurt their feelings, Pilate immediately releases notorious Roman-hating terrorist Barabbas for them, and reluctantly sends Jesus off to be flogged and crucified.

Again, the careful reader might find all this a tad unrealistic. Consider: the chief priests were hated Roman toadies, despised by the Jerusalem multitudes, who loved Jesus. But as I noted in *Nailed*, why were the hated priests ever afraid of a popular uprising? They could not only talk the crowd into choosing a murderer to be freed over their beloved miracle-working savior; *they could whip them up into a frenzied mob howling for Jesus' blood.* All it took was some spirited cheerleading.

More Problems

In real life, the Pharisees hated both the Romans and their Sadducee puppets – and would have approved heartily of a figure like Jesus, who taught much of the same things that they did. Although Matt. 7:29 tells us Jesus did not teach "like the scribes and Pharisees," he certainly does in the gospels. In *Deconstructing Jesus* (pp. 253-57), Robert Price lists numerous examples of Jesus giving teachings that actually come from the Pharisees themselves.

Another problem: why can't the Gospels agree on the rationale for his execution?

In Mark, Jesus heals a man with a withered hand early in his career and the Pharisees immediately (and inexplicably) begin plotting how they might destroy him (3:6). Robert Price has pointed out how odd this is, since Jesus doesn't get arrested until the end of the story, and when he does, the Pharisees have nothing to do with it (11:18). For Matthew, Jesus' fate is sealed in a secret meeting of the chief priests, scribes and elders two days before Passover, which the Evangelist somehow knows all the details of (26:2). Apparently-omniscient Matthew also knows the details of other secret meetings of Jesus' enemies (28:11-15), much like his insider knowledge of what angels tell Joseph in his dreams (1:20, 2:13, 2:19, 2:22).

In Luke, the last straw for the Jewish authorities is Jesus driving the moneychangers from the Temple (19:47-48). But for John, that Temple-cleansing incident occurred three years earlier, when Jesus kicked off his career. Instead, when John's Jesus infuriates the wicked Jews (11:43-53), it has nothing to do with the incident with the moneychangers or the Temple at all: it is because he raised Lazarus from the dead (11:43-53); an event that doesn't even occur in the other Gospels. And how could it? Remember, despite being the pivotal character in John's story, Lazarus doesn't even *appear* in the other gospels.[18]

Still another problem: Even if the crowd somehow preferred Barabbas to Jesus, why would Pilate ever feel compelled to offer to release a murderer and rebel in the first place? Perhaps it's plausible to imagine that the crowd was really filled with Roman-hating zealots who wanted Barabbas free; but if so, why didn't Pilate round them all up and massacre them there and then? (it wouldn't have been the first time[19])

The Biggest Problem
But unlike the apologists who struggle to make historical sense of Mark's scenario, we really don't need to waste much speculation trying to solve these difficulties – since there's a bigger problem with the entire set-up. Perhaps the single biggest historical difficulty with the customary releasing of a prisoner at Passover (Mark 15:6) ... is that we have no corroborating evidence whatsoever that this "custom" ever existed. Neither the Jews, the Romans nor Pilate himself ever had a custom of freeing prisoners on Passover (or any other day), not that an occupational governor would ever have

offered to release a convicted murderer and anti-Roman insurrectionist even if that *were* the case. Christians have spent years scouring Roman and Jewish records in search of supporting evidence to justify the historical veracity of this so-called *Privilegium Paschale*, to no avail (see *Nailed*, pp. 97-99). So where did Mark ever get the idea?

The answer to *that* question solves all the historical problems with this incident at once. It's no coincidence that the perfect and innocent Jesus is paired up with a criminal named Barabbas who is accused of murder and sedition, and that Barabbas is released unharmed. Even Barabbas' name is a clue to what Mark is doing here: *Bar-Abbas* means "Son of the Father" – in fact, in some early Syriac Christian manuscripts, his name is *Jesus* Barabbas.[20]

There was no tradition of releasing a prisoner, but there was a venerable Hebrew tradition Mark was drawing on: the Yom Kippur scapegoat. On the Day of Atonement, the high priest in the Temple took two goats. One of the goats, perfect and flawless, would be killed as a blood sacrifice to the Lord. The other would be released into the wilderness unharmed to carry away the sins of Israel, like murder and sedition, as a scapegoat (Leviticus 16: 5-10,15-22).

Likewise, Mark gives us two "sons of the father." Barabbas, the son guilty of murder and sedition, is nonetheless released unharmed into the wilderness, while the perfect and flawless son Jesus (whose name, after all, means "Yahweh Saves") is sacrificed so that his blood will atone for the sins of Israel. As history, Mark's Barabbas episode is ridiculous on multiple levels. As literary symbolism for the Jewish Day of Atonement ceremony, every detail comes together in a brilliant allegory.

Next (15:15-20), the soldiers then led Jesus into the courtyard and called together the whole cohort. They dressed him in a purple cloak, and twisted some thorns into a mock crown for his head. Then they knelt down in homage to him, saluting him with "Hail, King of the Jews!" before beating his head with a reed and spitting upon him. After mocking him, they stripped off the purple cloak and put his own clothes back on him

Then they led him out to crucify him.

***

For further reading:

Dr. Akiva G. Belk (Dean of Jewish Studies of the B'nai Noach Torah Institute in Cedar Hill, MO) gives a spirited argument for just how badly the gospels misunderstand and misrepresent what would have actually happened during Passover in his article "Chronology of Events, 1 Nisan through 16 Nisan: Many Proofs Why The New Testament is Unreliable," available online at:
http://www.jewishpath.org/hdshabbospesachwhyntisunre.html

---

[1] MacDonald, *The Homeric Epics and the Gospel of Mark*, p. 129
[2] MacDonald thinks that Paul objected to the metaphor (ibid.); but this doesn't seem the case in the verses where we see Paul employing it. In either case, it's clear the early Christians were quite familiar with the garment = body comparison.
[3] See HE&GoM, p. 234 n22 for still more examples.
[4] Wells, HEJ, p. 14
[5] Cohn, p. 98
[6] Ibid.
[7] Cohn, p. 359, n16
[8] Cohn, p. 112
[9] Carrier, *On the Historicity of Jesus*, p. 425 n73
[10] Ibid., p. 425 n76
[11] Helms, GF, p. 118
[12] Cohn, p. 130-31

[13] Cohn, p. 129
[14] Ibid.
[15] Maccoby, p. 23
[16] Cohn p. 149
[17] Philo of Alexandria, *Embassy to Gaius* 302-303
[18] Unless, of course, you count the fictional beggar Lazarus in a parable told by Luke's Jesus (16:19-31).
[19] See *Nailed,* pp. 94-97 for the grim details
[20] See Nailed, p. 219 n19

Chapter Ten: Crucify Him!

"What is truth? Is truth unchanging law? We both have truths. Are mine the same as yours?"

– *Jesus Christ Superstar*

O*r is* that how it happened? Mark tells us the soldiers then led Jesus into the courtyard of the *Praetorium*, the governor's headquarters, and called together the entire cohort – five hundred men. Mark probably intended for us to picture all the troops arrayed on either side at attention, mustered as they would be for a visiting dignitary.

There they dressed him in a purple cloak, the color of emperors and gods. Mark adds that they twisted some thorns into a mock crown for his head. Then they knelt down in homage to him, saluting him with "Hail, King of the Jews!" before beating his head with a reed and spitting upon him. Just as earlier, this same abuse is paralleled almost verbatim in Isaiah 50:6 and in Micah 5:1 ("with a rod they strike the ruler of Israel upon the cheek") After mocking him, they stripped off the purple cloak and put his own clothes back on him (15:15-20), and led him out to be crucified.

Or maybe not just yet... Luke complicates matters further by adding – unbelievably – yet *another* trial, one that none of the other Gospel writers know anything about. This trial is before the Jewish client-king, the Tetrarch Herod Antipas. Luke inserts it awkwardly into the middle of Pilate's trial (Luke 23:6-12). And pointlessly too, since Herod just returns Jesus to Pilate so that the story can continue - without skipping a beat! Interestingly though, in Luke's version (23:11), it is *Herod's* soldiers who dress Jesus in a king's robe and mock him, not the Roman soldiers, as in the other Gospels (Mark 15:16-20, Matt. 27:27-31, John19:2-5).

On a total side note, it's interesting to see what liberties Mel Gibson took when he gave us his cinematic torture-porn gospel, *The Passion of The Christ* (2004). He follows Luke's version and includes Jesus being taken before Herod Antipas – except where Luke has King Herod and his soldiers, Mel the evangelist presents a very gay, debauched Herod, in wig and mascara, with a bevy of boy-toys. One had to wonder why Gibson so often feels the need to invent and insert a gratuitous gay-bashing subtext where there is none in the original material – just as he did in *Braveheart* (1995), where the battle-axe-wielding English warrior-prince Edward II is portrayed instead as a soft fey Nancy boy, whose foppish boyfriend is tossed out a window to his death for comic effect.

Double Indemnity
Why would Luke clutter up his story with such a clunky addition, forcing Jesus to improbably bounce from Pilate, to Herod, then back to Pilate again? And why the switch from the Roman soldiers mocking Jesus to Herod's soldiers? Alfred Loisy, a Roman Catholic priest and theologian came up with an answer when he surmised that Luke (or a later editor) must have had access to a version of the Passion story in which Herod had Jesus killed, not Pilate.[1] And indeed, we do have exactly such a text. In the *Gospel of Peter,* a popular early Christian gospel later rejected by the Church, Pilate has a supporting role, but it is Herod who orders Jesus crucified.

Robert Price spots the problem Luke missed. To use both stories, Luke had to change Herod's verdict from guilty to innocent (otherwise Herod would be responsible for his crucifixion, just as in the *Gospel of Peter*). But Herod found Jesus innocent – so why send him back to Pilate? And if Pilate had already found Jesus innocent too (Luke 23:14-16), why did he hand Jesus off to Herod in the first place? And once Herod acquitted Jesus, why didn't Pilate just let him go there and then? Luke uses Mark's ludicrous plot device and has the bloodthirsty crowd push hapless Pilate around, demanding Jesus be crucified. But nothing in this entire scenario makes any sense; as Price aptly puts it, "Luke has too many cooks in the kitchen, and the stew is spoiled."[2]

The Mad King and the Mad Prophet

Intriguingly, this part of Mark's story shares interesting parallels with two other first century figures. Philo of Alexandria's popular historical work *Flaccus*[3], written decades before the gospels, describes the protests in the year 38 when Caligula made Herod the Great's grandson, Herod Agrippa I, his newly-minted client king. As the Emperor's new Jewish prince passed through Alexandria on his way home to Palestine, the unimpressed populace showed what they thought of him by staging an improv mock coronation in his honor - starring the local idiot as a mock King of the Jews. The unlucky vagrant was a madman named Carabas[4], well-known for sleeping naked in the streets, constantly abused by the elements and the cruelty of neighborhood children. Taken up to the public gymnasium and seated in view of all, the poor creature was crowned with a flattened out papyrus-leaf, dressed in a doormat for a robe and given a papyrus reed from out of the gutter for his royal scepter. With his majesty in place, street youths grabbed sticks and stood at attention by his side like royal bodyguards. Others acted like courtiers and came up to salute the gibbering lunatic, plead their cases and consult on affairs of state with their unfortunate new king. The amused multitude watching this little pageant broke out into spontaneous shouts of acclaim for the new King of the Jews.

There are even more parallels with another first-century Jesus: Jesus Ben-Ananias, a mad prophet active in Jerusalem during the 60s. Josephus gives his story in *The Jewish War*, a book written around the same time as Mark's gospel. Josephus' account could even be a direct inspiration for Mark's passion story. But unless the story is a complete fabrication of Josephus, there's no reason to think Mark couldn't have already heard about the famous doomsayer and his eerie death around the year 70, during the siege of Jerusalem:

"An incident more alarming still had occurred four years before the war at a time of exceptional peace and prosperity for the City. One Jesus son of Ananias, a very ordinary yokel, came to the feast at which every Jew is expected to set up a tabernacle for God. As he stood in the Temple he suddenly began to shout:
'A voice from the east,
A voice from the west,
A voice from the four winds,
A voice against Jerusalem and the Sanctuary,
A voice against the bridegrooms and brides,
A voice against the whole people.
Day and night he uttered this cry as he went through all the streets.

Some of the more prominent citizens, very annoyed at these ominous words, laid hold of the fellow and beat him savagely. Without saying a word in his own defense or for the private information of his persecutors, he persisted in shouting the same warning as before. The Jewish authorities, rightly concluding that some supernatural force was responsible for the man's behavior, took him before the Roman procurator. There, though scourged till his flesh hung in ribbons, he neither begged for mercy nor shed a tear, but lowering his voice to the most mournful of tones answered every blow with 'Woe to Jerusalem!' When Albinus – for that was the procurator's name – demanded to know who he was, where he came from and why he uttered such cries, he made no reply whatever to the questions but endlessly repeated his lament over the City, till Albinus decided he was a madman and released him.

All the time till the war broke out he never approached another citizen or was seen in conversation, but daily as if he had learnt a prayer by heart he recited his lament: 'Woe to Jerusalem!' Those who daily cursed him he never cursed; those who gave him food he never thanked: his only response to anyone was that dismal foreboding. His voice was heard most of all at the feasts. For seven years and five months he went on ceaselessly, his voice as strong as ever and his vigor unabated, till during the siege after seeing the fulfillment of his foreboding he was silenced. He was going round on the wall uttering his piercing cry: 'Woe again to the City, the people, and the Sanctuary!' and as he added a last word: 'Woe to me also!' a stone shot from an engine struck him, killing him instantly. Thus he uttered those same forebodings to the very end."

(Flavius Josephus, *The Jewish War* VI: 302)[5]

As Theodore Weeden and numerous other scholars[6] have recognized, there are far too many significant parallels between the careers and deaths of Jesus of Nazareth and Jesus of Jerusalem to be a coincidence – even the sequence of events in Mark follows that of the story in Josephus. See for yourself:

Parallels between Jesus of Nazareth and Jesus ben Ananias

Jesus of Nazareth in the *Gospel of Mark*	**Jesus ben Ananias In Josephus' *The Jewish War***
The main figure of the story is named Jesus.	The main figure of the story is named Jesus.
Jesus comes to Jerusalem during the time of a holy festival (Passover) (14:2).	Jesus comes to Jerusalem during the time of a holy festival (the Feast of Tabernacles). (J.W. VI 301).
Jesus enters the Temple and	Jesus enters the Temple and

suddenly begins to rant against practices in the Temple, loudly quoting Jeremiah 7:11 (11:15-17).	suddenly begins to rant against the Temple and the people of Jerusalem, loudly quoting Jeremiah 7:34 (J.W. VI 301).
Jesus teaches daily in the Temple (14:49).	Jesus preaches daily in the Temple (J.W. VI 306).
Jesus declares woe unto the people of Jerusalem/Judea (13:17).	Jesus declares woe unto the people of Jerusalem/Judea (J.W. VI 304, 306, 309).
Jesus predicts the Temple will be doomed (13:2).	Jesus predicts the Temple will be doomed (J.W. VI 300, 309).
Jesus is arrested by the Jerusalem leaders (14:43).	Jesus is arrested by the Jerusalem leaders (J.W. VI 302).
Jesus is accused of speaking against the Temple (14:58).	Jesus is accused of speaking against the Temple (J.W. VI 302).
Jesus made no defense for himself in face of these charges of speaking against the Temple (14:60).	Jesus made no defense for himself in face of these charges of speaking against the Temple (J.W. VI 302).
Jesus is beaten by the Jews (14:65).	Jesus is beaten by the Jews (J.W. VI 302).
Afterwards the Jerusalem authorities delivered Jesus to the Roman procurator, Pilate	Afterwards the Jerusalem authorities delivered Jesus to the Roman procurator,

Jesus: Mything in Action

(15:1).	Albinus (J.W. VI 302).
Jesus is interrogated by the procurator Pilate (15:2-4).	Jesus is interrogated by the procurator Albinus (J.W. VI 305).
During interrogation the Roman procurator asks Jesus to disclose his identity (15:2).	During interrogation the Roman procurator asks Jesus to disclose his identity (J.W. VI 305).
Jesus says nothing to the procurator in his own defense (15:3-5).	Jesus says nothing to the procurator in his own defense (J.W. VI 305).
Jesus is scourged by the Romans (15:15).	Jesus is scourged by the Romans (J.W. VI 304).
The procurator decides he should release Jesus (but doesn't) (15:6-15).	The procurator decides he should release Jesus (and does) (J.W. VI305).
Jesus is finally killed by the Romans (executed) (15:15).	Jesus is finally killed by the Romans (hit by catapult) (J.W. VI 308-9).
Jesus utters a woeful lament for himself just before his death (15:34).	Jesus utters a woeful lament for himself just before his death (J.W. VI 309).
Jesus dies with a loud cry (15:37).	Jesus dies with a loud cry (J.W. VI 309).

Richard Carrier concludes: "Given that Mark is essentially a Christian response to the Jewish War and the destruction of the Jewish temple, it is more than a little significant that he chose *this* Jesus to model his own Jesus after. This also tells us, yet again, how much Mark is making everything up."[7]

A Second Simon
As they march him off to his death, Mark tells us "They compelled a passer-by, who was coming in from the country, to carry his cross; it was Simon of Cyrene, the father of Alexander and Rufus" (15:21). At first glance this would appear to be Mark implying there were people still alive who could corroborate his story – though that would also seem to be another indication that his story was written a generation or more after the fact. But things don't appear to be that simple.

First of all, this brief sentence makes no sense, historically. Cohn points out that legally speaking, it was flatly forbidden to compel an innocent passer-by to bear a condemned convict's cross for him; that would be transferring part of the sentence to be served to a wholly blameless third party.[8] For this reason alone, many scholars dismiss the entire addition of Simon of Cyrene as a fictional touch; or as French archeologist Salomon Reinach put it, as "unhistoric, something that never happened and could not happen."[9]

Then there is the curious detail Mark provides: naming the oddly irrelevant sons of Simon the Cyrenaean. Carrier asks:

> "This is most bizarre, since Mark states no reason at all for doing so. Why do we need to know this information? Why does Mark think it's important? And why is this the only instance in his whole Gospel where Mark names the sons of *anyone* Jesus encounters? (One wonders why none of his disciples had sons worth mentioning) Mark does not even say these sons became Christians, and one would expect him to if that was the point; or they were his sources for the account (though again, one would expect

him to say so). So as history, this detail is just inexplicably weird."[10]

Once again, a feature of Mark's gospel makes no sense historically. And once again, by contrast, the whole troublesome passage in question can be easily explained theologically, as symbolic allegory.

A favorite motif of Mark is the reversal of expectations. As Carrier notes, it doesn't just guide his narrative construction; it embodies his gospel message, which is all about reversing expectations, such as "The least shall be first."[11] Carrier and many other scholars have demonstrated plentiful examples of the evangelist pulling the rug out from under his readers like this.[12]

Earlier, Mark goes out of his way to have Jesus rebuke Simon Peter, saying, "If any man would come after me, let him deny himself, and take up his cross and follow me." (Mark 8:33-34) In real life, this would be a very odd spoiler for Jesus to spill so early in his career; since at that time no one has any idea that Jesus will end up dying at the end of the book. But (yet) again, it makes perfect sense if the storyteller is engaged in the time-honored literary technique of foreshadowing. It is also a perfect example of Mark's patented reversals to have Simon Peter, the most loyal disciple, not only *not* deny himself, but deny Jesus three times – and to have another Simon: a foreigner and a perfect stranger, take up Jesus' cross instead. Mark even uses the same words in both cases: Simon of Cyrene is pressed in service "to carry his cross" (*arē ton stauron autou*); just as Simon Peter is told "to take up his cross" (*aratō ton stauron autou*).[13]

Cyrenaean & Sons

Questions remain. Why is Simon specifically a Cyrenaean? And what is the significance of his sons, Alexander and Rufus?

Cyrene was an ancient Greco-Roman port city on the Mediterranean, near present-day Shahhat, Libya. Carrier notes that coming from beyond Egypt (allegorically, the realm of slavery and death) held symbolic overtones of its own. But he suggests an even stronger metaphor. According to the Greek geographer Strabo,[14] the most famous Cyrenaeans were a sect of hedonistic atheist philosophers called the Cyrenaics. Precursors to the Epicureans, they rejected any hint of spirituality and declared that pleasure was the only intrinsic good. Though the sect itself appears to have been long gone by the first century, they and their philosophy remained legendary, and a perfect choice to symbolize the exact opposite of Mark's gospel: a complete rejection of the spiritual in favor of materialistic lusts and worldly wisdom.

What's more, as Mark and his readers would have been well aware, the Cyrenaean Jews had just staged a violent rebellion, which Rome crushed.[15] Which made Cyrene a perfect allegory for two things Mark opposed: worldly philosophy *and* the doomed path of war. By having his alternate Simon take up the cross, Mark seems to be implying that the two failed materialistic values he represented were then metaphorically crucified with Jesus.[16]

Likewise, Carrier finds the names of the "sons" of Simon/Cyrene corroborate this analysis, and submits that "Alexander" and "Rufus" are meant to refer to the most famous men in history to hold those names: Alexander the Great and Musonius Rufus. Alexander was of course the greatest conqueror of the ancient world and the quintessential military messiah. Musonius Rufus, a contemporary of Mark, is less known to us, but he was the ancient world's most famous pacifist, and a philosopher second only to Socrates.

Carrier presents a number of further insights in support of this idea;[17] but the basic idea behind Mark's analogy is not difficult to imagine: As Mark would see it, the "Cyrenaean" (that is, Cyrenaic) worldview with its attachment to materialism, fathered two worldly ways: "Alexander's" (war, military might) and "Rufus's" (reason, philosophy). But in Mark's gospel, war and relying on human reason always lead to ruin; only faith in God brings salvation. Carrier grants there is obviously no way to prove this was Mark's purpose to name Simon and his sons (seeing as he expected only his most sophisticated readers to make the connection anyway).

And there are other intriguing possibilities. Robert Price wonders if Mark's Simon might be a coded reference to the Anti-Peter Simon Magus,[18] an evil sorcerer who appears in Acts (8:9-24) and the apocryphal *Acts of Peter*. In the *Acts of Peter*, no. 1 disciple Simon Peter actually battles his evil twin. Simon Magus shows his might by magically flying up into the air, but the apostle downs him with the power of prayer. The arch-heretic promptly crashes to the ground and is swiftly stoned to death.

On the mythic front, Frank Zindler notes[19] there appears to have been a Samaritan god named Simon who, like Mithra, was given the nickname of Peter ("Rock"). He could walk on water and held the keys to the gates of heaven. In this regard, he was the equivalent of the Roman god Janus, whose cult was headquartered a short distance from the present-day Vatican (the site of an equivalent "Peter cult")."

Whatever Simon meant to Mark, later Christians had their own ideas. For the author of the Gospel of John, no other characters were going to help *his* triumphant Jesus bear his cross, so he changed the script (see *Nailed*, pp. 80-84). John edits out Simon of Cyrene entirely and has Jesus carry his cross by himself (19:17). Others took the opposite route and made Simon the central figure of the whole crucifixion. Heretics like the early second-century Alexandrian Gnostic Basilides taught that it was Simon, not Jesus, who wound up crucified on the cross.[20]

If all these sound unduly speculative, we should keep in mind there is every bit as much evidence for any one of these theories as for the notion that the names derive from authentic historical tradition. Mark gives no indication that any of these reasons is why these names are here; in fact, he gives no indication why they are here at all, any more than he did with any of the other allegorical features that pervade his entire Gospel.

The Crucifixion
"Then they brought Jesus to the place called Golgotha, which means the place of a skull. And they offered him wine mixed with myrrh; but he did not take it. And they crucified him, and divided his clothes among them, casting lots to decide what each should take. It was nine o'clock in the morning when they crucified him." (Mark 15:22-25)

The Place of a Skull
Then they brought Jesus to the place called Golgotha, which means the place of a skull. (15:22)

The Greek word *Golgothá* (or *Calvaria* in Latin, which gives us "Calvary") is indeed a transcription of the Aramaic word for "skull" (*Gûlgaltâ*). But there is little agreement on how it got that name – or where this place is, exactly. It's notable how many sites associated with Jesus share that problem... The early Church Father Origen thought it was so named because Adam's skull was buried beneath the cross – and why wouldn't it be? Jerome offered the Frank Frazettaesque suggestion that it was because the area was littered with the skulls of executed prisoners.[21] Some wondered if the name was actually *Gol Goatha*, meaning *mount of execution*, (or if it was even the same *Goatha* mentioned in Jeremiah 31:39), though few think so.

According to Eusebius' *Onomasticon*,[22] in his day, Golgotha was believed to be north of "Mount Zion." But where is that? Walter Zanger's "The Elusive Mount Zion,"[23] explains some of the problems in locating that site with any precision. Some used it in reference to the Temple Mount itself, though Josephus identified it as the Western Hill, which would put it south of the two main sites currently in competition to be Golgotha.

According to Melito (*Paschal Homily* 71), in 160 CE the local Christian community thought Golgotha was actually deep within the city of Jerusalem, not outside the walls. Nonetheless, in 325 Constantine's mother, the Empress Helena (apparently accompanied by Eusebius), "discovered" the True Site of Cavalry™ – right on top of a sacred shrine to Aphrodite[24] (it's also truly remarkable how often sacred sites do double duty for rival religions). Conveniently enough, just a few yards away, she also found the True Tomb of Jesus™ – as well as the True Cross™ in its entirety, and those of the two thieves crucified with him, too. (Incidentally, by the end of the Middle Ages, so many churches claimed to have a fragment of the True Cross that John Calvin quipped if you gathered them all, there would be enough lumber to fill a ship's hold.[25]) The Empress' fortuitous discoveries also launched the booming Christian pilgrimage industry, which immediately took off and is still a winning income generator today.

But oddly enough, despite all that, there was (and is) *still* dispute over the location of Jesus' crucifixion. Since the mid 19th century, the Garden Tomb area, a limestone outcropping just north of the Old City, has been identified as the Real True Site of Cavalry™ as well as the Real True Tomb of Jesus.™ Though it should be noted that according to missionary Rodger Dusatko, who claims "Jesus spoke to me in a special way,"[26] the Actual Real True Site of Cavalry™ is clear on the other side of Jerusalem from the other proposed sites, on a cranium-shaped hill just outside the eastern wall, northeast of the Temple Mount.

Myrrhed Wine
And they offered him wine mixed with myrrh; but he did not take it. (15:23)

In the ancient world, wine mixed with grains of myrrh resin was a painkiller. According to a Rabbinic gloss on Proverbs 31:6 ("Give strong drink to him that is perishing, and wine to those whose soul is in bitterness") it was Jewish custom to give myrrhed wine to victims of crucifixion to ease their suffering.²⁷ Prov. 31:6 also appears to be Mark's inspiration for this verse, but it wouldn't serve his literary or his theological aims to give his Jesus an easy way out of the suffering to come. So he has already had Jesus at the Last Supper tell his disciples, "Truly I tell you, I will never again drink of the fruit of the vine until that day when I drink it new in the kingdom of God" (14:25).²⁸

Randal Helms shows that Matthew makes changes to Mark's story, based on a different psalm: "They gave (*edōkan*) me also gall (*cholēn*) for my food, and made me drink vinegar (*oxos*)." (Ps. 69:21) In Matthew's hands, that psalm now becomes a prophecy, and an act of mercy becomes a cruel joke instead: "They gave (*edōkan*) him wine to drink, mixed with gall (*cholēs*); but when he tasted it, he refused to drink" (Matt. 27:34).²⁹

Remarkably (though not likely coincidentally), Luke picks precisely the same source psalm (69:21) as Matthew, but he focuses on the other half of the verse: "They ... made me drink vinegar (*oxos*)." As his gospel has it: "The soldiers joined in the mockery and came forward offering him their sour wine (*oxos*)" (Luke 23:36). Like Matthew, Luke drops Mark's line about myrrhed wine altogether.³⁰ For John's part, he blends in yet another scripture, Psalm 51:7 ("Sprinkle me with hyssop") by having them offer Jesus a sponge of sour wine on a stalk of hyssop (19:28-29) . There is further symbolism for John here) as we'll soon see...

Casting Lots, Divided Clothes... and Bulls of Bashan?
And they crucified him, and divided his clothes among them, casting lots to decide what each should take. (15:24)

Many gospel readers take incidental details like these to be indications that the story is true:

"And they crucified him, and divided (*diamerizontaí*) his clothes (*himatia*) among them, casting lots (*ballontes klēron*) to decide what each should take."

But verses like these are nothing of the kind. In fact, this line is completely
structured from the 22nd Psalm:
"They parted my garments (*Diemerisanto ta himatia mou*) among themselves, and cast lots (*ebalon klēron*) for my raiment." (Ps. 22:18)[31]

And if there was any doubt that this was taken from Psalm 22, John removes it by explicitly telling us so (John 19:23-24). He also goes out of his way to bring up an oddly specific detail about Jesus' seamless tunic ("They also took his tunic; now the tunic was seamless, woven in one piece from the top.") in order to echo Leviticus 16:4 and Exodus 28:32, which state that when the high priest enters the Holy of Holies, the inner sanctuary of the temple, he shall put on the consecrated linen tunic, which must be seamless.[32]

Christians love to answer critics of the more horrible bible verses by protesting, "You're taking that out of context!" If you ever get hit by this particular cloud of apologetic squid ink, be sure to ask them, "Well, what *is* the context?" I have never yet found a believer who can tell me the correct context for anything in the bible – they only know that nonbelievers are wrong about it...

So let's look at the context here. Just to be clear, Psalm 22 is *not* a prophecy of the coming messiah, as even a casual reading of the song shows. It is ostensibly a psalm by David, and perhaps it really is, but whoever the true author is, this song is the lament of a man who feels surrounded by enemies and abandoned by God. Certainly that sounds appropriately Jesus-like, but does any of the rest of the song? Such as when he complains: "Many bulls encircle me, strong bulls of Bashan surround me..." (22:12) Hear what else the psalmist has to say:

"Deliver my soul from the sword, my life from the power of the dog! Save me from the mouth of the lion! From the horns of the wild oxen you have rescued me. I will tell of your name to my brothers and sisters; in the midst of the congregation I will praise you... From you comes my praise in the great congregation; my vows I will pay before those who fear him." (22:20-22, 25)

Following his rescue from perils like the strong bulls of Bashan, the sword, the power of the dog, the mouth of the lion and the horns of the wild oxen, the singer makes good on his vow to go to the Temple to sing praises to the Lord before his brothers and sisters in the congregation for his deliverance, which constitutes a third of the song (verses 22-31). But this happy ending didn't stop cherry-picking Christian writers like Mark from repeatedly quote-mining the 22nd Psalm for proof texts of their suffering messiah.

Christ, I'm Late
And it was the third hour, and they crucified him. (15:25)

Even if we were to ignore all the allegorical elements and literary clues, another serious credibility problem with the crucifixion account is simple logistics. Just from the timeline alone, the events are impossible; many scholars have noted that if this game of musical chairs really had occurred, Jesus would have been so busy being shuffled from interrogation to interrogation that he could barely have had time to get crucified! The logistical crunch is not as apparent in Mark's original story. He keeps the story relatively simple and even divides up the day into handy (if suspiciously convenient) 3-hour increments:

6:00 a.m. Dawn
    Jesus is taken to Pilate (Mark 15:1)
9:00 a.m. ("the third hour")

> Jesus is crucified (15:25)
> 12:00 p.m. ("from the sixth to the ninth hour")
> > Supernatural darkness (15:33)
> 3:00 p.m. ("the ninth hour")
> > Jesus cries out and dies (15:34-37)
> 6 p.m. Dusk ("when darkness had come")
> > Joseph asks for his body (15:42)

However, by the time we get to Matthew and Luke, things have grown just a smidge more complicated. Mark says events began at 6:00 a.m. and by "the third hour" (i.e. nine a.m.) Jesus was crucified. If just the three Synoptic Gospel accounts were true, that meant Jesus had just three hours in the morning to carry out all these errands of this busy schedule:

> 6:00 a.m.
> > The elders, chief priests and scribes begin to gather. Jesus is then:
> > > Taken to the Sanhedrin council (Luke 22:66)
> > > Interrogated by the council (22:66-71)
> > > Taken to Pilate (23:1)
> > > Accused by the Jews and questioned by Pilate (23:2-6)
> > > Taken to Herod (23:7) *
> > > Questioned by Herod (23:9) *
> > > Dressed in a robe and mocked by Herod's Soldiers (23:11) *
> > > Taken back to Pilate (23:11) *
> > > Pilate calls together "the chief priests, the rulers, and the people." (23:13)
> > > Pilate speaks and offers to release either Jesus or Barabbas (23:14-18)
> > > Pilate tries to convince the crowd to choose Jesus (23: 20-23)
> > > Pilate gives up and condemns Jesus (23:24)

> Jesus was then scourged – but not in Luke (Matt 27:26, Mark 15:15)
>
> Taken to the Praetorium and the Roman garrison is called together (Matt 27:27, Mark 15:16)
>
> Dressed in a robe and mocked (again!) by the Roman Soldiers (Matt. 27:28-30, Mark 15:17-19)
>
> Redressed and led out to be crucified (Matt. 27:31, Mark 15:20)
>
> Marched up to Golgotha; has to be helped by Simon but not according to John (Matt. 27:32, Mark 15:21, Luke 23:26)
>
> Jesus gives a farewell speech to the crowd following him * (Luke 23:28-31)
>
> 9:00 a.m.
>
> Jesus is crucified (Mark 15:25)
>
> * only according to Luke, that is.

This already gives us three different interrogations, two different episodes of identical mockery, a scourging, at least five different foot trips (one while carrying a cross uphill!), and an exchange between the Governor and the city of Jerusalem – all in the three hours between dawn and 9:00 a.m. ("the third hour") on the Day of Passover, the 15th of Nisan on the Jewish calendar, when Jesus is crucified (15:25).

Meanwhile, in a Parallel Universe...

However, this is only taking into account the first three gospels. John disputes all the others by telling us at noon, "about the sixth hour" (19:14), Pilate was still pleading with the crowd to save Jesus! That would seem to give Jesus a little more wiggle room, but in fact just makes the problem worse. Because John doesn't actually have Jesus crucified three hours later than the Synoptics – he has Jesus crucified on the day *before* the other gospels. His Jesus dies (19:30) some time after the sixth hour (19:14); but on the Day of Preparation for the

Passover – the 14th of Nisan on the Jewish calendar, as John explicitly makes clear, repeatedly (19:14, 19:31).

As blatant as this discrepancy is, John actually contradicts the other Gospels far worse than that. As mentioned earlier, none of the events of the Passion – Jesus' triumphant entry, last supper, trial(s), his death – occur within the same timeframe as the other gospels. When Jesus goes after the greedy moneychangers and drives them from the temple, the Synoptic Gospels tell us *this* is what enrages the Jewish leaders and leads to his death within a few days (Mark 11:18, Matt. 21:15, Luke 19:47). But not in John's world. The Temple cleansing incident isn't the end for Jesus in John's gospel - it *launches* his whole career, three years beforehand (2:15-16). In John, raising Lazarus from the dead is what leads to Jesus' death (11:45-53;12:9-11); in the other gospels, Lazarus doesn't even exist.

In fact, a quick comparison of the gospels shows that while all offer very detailed accounts, the details of Jesus' final Passover trip to Jerusalem (or in the case of the Synoptics, his first and last trip) don't synch up – at all:

Mark has Jesus making his way towards Jerusalem (10:32 - 33), followed by adoring throngs of people (10:1). This triumphant victory tour takes him from the Galilee (9:30) to Capernaum (9:33); across the Jordan into Judea (10:1), then to Jericho (10:46), Bethphage and Bethany (11:1), before he will seal his fate by clearing out the temple, which enrages the scribes and the chief priests.

But again, not in John's world; where Jesus has just raised Lazarus from the dead, enraging the chief priests and the Pharisees. "From this day on" they plot to kill him (11:53). He stops traveling openly and immediately goes into hiding, holing up with his disciples in the Judaean wilderness, in a hill town called Ephraim before slipping off to Jerusalem (11:54).

Finally, to tie a bow on an already unsolvable Gordian knot of contradiction, all four Gospels say Jesus died on a Friday (that is, the day before the Sabbath). So by changing the date, John has also changed the *year* of his crucifixion,[33] which now could never be the same as in the Synoptics.

Shepherding the Lamb of God

Why all the confusion? It's no accident. It's because there are two dueling metaphors at play here: John prefers to have his Jesus executed on the afternoon when the Passover lambs were sacrificed in the Temple. This is why John's is the only gospel that calls Jesus "the Lamb of God" (1:29; 1:36). John also says (19:31-36) that the Romans broke the legs of the two robbers crucified alongside Jesus to finish them off, but when they saw that he was already dead, they did not break his legs.

This, we are told, was to fulfill the prophecy, "Not one of his bones shall be broken." However, there is no such prophecy. John said this because the Torah forbids breaking the bones of the Passover lamb (Exodus 12:46, Numbers 9:12) and for John, Jesus *is* the Passover lamb: he will die at the same time (on the afternoon of the Day of Preparation), in the same place (Jerusalem), and at the hands of the same people (the Temple priests) as the Passover lambs do.[34] The reason John has the Romans offer him sour wine on a stalk of hyssop (19:28-29) is because in the Exodus story (Ex.12:22) sprigs of hyssop are what the Israelite slaves used to brush the doorposts and lintels of their homes with the lamb's blood. So touching Jesus with hyssop underscores one more allegorical reference to Passover, and to Jesus as the Passover lamb.[35]

But you can't have your Lamb of God and eat it too. Mark and the other Synoptic Gospels need their Jesus to survive the Day of Preparation on Nisan 14th so they could transform the symbolism of the Jewish Passover meal into the Christian Lord's Supper ritual described in Paul's writings. Though they don't explicitly call him that in the Synoptics, they also saw Jesus as the Lamb of God; but had a slightly different take on the idea. To them, it was impossible for Jesus to be both the Passover Lamb and at the same time eat the Passover meal. So Mark and the Synoptics have Jesus die the following day,

Nisan 15th, after the lambs had been eaten, but at the exact same hour that the lambs were slaughtered the day before, "the ninth hour," or 3 p.m.[36] Randel Helms notes another theological allusion at work here: Mark & Co. have their Jesus suffer for six hours (from 9 a.m. to 3 p.m.) so that on the seventh hour (or the Sabbath hour, if you will) he could rest, just as his Father did after the six days of creation.[37] Carrier finds poetry in Mark's artful arrangement of the twelve hours of the day into four triads of
3-hour time blocks.[38]

Even if we still insist there once was a real Jesus somewhere under all these layers of allegory and symbolism, any idea that any of the evangelists are faithfully recording Jesus' biography as it really happened goes out the window when you see how freely all four felt to invent events and shuffle them around in time and space. This is theology, not history.

***

---

[1] Price, DJ, p 249
[2] Ibid.
[3] Philo, *Flaccus*, Book 6. 36-39
[4] It's tempting to see a parallel between the names Carabas and Barabbas, but personally, I'm not convinced this isn't merely an etymological coincidence. Certainly the Carabas incident *could* have inspired Mark; especially considering some of the intriguing similarities. In any case, the symbolism of the name Barabbas ("Bar-Abbas") fits the Yom Kippur scapegoat ritual so perfectly – and that parallel is indisputable.
[5] Flavius Josephus, *The Jewish War*, G. A. Williamson translation pp.327-8, Penguin Classics, 1959
[6] Theodore Weedon (Weeden, pp. 137-341). For other examples, see also: Richard Carrier, *On the Historicity of*

Jesus, pp. 428-430); Craig Evans "Jesus in Non-Christian Sources," pp. 443-78 (475-77) in Chilton and Evans, *Studying the Historical Jesus: Evaluations of the State of Current Research*; Robert Price, *The Incredible Shrinking Son of Man*, p. 314.

[7] Carrier, op. cit., pp. 430
[8] Cohn, p. 205
[9] Salomon Reinach cited in Cohn, p. 378
[10] Carrier, op. cit., p. 444
[11] Ibid., p. 445
[12] Richard Carrier gives several examples of this in "The Spiritual Body of Christ and the Empty Tomb," (Price & Lowder, pp. 163-65); see also: Jerry Camery-Hoggatt, *Irony in Mark's Gospel: Text and Subtext* (New York: Cambridge University Press, 1992); Paul Danove, *The End of Mark's Story: A Methodological Study* (New York: E.J. Brill, 1993) Adela Collins, "The Empty Tomb in the Gospel According to Mark," in Eleonore Stump and Thomas Flint, ed., *Hermes and Athena: Biblical Exegesis and Philosophical Theology* (Notre Dame, Indiana: University of Notre Dame Press, 1993), pp. 107-40; Deborah Krause, "The One who Comes Unbinding") etc.
[13] see Helms, GF, pp. 121
[14] Strabo, *Geography* 17.3.22; Diogenes Laertius, *Lives of Eminent Philosophers* 2.65-104
[15] Josephus, *Life* 76.424-25
[16] Carrier, op. cit., pp. 446-7
[17] Ibid., pp. 447-451
[18] Price, *The Incredible Shrinking Son of Man*, pp. 319-320
[19] "The Twelve: Further Fictions from the New Testament," by Frank R. Zindler, available online at: http://www.atheists.org/christianity/twelve.html
[20] Price, op. cit., p. 320
[21] Jerome, *Comm. in Matt* 27:33; see "Golgotha" Eerdmans Dict. p. 519

[22] Eusebius, *Onomasticon*, 365
[23] Zanger, Walter, "The Elusive Mount Zion," *Jewish Bible Quarterly*, Vol. 30, No. 3, 2002
[24] Eusebius, *Life of Constantine*, 3:26
[25] Calvin, *Traité Des Reliques*
[26] "Golgotha Rediscovered" http://www.golgotha.eu
[27] Commentary on Mark, *The Cambridge Bible for Schools and Colleges*, Cambridge University Press
[28] Helms, GF, p. 123
[29] Ibid.
[30] Ibid.
[31] Helms, GF, p. 125
[32] Ibid.
[33] See "When did Jesus Die?" in *Nailed*, p. 88
[34] Ehrman, *Jesus: Apocalyptic Prophet*, p. 35
[35] Helms, GF, p. 124
[36] Josephus reports this in *The Jewish War*, 6.423
[37] Helms, GF, p.126
[38] Carrier, op. cit., p. 424, n74

Chapter Eleven:
The Crucial Moment

"Scripture contains many contradictions, and many statements which are not literally true, but must be read spiritually and mystically."
– Origen of Alexandria[1]

Jesus Rex
The inscription of the charge against him read, "The king of the Jews." (15:26)

Or did it? Perhaps it's not a big deal, but it is slightly odd that no two Gospels agree on the exact wording:

Mark: "The king of the Jews." (15:26)
Matt: "This is Jesus, the king of the Jews." (27:37)
Luke: "This is the king of the Jews." (23:38)
John: "Jesus of Nazareth, the king of the Jews." (19:19)

John adds that this was written in three languages, Hebrew, Greek and Latin (19:20). The Latin portion, IESVS·NAZARENVS·REX·IVDÆORVM (Iesus Nazarenus, Rex Iudaeorum), is where we get the little "INRI" sign in medieval art. Incidentally, you'll be glad to know that the Empress Helena also discovered this very same True Little "INRI" Sign of Jesus™ back when she found all her other fabulous True Jesus™ artifacts in the year 325 – though for some reason the "INRI" tablet wasn't discovered (sorry, re-discovered) until 1492 in Rome.[2]

Verse Not Found
"..." (15:28)

If you're reading a modern bible translation, at this point you may now be wondering: *where did Verse 15:28 go?* Take another look; the verses run fine up to verse 27 – and then it

skips to verse 29. What happened? It's not missing from older bible translations like the New King James Version, which reads:
> "So the Scripture was fulfilled [a] which says,
> 'And He was numbered with the transgressors.'[b]"

A quick look at footnote [a] tells us that this scriptural fulfillment is referring back to Isaiah 53:12. Footnote [b] is more cryptic, saying: "NU-Text omits this verse." What does *that* mean? The NU-Text generally represents the Alexandrian or Egyptian family of text types; our oldest, but sometimes questioned, text. These texts are in the Critical Text of the Nestle-Aland Greek New Testament, 26th ed. (N) and the United Bible Society's third edition (U), hence the acronym "NU-text." Mark 15, verse 28 isn't found in these biblical texts, and neither of our oldest complete (but not identical) New Testaments, the codices *Vaticanus* and *Sinaiticus* contain the verse either. The standard work, Aland & Aland's *The Text of the New Testament* points out that 15:28 derives from Luke 22:37, and that the external textual evidence clearly demonstrates that it is a later interpolation that should be omitted.[3] As it turns out, there are several other verses that modern bible translations reject for similar reasons.[4]

Cross Purposes
And with him they crucified two bandits, one on his right and one on his left. Those who passed by derided him, shaking their heads and saying, "Aha! You who would destroy the temple and build it in three days, save yourself, and come down from the cross!" In the same way the chief priests, along with the scribes, were also mocking him among themselves and saying, "He saved others; he cannot save himself. Let the Messiah, the King of Israel, come down from the cross now, so that we may see and believe." Those who were crucified with him also taunted him. (15:27-32)

Three is a magic number for Mark. Triads fill his passion narrative, which alone may account for why he has two more victims crucified alongside Jesus. But as later editors also noted (see above), there is also a scriptural passage to inspire it: "And he was numbered with the transgressors." This is from verse 12 of Isaiah 53, the famous "Suffering Servant" passage; a gold mine for the evangelists and others searching for traces of the messiah in the writings of the Hebrew prophets:

> "… he poured out his life unto death, and was numbered with the transgressors. For he bore the sin of many, and made intercession for the transgressors."
> (Isaiah 53:12)

We know Luke certainly recognized its messianic potential of verse 53:12, because he has his Jesus say as much. At the Last Supper, Jesus tells his disciples, "For I tell you, this scripture must be fulfilled in me, 'And he was counted among the lawless;' and indeed, what is written about me is being fulfilled." (Luke 22:37)

Other details in this part of the passion story also come straight from this and other Old Testament passages. Take the mockery Jesus endures from everyone while on the cross, despite the fact that mere days ago he had been followed all the way across the Holy Land by multitudes of worshipful followers and greeted by everyone in Jerusalem as their promised messiah. Almost two centuries ago, David Friedrich Strauss' classic *Das Leben Jesu, Kritisch Bearbeitet* (*The Life of Jesus, Critically Examined*) pointed out just how ridiculous this scene is, and Haim Cohn concurred:

> "It simply will not bear belief that priests or scribes or elders or rulers or any commoner should mock and curse a fellow Jew hanging on a Roman cross, whatever his crime was. Hence the theory that scripture had to be fulfilled; and that, by the same stroke, the Jews could be presented

as the cruel and inhumane creatures, lacking the least decency, and true to the vileness of character portrayed throughout the Passion story, was only a further and more welcome ground for arranging that scripture fulfill itself."[5]

Cohn argues such a wildly improbable report could only be inserted into Mark's gospel story for one purpose, to contrive just such "fulfillment" of scriptures like this:

"All who see me mock at me; they make mouths at me, they shake their heads..." (Psalms 22:7-8)[6] Matthew found more to add from Psalm 22 and inserted his version of verse 8 ("He trusts in the Lord," they say, "let the Lord rescue him. Let him deliver him, since he delights in him") into verse 31 of Mark's narrative above (15:27-32), which he otherwise copies almost word for word:

> "Then two bandits were crucified with him, one on his right and one on his left. Those who passed by derided him, shaking their heads and saying, 'You who would destroy the temple and build it in three days, save yourself! If you are the Son of God, come down from the cross.' In the same way the chief priests also, along with the scribes and elders, were mocking him, saying, 'He saved others; he cannot save himself. He is the King of Israel; let him come down from the cross now, and we will believe in him. **He trusts in God; let God deliver him now, if he wants to; for he said, "I am God's Son."**' The bandits who were crucified with him also taunted him in the same way." (Matt. 27:38-44)

In Mark and Matthew, their message is that Jesus is totally abandoned; even the thieves crucified alongside him take time out from their own agonizing deaths to taunt him, too.

Luke has a different theological point to make – that any sinner can be saved if they but ask Jesus – so he changes the story so that only one thief taunts him. The other crucified criminal chides his friend with a suspiciously eloquent and sensitive speech:

> "One of the criminals who were hanged there kept deriding him and saying, "Are you not the Messiah? Save yourself and us!" But the other rebuked him, saying, "Do you not fear God, since you are under the same sentence of condemnation? And we indeed have been condemned justly, for we are getting what we deserve for our deeds, but this man has done nothing wrong." Then he said, "Jesus, remember me when you come into your kingdom." He replied, "Truly I tell you, today you will be with me in Paradise"[7] (Luke 23:39-43).

Price observes that the thief's plea, "Remember me when you come into your kingdom," is a line taken verbatim from the Greek historian Diodorus Siculus.[8]

Darkness at Noon
When it was noon, darkness came over the whole land until three in the afternoon.

It should be immediately obvious to Christians and heretics alike that this never happened. There have been several attempts to link it to ancient eclipse accounts – but this isn't a solar eclipse, contrary to some of our texts of Luke that now say "the sun was eclipsed" (23:45).[9] Eclipses never last longer than a few minutes, certainly not for three hours; and are localized to a relatively narrow track along the earth, not the whole world. Besides, Passover always falls during the full moon, when the moon is on the wrong side of the planet to block out the sun.

Perhaps we might dream up some other natural explanation; something more spectacular than just a particularly overcast day: some sort of freak sandstorm, say, or any other weird atmospheric anomaly you please, occurring for three hours over Jerusalem. But however we try to explain it, if anything of the sort happened, how do we explain why no one noticed it? There were plenty of astronomers and sky-watchers then (Seneca and Pliny the Elder, just to name two) recording and commenting on similar phenomena.

There is no mention of it anywhere until Mark writes his gospel decades later, and even then it only appears in the three Synoptic gospels; not in John's gospel or any other New Testament book, apart from later (2nd century) apocryphal gospels (or the still-later *Gospel of Nicodemus*) that borrow or even embellish Mark's darkness story.[10]

One possibility explains both problems nicely, however: Mark just made it up. The 6th-century Byzantine classicist John Lydus (a.k.a. John the Lydian) reported that in ancient times it was common lore that the sun would be eclipsed at the death of a great king;[11] and Carrier has listed several examples.[12] But even if that weren't the case, Mark's usual m.o. of covertly sourcing his story details from Hebrew scripture already provides abundant historical precedent. He only need turn to prophets like Amos: "I will cause the sun to go down at noon, and I will darken the earth in the clear day" (Amos 8:9).[13]

"My God, my God, why have you forsaken me?"
> *At three o'clock Jesus cried out with a loud voice, "Eloi, Eloi, lema sabachthani?" which means, "My God, my God, why have you forsaken me?" When some of the bystanders heard it, they said, "Listen, he is calling for Elijah." And someone ran, filled a sponge with sour wine, put it on a stick, and gave it to him to drink, saying, "Wait, let us see whether Elijah will come to take him down."* (Mark 15:34-36)

Fifteen-plus years ago, as an atheist who still believed there had been a real Jesus, I used to find it unbelievably sad that his last words were such an agonized cry of despair. Yes, I knew that Luke had said Jesus signed off with a gentle "Father, into thy hands I commend my spirit" (Luke 23:46); and that John's badass Jesus, with his usual bluster, simply gave a terse "It is finished" (John 19:30) and dropped the mike. But it was hard to take either of those seriously. I found Mark and Matthew's anguished "My God, my God, why have you forsaken me?" all too heartbreakingly believable.

Still, I puzzled over why Mark's Jesus cried out "*Eloi, Eloi,*" when Matthew's said "*Eli, Eli.*" Much later I was shocked to learn that the entire line, like so many other realistic-seeming details of Mark's passion story, is taken from the opening line of the 22nd Psalm (and for Luke's part, he took his Jesus' serene last words from another Psalm, 31:5). But why the change in spelling? It's because Mark is translating the line into Aramaic, which is what Jews of the time would have spoken. Mark wanted the bystanders to think Jesus is calling for the prophet Eli (Mark 15:34-35) but that makes no sense if Jesus was saying "Eloi." His play on words only works in Hebrew, not in Aramaic. So Matthew corrects him (again!) and switches Jesus' lasts words from Aramaic to Hebrew; this is historically incorrect for Jesus to have spoken, but at least it makes the pun work (27:46).

It's Curtains for Jesus

Then Jesus gave a loud cry and breathed his last. And the curtain of the temple was torn in two, from top to bottom. Now when the centurion, who stood facing him, saw that in this way he breathed his last, he said, "Truly this man was God's Son!" (15:37-39)

At the moment of Jesus' death, even more spectacular supernatural events occur. Exactly *what* happened depends on who's telling the story, but one would think any were noteworthy enough for contemporary historians – apparently not...

Mark and Luke only give one: the tearing of the temple veil ("the curtain of the temple") from top to bottom. This heavy curtain of fine linen, richly embroidered with angelic cherubim in blue, purple and scarlet, separated the Holy of Holies – the sacred sanctuary, the center of the world, the very presence of God – from the rest of the temple[14] - and separated heaven and earth/God and man as well. So when Mark has God almighty rip it in half, the symbolism is unmistakable; he's turning a first-century theological concept into an historical event[15] to announce that the old temple system is over. Oddly, Luke has the temple curtain rip just *before* Jesus' death (Luke 23:45–46), which makes apologists squirm a bit. But in any case, no one but the Synoptic authors seem to know about this incident – not Paul, not John, not anyone else in Jerusalem; not even the temple priests whose sole job was caring for that curtain...[16]

Shall Not the Land Tremble?

Matthew has more miracles for us. It's a shame that apparently no one else in human history seemed to notice any of them, because they are doozies. The first is a mighty earthquake: "The earth shook, and the rocks were split" (27:51). Later he'll throw in a second "great earthquake," when the Angel of the Lord appears at the tomb (28:2). Both seismic events are problematic, having neither written evidence nor archaeological support.

There *is* evidence for earthquakes in the area during the first century; Josephus reports one that hit Palestine in 31 BCE and the surviving physical evidence, including cracked rocks and damaged man-made structures, extensively confirms it.[17] By contrast, the only confirmed earthquake in Palestine between 26 and 36 CE was "not energetic enough to produce" visible effects of this magnitude, according to the *International Geology Review.*[18]

Nonetheless, many apologists have tried to rescue Matthew's quakes by citing medieval reports like this:

"Bithynia was struck by an earthquake, and in the city of Nicaea many buildings fell."[19] But they don't seem to realize this only makes things worse. Since Bithynia and Nicaea were over 600 miles away in Asia Minor, *that* quake couldn't have been either of the two that struck Jerusalem in Matthew's story; it only demonstrates what we already knew: that people *were* keeping accounts of earthquakes then, and nobody noticed Mathew's...

Where did Matthew get the idea to throw in a pair of earthquakes to his story? From the very same place Mark found his darkness at noon: Amos, chapter 8 – in fact, just one verse away:

> "Shall not the land tremble on this account,
> and everyone mourn who lives in it?
> and all of it rise like the Nile,
> and be tossed about and sink again,
> like the Nile of Egypt?" (Amos 8:8)

The Gospel According to George Romero

If it seems unrealistic to accept that everyone in the ancient world could miss supernatural darkness, the tearing of the temple veil, and not one but two rock-shattering earthquakes hitting Jerusalem – I'm afraid this will only further strain your suspension of disbelief. Matthew reports one last miracle, live from Jerusalem cemetery:

> "The tombs also were opened, and many bodies of the saints who had fallen asleep were raised. After his resurrection they came out of the tombs and entered the holy city and appeared to many." (Matt. 27:52-53)

For sheer unbelievability, few Bible passages make Christians squirm like this one. I have had believers try to tell me this holy zombacalypse may have not been in the original text, or that this was probably a very localized event, only

David Fitzgerald

witnessed by a handful of people (forgetting what the word "many" means; or that this is describing *a mass resurrection of famous dead people in downtown Jerusalem*); I have even been accused of making a straw man argument – just for repeating what Matthew's Gospel says *word for word.* As we already saw (see case study no.1 in ch. 2) evangelical bible scholar Mike Licona got into hot water for merely suggesting that it might – just might – be a case of apocalyptic imagery. It does seem to be inspired by passages like Isaiah 26:19 ("Thy dead men shall live, together with my dead body shall they arise."), or as Robert Price suggests, the idea expressed in 1 Cor. 15:20-23 that Jesus was the first fruits of a general resurrection of the dead.

Women Witnesses
> *There were also women looking on from a distance; among them were Mary Magdalene, and Mary the mother of James the younger and of Joses, and Salome. These used to follow him and provided for him when he was in Galilee) and there were many other women who had come up with him to Jerusalem.* (15:40-41)

As mentioned before (See "Embarrassment no. 2: Jesus' Female Witnesses," in ch. 5), even the names Mark provides (here and in verse 16:1) all conveniently have rich symbolism, as many scholars have noted.[20] In his version (unlike the later gospels) there are three women coming to anoint Jesus: Mary Magdalene, Mary the mother of James, and Salomê. None of the three appear anywhere else in Mark's story until the three symbolic times of Jesus' death, burial and resurrection. Salomê is the feminine form of Solomon, an obvious symbol of both wisdom and kingship. Mary/Mariam is the sister of Moses and Aaron who led the Hebrew women in song after their delivery from Egypt. In Jewish symbolism, Egypt represented death, slavery, and oppression.[21] The "Magdala" in "Magdalene" is a Greek cognate of the Hebrew for "tower," given in the

Septuagint (the Greek translation of the Jewish scriptures) as *Magdôlon*; in other words, the biblical tower Migdol, which represented the border between Egypt and the Promised Land, i.e. between death and deliverance.[22] "James" is just the English form of the Hebrew name "Jacob," so "Mary the mother of Jacob" is an obvious reference to *the* Jacob, a.k.a. Israel (Genesis 32:28-29; 35:10). Mark revels in concealing symbolic meanings in plain sight throughout his narrative, and the names and events of this incident at the tomb don't all come together by accident;[23] the symbolic double meanings are woven as tightly as a basket.

John, as usual, has different symbolism in mind, so first, he brings the three women boldly to the foot of the cross (19:25) instead of watching from a safe distance, as Mark does (also Matt. 27:55 & Luke 23:49). He also changes up the cast of characters; trimming Mary Magdalene, the other Mary, Salomê and a crowd of many other women, down to only a trinity of Marys: 1) his mother, the Virgin Mary; 2) his mother's sister, Mary the wife of Cleophas) and 3) Mary Magdalene (John 19:25).

Broken Bones / Blood and Water
Like Matthew, John has other bits of scripture he wants to bring into play for this scene. So he has the Jewish leaders ask Pilate to break the legs of the crucified men to finish them off and remove the bodies. The soldiers dutifully break the legs of the two thieves, but when they get to Jesus, they see he is already dead and do not break his (John 19:31-33). As mentioned before, though John says this was to fulfill (a non-existent) prophecy; in reality, it comes from the Torah's rule against breaking the Passover lamb's bones, since for John, Jesus *is* the Passover lamb.

For his next trick, John has another scriptural passage in view: "They will look on the one whom they have pierced," taken from Zechariah (12:10), albeit out of context. There it is talking about Judea's victory over its enemies. John, however, declares it a prophecy (19:37) of this line in his story:

> "Instead, one of the soldiers pierced his side with a spear, and at once blood and water came out." (19:34)

Medically speaking, of course, this fails the reality check. If you poke a corpse, blood and water won't come spilling out together (and if they did, how would you be able to tell them apart just by sight, anyway?). Does it make sense as theological allegory? You already know the answer; of course it does: Not only were blood and water interpreted as symbols of the Eucharist and Baptism,[24] Christians said Jesus came "by water and blood," as in: "This is the one who came by water and blood, Jesus Christ; not with the water only, but with the water and the blood" (1 John 5:6).

Not convinced? Put your mind at ease. Although this blood-and-water business may sound far-fetched, the text of John assures us that "He who saw this has testified so that you also may believe. His testimony is true, and he knows that he tells the truth." (19:35) Still, if *that* assurance sounds suspicious, there were early Christian scribes who agreed with you. A variant of this verse reads "… His testimony is true, and there is one who knows that he tells the truth." Better now?

Then again, it could be pointed out, as Price does,[25] that according to Plutarch, the divine portents at Jesus' death serve the same purpose as those at the crucifixion in Alexandria of the rebel king Cleomenes of Sparta in 219 B.C.E. In both cases, omens[26] cause onlookers to declare the crucifiee is a son of god. And like Cleomenes, Jesus is stabbed to make sure he is dead.

Jesus is dead.

---

[1] *Commentary on John*, vol. 10, ch. 4

[2] Roberto Lanciani, *Storia degli scavi di Roma*, vol. I, 79, noted by Roberto Weiss, *The Renaissance Discovery of*

Classical Antiquity 1969:102
³ Aland & Aland, p. 302
⁴ For instance, see Wikipedia's handy list of Bible verses not included in modern translations; available online at: http://en.wikipedia.org/wiki/List_of_Bible_verses_not_included_in_modern_translations
⁵ Strauss pp. 136-7, Cohn p. 223
⁶ Possibly Lamentations 2:15 as well: "All who pass along the way clap their hands at you; they hiss and wag their heads..."
⁷ Here's a little-known fact: "Paradise" is actually a Persian word (*pairi-daēza,* "Garden of Delights") that came into Judaism from the older Zoroastrian religion of Babylon. (*Eerdmans Dict.*, p. 1008-9) Before the Babylonian captivity, the ancient Hebrews believed the dead, good and bad alike, all simply went to Sheol, the gloomy underworld of the grave. Judaism acquired several other new religious ideas from Zoroastrianism as well: Heaven and Hell, the idea that the world would come to an end, an expanded angelology and demonology, and more.
⁸ Diodorus Siculus, *Bibliotheca Historica* 34:2,5-8. Cited in Price, *DJ*, p. 205
⁹ Other Lukan manuscripts say "the sun's light failed," or "the sun was darkened."
¹⁰ See ch. 18 for details on Thallus and Phlegon, two ancient writers frequently alleged to have commented on the supernatural darkness.
¹¹ John Lydus, *De Ostentis* 70a
¹² For example, Herodotus, *Hist.* 7.37; Plutarch, *Pel.* 31.3 and *Aem.*17.7-11; Dio Cassius, *Hist. rom.* 55.29.3. I am indebted to Richard Carrier's "Thallus and the Darkness at Christ's Death," *Journal of Greco-Roman Christianity and Judaism*, vol. 8 for all the examples and citations in this section. Reproduced in Carrier, *Hitler Homer Bible Christ*, pp. 327-35.

¹³ This verse was hardly Mark's only option; there are others that employ the motif of darkness descending upon the earth, or the sun turning to darkness:

> Amos 5.20: "Is not the day of the Lord darkness, not light, and gloom with no brightness in it?"

> Joel 2.31: "The sun shall be turned to darkness, and the moon to blood, before the great and terrible day of the Lord comes."

> Ezek. 32.7-8: "When I blot you out, I will cover the heavens, and make their stars dark; I will cover the sun with a cloud, and the moon shall not give its light. All the shining lights of the heavens I will darken above you, and put darkness on your land, says the Lord God.

> Isaiah 60.1-2: "For darkness shall cover the earth, and thick darkness the peoples; but the Lord will arise upon you, and his glory will appear over you."

¹⁴ Shek. viii. 5; see *Jewish Encyclopedia*, "Holy of Holies"
¹⁵ Helms, GF, p128
¹⁶ Mishnah, *Sheqalim, Yoma* 5:1 and *Middot* 1:1h
¹⁷ Jefferson B. Williams, Markus J. Schwab and A. Brauer, 'An Early First-Century Earthquake in the Dead Sea', *International Geology Review* 54.10 (May 2012), pp. 1219-28 (cited in Carrier, "Thallus and the Darkness at Christ's Death")
¹⁸ Ibid.
¹⁹ George Syncellus, *Chron.* 394
²⁰ see Carrier, NtIF, pp. 314-15
²¹ Elwell, Walter A., "Egypt," *Evangelical Dictionary of Theology*, 1996
²² Carrier, op. cit.
²³ Ibid., pp. 316

[24] Goguel, vol. II, p. 462

[25] Price, *Deconstructing Jesus*, pp. 244-45

[26] For Jesus, the omens are darkness and the tearing of the temple curtain. For Cleomenes, a large serpent climbs covers his face, protecting his body from birds of prey, which makes the king superstitiously afraid and the Alexandrians believe "he had been some extraordinary being, and one beloved by the gods." They hold processions in his honor, and give Cleomenes the title of "hero, and son of the gods." (Plutarch, *Lives of the Noble Grecians and Romans, Cleomenes,* Dryden trans.)

Chapter Twelve: Jesus is Dead

"No, our discussion will show in a thousand ways, great and small, how every failure of the apologetical argument scores a point in favor of a genuine alternative: the literary, fictive character of the resurrection narratives. Not <u>bad</u> history because <u>not history at all</u>. Rather, good storytelling."

– Robert M. Price

Joseph of Arimathea

When evening had come, and since it was the day of Preparation, that is, the day before the Sabbath, Joseph of Arimathea, a respected member of the council, who was also himself waiting expectantly for the kingdom of God, went boldly to Pilate and asked for the body of Jesus. (15:42-43)

As we saw earlier, Mark forgot that he had the Sanhedrin council unanimously condemn Jesus to death when he introduces Joseph of Arimathea as both a respected member of the council and an eager fan of Jesus. The other gospel writers each try to fix this mistake in their own way:

> Matthew changes Joseph from a council member to just "a rich man from Arimathea, who was also a disciple of Jesus." (Matt. 27:57)
> Luke's Joseph is still a member of the Sanhedrin, waiting expectantly for the kingdom of God. But he changes Mark's unanimous verdict by adding: "who, though a member of the council, had not agreed to their plan and action." (Luke 23:50)

John says nothing about Joseph of Arimathea being a member of the Sanhedrin Council. His Joseph is only described as: "a disciple of Jesus, though a secret one, because of his fear of the Jews." (John 19:38)

Who to believe? None of them, apparently. Price points out that like Judas, Joseph of Arimathea is a fictional character who grows in the telling.[1] Dennis MacDonald has shown numerous parallels between Mark's gospel and the *Iliad*, and argues that Joseph of Arimathea is based on Hector's father, King Priam who begs Achilles for the body of his son, adding that he is named Joseph because he corresponds to the slain hero's father.[2] Carrier adds "Joseph of Arimathea exists only as a literary device, instantly produced on the stage when he is needed, without explanation or introduction, and then instantly removed when his role is done, just as inexplicably, never to be heard of again, not even in Acts."[3]

Arimathea itself is just as fictional as Joseph, it would seem.[4] There is no record of it anywhere in the ancient world outside of these four references in the Gospels. Even today archeologists cannot agree where it ever was, though there have been several hopeful attempts to link it to various sites with similar-sounding names. But the name alone should have been a clue to investigators. Richard Carrier has confirmed that the name "Arimathea" is a pun in Greek: *ari-* (best) *math-* (disciple) *–aia* (town/place).

> "the *ari-* prefix, meaning "best," appears in such words as *aristocracy* (rule of the best), *aripikros* (best in bitterness, hence bitterest), *arideiketos* (best in display, hence glorious), as explained in standard Greek lexicons. The *math-* root forms the verb *mathein*, to teach, and the nouns *mathê*, lesson or doctrine, and *mathêtês*, disciple. The *-aia* suffix as town or place appears for such regions as Galilaia (Land of the Galiyl) and Judaia (Land of the Jews), and such actual cities as Dikaia (Justice Town) and Drymaia (Thicket Town)."[5]

With that said, I asked in *Nailed*: Could it be mere coincidence that this follower of Jesus comes from Bestdiscipleville, Judea – or was Mark just being clever?"[6] As it happens, there are quite a lot of instances in his gospel where it appears Mark is indeed being clever; giving suspiciously apt names to characters and locales in his story, and dropping classical ancient literary references when he can (See "The Name Game" below).

The Name Game
(Suspiciously apt character & place names)

For a presumed work of nonfiction, many of the people and places in the Gospels have suspiciously apt names. Is it a coincidence:

- That Nicodemus (whose name means "ruler of the people") is a ruler of the Jews? (John 3:1)

- That Jairus, whose name means "awaken" (*yair*, "to bring light, enlighten, awaken" in Hebrew), has his dead child resuscitated by Jesus, who tells him "She is not dead, but only sleeps"? (Luke 8:40-56)

- That Martha (whose name means "Lady of the House") is Jesus' hostess? (Luke 10:38)

- That Zacchaeus (from the Aramaic *zakki*, "to give alms") gives half of all he owns as alms to the poor? (Luke 19:8)

- That Theophilus (whose name means "Lover of God") is the patron that Luke/Acts is addressed to? (Luke 1:3, Acts 1:1)

- That Barabbas (whose name means "Son of the Father") is exchanged for the Son of Man? (Matt. 27:17, et al.)

- That among Jesus' twelve disciples we have zodiacal references? Thomas Didymus (Thomas was not originally a proper name; it means "twin" – as does "Didymus" – and was the Hebrew word for the constellation Gemini). James and John, the sons of Zebedee, nicknamed "Boanerges" or "Sons of Thunder"

(like the Roman Twins Castor and Pollux, one mortal and one the son of the Thunder god Zeus). See *Nailed*, pp. 159-60 for more.
- That "Arimathea," the town of the disciple Joseph of Arimathea (which has never been found, despite much guesswork) sounds in Greek like 'Town of the Best Disciple'?
- That one variant of Judas Iscariot's surname is *Ishqarya*, "man of falsehood, betrayer"? (Mark 3:19), or that Judas itself means "Jew" (in fact, almost literally 'Judea')?
- That Emmaus, where Jesus returns in disguise and reveals himself, is a pun on Eumaeus, the servant to whom Odysseus returns in disguise and reveals himself in the Odyssey?
- Or that the name of Cleopas, the follower to whom Jesus appears, means "all the glory" or "All the good news (gospel)" in Greek?
- That Bar-Timaeus, ("Son of Timaeus") the blind beggar who is the only one in a crowd to recognize Jesus (Mark:10 46-52) shares his name with Plato's book *Timeaus*, where we read of having true vision as opposed to going along with the crowd? (See Price, *The Incredible Shrinking Son of Man*, pp. 147-48 for more)

See Price; *The Incredible Shrinking Son of Man* and *Deconstructing Jesus*; and Patella, *Lord of the Cosmos*.

See also: "The Twelve Disciples: their names, name-meanings, associations, etc."http://vridar.org/2008/07/13/the-twelve-disciples-their-names-and-their-meanings-associations-etc/

"More Puns in the Gospel of Mark: People and Places" http://vridar.org/2010/12/12/more-puns-in-the-gospel-of-mark-people-and-places/

Dead So Soon?
> *Then Pilate wondered if he were already dead; and summoning the centurion, he asked him whether he had been dead for some time. When he learned from the centurion that he was dead, he granted the body to Joseph. Then Joseph bought a linen cloth, and taking down the body, wrapped it in the linen cloth, and laid it in a tomb that had been hewn out of the rock. He then rolled a stone against the door of the tomb. Mary Magdalene and Mary the mother of Joses saw where the body was laid.* (15:44-47)

There are many less-obvious plot problems with the whole passion scenario which anxious biblical scholars have been gnawing on for centuries.[7] Here's another. Normally, crucifixion was not a rush job. The Romans usually let their condemned hang on their crosses for days and days, to be exposed to the elements and finally, jackals and vultures. So why does Mark go out of his way to kill off Jesus in a mere six hours, when it should have taken days?

Robert Price looks at this and other clues (Jesus asking God to allow him to escape death in Gethsemane, the bystanders jeering at him to come down from his cross, Pilate surprised that Jesus is already dead so quickly, the rapid burial in a rich man's tomb; and wonders if this isn't reflecting an original ending to the story where Jesus *does* escape. Jesus' story does match that of many other innocent-but-persecuted Old Testament figures like Joseph, Daniel, Isaiah's Suffering Servant, and more. It also matches a common literary device found in ancient novels, of a comatose victim being entombed alive and accidentally rescued when grave robbers break in later to steal the riches.[8]

The protagonist of Psalm 22, which inspired so much of Mark's story, does get a rescue at the last minute (Ps. 22: 22-24), which has made some scholars wonder if there was originally a happy ending for Jesus as well. The "Swoon" theory (that Jesus was taken down while he was only *mostly* dead, à la *The Princess Bride*), has been a recurring trope throughout Christian history. Ahmadiyya Muslims still believe that Jesus survived the cross this way.

Like a Rolling Stone
> *When the Sabbath was over, Mary Magdalene, and Mary the mother of James, and Salome bought spices, so that they might go and anoint him. And very early on the first day of the week, when the sun had risen, they went to the tomb. They had been saying to one another, "Who will roll away the stone for us from the entrance to the tomb?" When they looked up, they saw that the stone, which was very large, had already been rolled back.* (16:1-4)

Mark's entire story of the empty tomb is predicated on a mistake: the women visiting the tomb in order to anoint Jesus' body for preservation. As Price points out, in the Middle Eastern climate, no one would wait two days after death to start preserving the body.[9] Careful historian Luke unblinkingly repeats Mark's error (Luke 24:1). Here yet again, Matthew corrects Mark's mistake, and omits the anointing entirely; he has the women coming merely to see the sepulcher (Matt. 28:1) John fixes it his own way, as usual; he has the body already anointed ahead of time by Joseph of Arimathea and Nicodemus instead (John 19:38-40). Who's Nicodemus? Like Lazarus, Nicodemus is a character that only shows up in John's gospel; a Pharisee who secretly meets with Jesus by night (3:1-21) and later tries to defend him to his Sanhedrin colleagues (7:50-52) – so where was he at Jesus' trial? Nicodemus has Jesus' body wrapped in linen cloth with around one hundred pounds of myrrh and aloes spice, an extraordinarily exorbitant amount, fit for a king.

Oddly, the women only wonder how they will ever move the stone blocking Jesus' tomb in Mark's gospel (16:3). The women are right to ask, since a stone like this should have weighed between 1½ to 2 tons, about the same as a mid-sized car. So if the women had already realized this, why would they have gone to the tomb by themselves in the first place? Matthew compounds the problem by adding that it was secured with a Roman seal to boot (Matt. 27:66), so opening it would have been a capital crime in any case.

There is an anachronism here as well. Round blocking stones like the kind described in the Gospels weren't used in the time of Jesus, but were commonly used after 70 CE. Mark mistakenly projected his knowledge of tombs in his own day back into the early first century.[10] Luckily for the women, they arrive to find that the stone has already been rolled away for them. So they enter...

In the Tomb

As they entered the tomb, they saw a young man, dressed in a white robe, sitting on the right side; and they were alarmed. But he said to them, "Do not be alarmed; you are looking for Jesus of Nazareth, who was crucified. He has been raised; he is not here. Look, there is the place they laid him. But go, tell his disciples and Peter that he is going ahead of you to Galilee; there you will see him, just as he told you." (16:5-7)

Surprise! It's the youth from the arrest scene back in Mark 14:51-2, who slipped out of his flimsy linen cloth and ran away naked (see "The Streaker in the Garden," ch. 9). In that scene, the youth serves as a metaphor for Jesus losing his life. As we've already seen, equating the body with a garment was an ancient literary trope[11] and a popular metaphor for early Christians. The young man losing his clothes equals Jesus losing his life. But now, the mysterious unnamed youth reappears, in new and brilliant raiment, just as Jesus' life has returned in a new and glorious form. A perfect and beautiful allegory... just like everything else in Mark's gospel.

David Fitzgerald

The End
So they went out and fled from the tomb, for terror and amazement had seized them; and they said nothing to anyone, for they were afraid. (16:8)

Once again, Mark employs a reversal of the reader's expectations and ends his gospel with a shocker ending. The women ran screaming from the tomb in terror, and never told anyone that Jesus had risen. As noted before (see "Embarrassment no. 2: Jesus' Female Witnesses", in ch. 5), far from corroborating Mark's story, this detail is a clever device to explain why no one had ever heard the story before now, decades later. And that is where his story ends.

But not where the others end...

(left) The original ending of Mark at verse 16:8 in the Codex Vaticanus, one of our two oldest complete New Testament texts.

Codex Vaticanus Graecus 1209, from the Vatican Library. *Uncial 059 (Gregory-Aland)*

Other Endings
The other evangelists were quite dissatisfied with Mark's ending, and set out to fix it, as each saw fit. However, none of them end it the same way; watch for where they differ.

Matthew says: Mary Magdalene and the other Mary come to see the tomb. It is closed by the heavy stone. Suddenly **a great earthquake** occurs, and then **an angel descends from heaven**, his face blazing like lightning and his clothing white

Jesus: Mything in Action

as snow. A squad of **Roman guards** assigned to the tomb are utterly terrified and all faint dead away. The angel **rolls away the stone** and sits on it, instructing the women to tell the disciples Jesus is risen and he will see them **in Galilee**. As the two Marys run to tell the good news, **Jesus meets them**, saying "Rejoice!" They hold him by his feet and worship him. The disciples go to the mountain in Galilee where Jesus told them to go. When they see him they worship him, but some doubt. He tells them all authority has been given to him in heaven and on earth, and sends them out to spread the Gospel to all nations. There is no ascension in Matthew's Gospel. It ends with **Jesus still on the mountain, telling his disciples he is with them always.** (Matt. 28:1-20)

Wait, where did these Roman guards come from? One indication that Matthew is writing after Mark is that he is countering what must have been a common retort to Mark's original story: that the disciples simply stole the body. So he has the Jews explicitly point out this potential plot hole (27:62-66) and adds the guards; a feature found in no other canonical gospel. Unfortunately, his workaround doesn't work. He says:

> "…some of the guard went into the city and told the chief priests everything that had happened. After the priests had assembled with the elders, they devised a plan to give a large sum of money to the soldiers, telling them, "You must say, 'His disciples came by night and stole him away while we were asleep.' If this comes to the governor's ears, we will satisfy him and keep you out of trouble." So they took the money and did as they were directed. And this story is still told among the Jews to this day." (28:11-15)

But this makes no sense, since dereliction of duty was a serious offense for a Roman soldier (as were taking a bribe and giving false witness, for that matter), usually punished by *Fustuarium*, i.e., having the entire legion beat them to death;[12]

we also have records of soldiers asleep on duty being hurled off the cliff of the Capitolium.[13] And no one would be able to save them from that, least of all Jewish religious authorities under occupation. And what were Roman soldiers doing secretly reporting to the priests in the first place? And even if they had, how would anyone else know the details of their secret meeting? Besides, their supposed cover story doesn't even hold together: if they were asleep, how were *they* supposed to know the disciples stole the body while they slept? No matter how you slice it, Matthew's add-on fails. And incidentally, that last line ("And this story is still told among the Jews to this day") is another giveaway that Matthew is writing long after the supposed events.

Luke says: Sunday morning **Mary Magdalene, Joanna, Mary the mother of James, and "certain other women"** having **already seen the tomb**, come to **anoint Jesus' body**, with **no thought of how they are going to roll away the stone.** Luckily, they find **the stone already rolled away**. They enter the tomb and cannot find Jesus' body. Suddenly **two men** appear standing beside them in shining garments. **"Why do you seek the living among the dead?"** the men ask them. They tell the women that Jesus is risen and reminds them what he told them: that he would be crucified and on the third day rise again. The women tell the disciples, who do not believe them, except **Peter, who runs to the tomb** and sees the empty burial cloths (24:12).

Jesus appears to two men (Luke identifies one of the men as "Cleopas") walking **on the road to Emmaus**, but they do not realize it is him until that evening, when he then vanishes before their eyes. They run all the way back to **Jerusalem** to tell the eleven remaining Disciples (who, oddly enough, tell them in turn that Jesus has appeared to Simon Peter, even though Luke says that Peter only saw the empty burial cloths). As soon as they finish, **Jesus re-appears** and says "Peace to you." They are terrified, thinking it is a ghost.

Jesus: Mything in Action

Jesus reassures them, inviting them to touch him, and showing his hands and feet. Jesus asks "Have you any food here?" and eats a piece of broiled fish and some honeycomb. **He tells them to wait in Jerusalem** until they are filled with "power from on high" later. After dinner **(this is all still on Sunday)** he leads them out to Bethany and lifts his hands to bless them. While he is blessing them, **he is carried up into heaven**. (Luke 23:55 - 24:51)

John says: With Jesus' body **having been anointed by Joseph and Nicodemus** shortly after his death, **Mary comes alone** on Sunday morning, and **finds the stone rolled away**. **She runs to Simon Peter and the unnamed "disciple that Jesus loved"** (traditionally John, but the text never says so) and tells them Jesus' body has been stolen. The **"Other Disciple" outruns Peter to the tomb**, and both men see the burial cloths and "the handkerchief that had been around his head" folded neatly. They go home, but **Mary stays behind weeping**. She suddenly sees **two angels** in white, one sitting at the head and the other at the foot of the tomb. **"Woman, why are you weeping?"** they ask her. "Because they have taken away my Lord, and I do not know where they have laid him," she replies. She turns and sees Jesus standing there, but does not know it is Jesus. He says to her "Woman, why are you weeping? Whom are you seeking?" Thinking he is the gardener, she sniffs, "Sir, if you have carried him away, tell me where you have laid him, and I will take him away." Jesus says to her "Mary!" At this she turns (again[14]) and finally recognizes him, cries out "Rabboni!" ("Teacher") and runs into his arms. He tells her not to cling to him, for "I have not yet ascended to my Father," but to tell the disciples that "I am ascending to my Father and your Father, and to My God and your God."

That same evening (still Sunday), while the disciples are hiding out from the Jewish authorities behind locked doors, Jesus appears, saying "Peace be with you!" He shows them his hands and his side, and the disciples are glad. Jesus breathes on them, giving them the Holy Spirit, so that they can now forgive – or retain (?) - anyone's sins. He then apparently vanishes. Doubting Thomas somehow wasn't there for any of this (no Holy Spirit powers for him, then!), and doesn't believe the others when they later tell him they saw the risen Jesus last Sunday. Presumably, the other disciples showed him their newfound ability to forgive or retain his sins, but Thomas apparently remains unimpressed. He contends that until he can put his finger in the nail prints and his hand into Jesus' side he will not believe. **Eight days later,** Jesus re-appears and invites Thomas to do just that, but he passes on the offer. After this Jesus vanishes again but **re-re-appears** to them some time later at the sea of Tiberias while the disciples are fishing. The Gospel states explicitly (John 21:14) that this is the third time Jesus appears to his disciples. With his help, they catch exactly 153 fish and have breakfast with Jesus. This Gospel ends with Jesus and his disciples **on the shore of the Sea of Tiberias**, and even though John already has Jesus sticking around longer than Mark and Luke, he seems to further imply that Jesus continued to have jolly adventures with his chums long after the book ends: "And there are also many other things which Jesus did, the which, if they should be written every one, I suppose that even the world itself could not contain the books that should be written." (John 20:1 - 21:25)

Interestingly enough, John already has a very similar sign-off at the end of the chapter just preceding this: "And truly Jesus did many other signs in the presence of his disciples, which are not written in this book; but these are written that you may believe that Jesus is the Christ, the Son of God, and that believing you may have life in his name." (John 20:30-31) This strongly suggests that the Gospel originally ended here, after the anecdote about Thomas, with Jesus giving a little blessed thumbs up to the faithful readers out there who, unlike Thomas "have not seen, and yet have believed." This would further mean that the last chapter of John, with its story of the

Fishing Disciples was tacked on later, as the majority of scholars have long recognized.[15]

The End, Part II
But wait – let's go back to that abrupt ending at Mark 16:8. You say your Gospel of Mark didn't end there? Yours goes on for another twelve verses? If you look closer, you may find a footnote or a pair of brackets telling you verses 16:9-20 are not found in "some of the oldest manuscripts," and that the translation team (along with most biblical scholars today) believe they were not part of the original text. At least, that's what you'll find if the translators are being honest; and not all of them are.

The Original Ending (OE)
Verses 16:1-8 are referred to as the Original Ending (OE). The verdict is still out whether the OE *is* in fact the original ending, or if there was more to it that was lost. Nonetheless, among biblical experts the most common, if not universal, opinion remains that Mark ended his gospel with verse 8. Original or not, that ending was completely unsatisfying to later Christians. And so expanded, alternate endings began to appear.

The Long Ending (LE)
One of them can still be found in our modern bibles today. Verses 9-20 of Mark 16 are collectively the so-called Long Ending (LE). Here is how it reads in the New American Standard Bible (NASB), complete with Jesus-related he's and him's always capitalized:

> Now after He had risen early on the first day of the week, He first appeared to Mary Magdalene, from whom He had cast out seven demons. She went and reported to those who had been with Him, while they were mourning and

weeping. When they heard that He was alive and had been seen by her, they refused to believe it.

After that, He appeared in a different form to two of them while they were walking along on their way to the country. They went away and reported it to the others, but they did not believe them either. Afterward, He appeared to the eleven themselves as they were reclining at the table; and He reproached them for their unbelief and hardness of heart, because they had not believed those who had seen Him after He had risen.

And He said to them, "Go into all the world and preach the gospel to all creation: He who has believed and has been baptized shall be saved; but he who has disbelieved shall be condemned. These signs will accompany those who have believed: in My name they will cast out demons, they will speak with new tongues; they will pick up serpents [in their hands][16], and if they drink any deadly poison, it will not hurt them; they will lay hands on the sick, and they will recover."

So then, when the Lord Jesus had spoken to them, He was received up into heaven and sat down at the right hand of God. And they went out and preached everywhere, while the Lord worked with them, and confirmed the word by the signs that followed. (16:9-20)

Biblical scholars are in virtually unanimous agreement that all those verses were either forged, or taken from some other text altogether, and inserted long after the original author composed the Gospel. It is difficult to say exactly when this new and improved ending was created; Irenaeus may have been the first to quote from the extended ending, which would place it sometime in the late 2nd century, but this is uncertain. The earliest surviving manuscript to include it is not Greek at all, but Coptic, from the 4th century. According to some scholars, even Eusebius doubted its authenticity. Several scholars argue that the LE was composed around 120-150 CE and inserted into a copy of Mark sometime in the 2nd century, or at least by the end of the 3rd century.[17]

There is persuasive evidence, both internal and external, to think so. For example, the LE betrays knowledge of all four Gospels and Acts, books that didn't exist when Mark wrote his. The vocabulary and syntax of the LE could hardly be further from the style of Mark's Gospel. This has been known for over a hundred years, since Ezra Gould famously demonstrated stylistic incongruities to devastating effect in 1896, an analysis repeated by several scholars since.[18] Individually, the LE's style, logic, and content all argue decisively against Markan authorship; taken together, the conclusion is undeniable.

Now add the manuscript evidence and patristic evidence: not only is the ending of Mark absent from the *Codex Vaticanus* and *Codex Sinaiticus* (our oldest Greek manuscripts of Mark), it was also unknown to many of the early Church Fathers.[19] Thus, all the leading experts agree the case is ironclad: There is simply no rational basis to believe the LE is genuine.[20]

The Shorter Ending (SE)
So much for the Long Ending found in some of our bibles. But it's not the only ending Christians later created for Mark. In some manuscripts of Mark, the Long Ending is preceded by, or even completely replaced, by this ending:

> And they promptly reported all these instructions to Peter and his companions. And after that, Jesus Himself sent out through them from east to west the sacred and imperishable proclamation of eternal salvation. Amen.

This is called the "Shorter Ending" of Mark (SE). Unfortunately, some scholars confuse the "Original Ending" (OE) (which may or may not have been the actual original ending) with the "Shorter Ending" (SE). Although the OE *is* the shorter ending to Mark, the SE is in fact another textual variant altogether.

The SE fails on several levels: it doesn't match Markan style; it's painfully inept (seeing as it immediately and inexplicably contradicts the sentence before it) and is implausibly brief. Like the LE, it's obviously written to "fix" the disappointing original ending and shows a familiarity with writings that came after Mark – in this case, Acts (e.g. Acts 1:8) and Luke (e.g. Luke 1:77). So from internal evidence alone, it's clearly a forgery.

Double Ending (DE)
Both the LE and SE show up in various manuscripts, sometimes singly and sometimes combined into a Double Ending (DE), even though they make no sense together. Since they are incompatible, both logically and narratively, they could not have come from the same author. And it is manifestly apparent that Mark wrote neither.

Other Endings
There is also a third ending found in one surviving manuscript which some have called the **Freer Logion**. Carrier calls it the **Very Long Ending (VLE)**, since it is an extension of the LE, which also clinches the fact that it is a forgery. Likewise, the **Bobbio Ending (BE)**, also only found in a single manuscript (the *Codex Bobiensis*, a pre-Vulgate Latin translation). It intrudes into verses 16:3 & 4:

³They were saying to one another, "Who will roll away the stone for us from the entrance of the tomb?" **Then all of a sudden, at the third hour of the day, there was darkness over the whole earth, and angels descended from heaven and [as he] rose up in the splendor of the living God they ascended with him, and immediately it was light.** ⁴Looking up, they saw that the stone had been rolled away, although it was extremely large.

The codex itself physically dates from the 4th or 5th century, with a text dated no later than the 3rd century and some evidence suggesting it ultimately derives from a lost 2nd century manuscript.[21] Although it must be quite ancient, no authorities accept the Bobbio Ending (BE) as genuine.

Lost Original Ending (LOE)
Some scholars theorize there was more to Mark's original ending, but it was accidentally (or deliberately) lost. While there are many intriguing arguments for a "Lost Original Ending" (LOE), none are conclusive. No actual texts of such an ending (if it existed) have been found, nor can scholars agree which ending it should be. Some suggest it became one of the endings in the other gospels (Matthew's appearance in the mountains of Galilee, Luke's Road to Emmaus appearance, John's Sea of Tiberias fishing scene) and still others in the SE or LE itself, and so on.[22] The fact remains: no matter how Mark originally ended his Gospel, all experts agree it was not the ending we have now. Those verses in our modern bibles (9-20) are forgeries, just like all these variant endings we have uncovered since.

This means that by all indications, our original gospel (and the one from which all subsequent gospels derived), did indeed end at verse 8: an abrupt surprise ending, without any appearance of the risen Jesus, or his ascension into heaven, or promises that his followers would be able to take up venomous serpents without harm (sorry to be the one to tell you, fundamentalist Appalachian snakehandlers). Granted, it is an unconventional way to end a book; though not without precedent. What's more, his approach does make more literary sense than most commentators appreciate, a fact Daniel Wallace illustrates well in David Alan Black's *Perspectives on the Ending of Mark: Four Views* (2008).[23]

David Fitzgerald

The Verdict
It will not make Christians happy to hear this, but there is no other way to say it: the existence of all these variant endings clearly demonstrates that early Christians felt free to doctor manuscripts of the Gospels. What's more, as we have ample evidence to confirm canonical Mark contains a forgery, this further conclusively proves the Bible is not inerrant; since we know it contains at least this one indisputable interpolation, falsely represented as original text, which can be neither true nor inspired.

But of course, believers are going to go down swinging. Incredibly, some Christians (mainly Pentecostals who desperately need the snake handling pronouncement to be true) agree that the evidence that Mark 16:9-20 is a forgery is undeniable – but then turn around and declare that the *forgery* is inspired, too![24] Why the Holy Spirit didn't just inspire it right the first time, and needed to bring in a forger to fix his omission is a different theological conundrum... As Wilbur Pickering asked: "Are we to say that God was unable to protect the text of Mark or that He just couldn't be bothered? I see no other alternative: either He didn't care or He was helpless. And either option is fatal to the claim that Mark's Gospel is 'God-breathed.'"[25]

The Chances of Changes
Carrier remarks this is one of the clearest examples of Christians meddling with the manuscripts of the canonical Bible, inserting what they wanted their books to have said (and possibly even subtracting what they didn't want it to have said).[26] He also points out some troubling implications: since we are actually *lucky* the evidence of this meddling survived, we should expect that other instances of meddling have occurred for which the evidence *didn't* survive, calling into doubt the rest of the New Testament.

In fact, we can expect that many other changes could have survived undetected.

We have scarce reliable testimonies, few to no manuscript fragments and no complete NT texts before c. 150 CE (fifty to eighty years after the NT books were supposedly written). All this means the survival of evidence is highly unlikely for any changes made before then – and in some cases even for changes made before c. 250 CE (well over a hundred more years later).

And yet this early blackout period is exactly the time when alterations are the most likely. The fewer copies in existence, the greater a forger's chance of success. This was the case for all other books, so we should expect it for the Gospels as well.[27] In fact, we know very well forgery was happening then, not least because we have plentiful ancient writings of early Christians themselves complaining about their fellow Christians tampering with scripture.[28]

Not even the New Testament is immune to the problem; as we'll see in chapter 16, the majority of the epistles are forgeries, including half of those attributed to Paul. The second letter to the Thessalonians (2 Thess. 2:2, 3:17) repeatedly warns Christians to beware of letters forged in Paul's name – ironically enough, most scholars agree that this letter is itself a forgery. This is a no-win situation for believers: either *this* letter is a forgery, or it is authentic and Paul really is warning us that forgers are out there – in any case, it's inescapable that people *were* forging letters in Paul's name.[29]

Helmut Koester recognized the dilemma decades ago: "Textual critics of classical texts know that the first century of their transmission is the period in which the most serious corruptions occur," and yet "textual critics of the New Testament writings have been surprisingly naive in this respect," despite the fact that they all agree 'the oldest known archetypes' we can reconstruct from surviving manuscripts "are separated from the autographs by more than a century."[30]

***

David Fitzgerald

For further reading:

For further discussion of early Christian forgeries and interpolations:

Bart Ehrman, *Forgery and Counterforgery* (2013); see also his *Jesus, Interrupted* (2009) and *Misquoting Jesus* (2005)

---

[1] Price, *The Incredible Shrinking Son of Man*, p. 327
[2] MacDonald, *The Homeric Epics and the Gospel of Mark*, p. 154-55. Note: this corrects *Nailed*, p. 107.
[3] Carrier, *On the Historicity of Jesus*, p. 439, n108
[4] For various perspectives on Joseph's historicity, see Lyons, "On the Life and Death of Joseph of Arimathea," (with updated remarks in Lyons, "Hermeneutics").
[5] Richard Carrier, e-mail to the author, 8/10/10
[6] *Nailed*, p. 107
[7] See Cohn, pp. 229-232 for in-depth analysis of still *more* story problems here, particularly with plot holes and contradictions between Mark and John's accounts.
[8] e.g., Chariton of Aphrodisias' *Chaereas and Callirhoe*, Iamblichus' *Babylonian Story*, Xenophon's *Ephesian Tale*, and more. For more discussion, see Price, *DJ*, pp. 214-221.
[9] Price, op. cit., p. 333
[10] Richard Carrier, "Craig's Empty Tomb and Habermas on the Post-Resurrection Appearance of Jesus," Secular Web, 1999 (cited in *The Empty Tomb*, p. 258)
[11] MacDonald,. p. 129
[12] Polybius, *The Histories*, vol. VI, Ch. 36-37
[13] Flavius Petrus Sabgatius Justinianus, (*Pandecta*) *Digesta*, 49.16.3.6; -10.1
[14] Verse 14 says Mary turned around and spoke to Jesus; then in verse 16, has her turn around and speak to him – again! Price and others have suspected this odd little double-take of Mary's is a literary seam; that is, an indication of where

outside material has been inserted into the text. John's gospel is rife with these signs of tampering and/or borrowing (see "the Lost Supper" in ch. 8 for more examples).

[15] Bauckham, 2007, p. 271

[16] Many manuscripts omit "in their hands" in this verse (16:18); one very late manuscript even omits the entire reference to serpents altogether, showing that even these endings continued to mutate over time. For further details, see Carrier, "Mark 16:9-20 as Forgery or Fabrication" in *HHBC*, p. 237n5.

[17] Carrier, "Mark 16:9-20 as Forgery or Fabrication" in *HHBC*, pp. 311 - 312

[18] Ibid., p. 251, n18

[19] Metzger, *The Text of the NT*, pp. 226 ff.

[20] Carrier, op. cit., pp. 311 - 312

[21] Ibid., pp. 240 -241

[22] Ibid., p. 241

[23] See Daniel Wallace, in David Alan Black, ed., *Perspectives on the Ending of Mark: Four Views*, section 3, pp. 33-38

[24] e.g., see "'And the Signs Are Following': Mark 16.9-20, A Journey into Pentecostal Hermeneutics," John Christopher Thomas and Kimberly Ervin Alexander, *Journal of Pentecostal Theology* 11.2 (2003): pp. 147-170.

[25] Quoted by Daniel Wallace, "Inspiration, Preservation, and New Testament Textual Criticism," *Grace Theological Journal* 12.1 (1992): p. 44 [pp. 21-50]

[26] Carrier, op. cit., p. 233

[27] Ibid., p. 234

[28] See *Nailed*, pp. 110-113. For other common examples of forgeries and interpolations, see the relevant sections of Bart Ehrman's *Forgery and Counterforgery* (2013), *Jesus, Interrupted* (2009) and *Misquoting Jesus* (2005); and Paul Tobin, *The Rejection of Pascal's Wager: A Skeptic's Guide to the Bible and the Historical Jesus* (2006).

[29] *Nailed,* p. 110
[30] Helmut Koester, "The Text of the Synoptic Gospels in the Second Century," in William Petersen, ed., *Gospel Traditions in the Second Century: Origins, Recensions, Text, and Transmission* (1989), pp. 19-27.

Index

1

1 Corinthians	160, 165, 174, 201
1 Kings	231, 249
1 Peter	204

2

2 Kings	229
2 Thessalonians	192, 331

A

Abgar	109
Abraham	39, 53, 72, 81, 261
Acts	105, 113, 115, 136, 138, 151, 152, 166, 189, 197, 204, 205, 214, 219, 241, 242, 250, 255, 262, 283, 314, 327, 328
ad hominem	36, 83, 88
Adam and Eve	70, 257
Aesop	80, 232
affective criterion	139
agnosticism	21, 30, 37, 39, 78, 85, 180
Akenson, Donald	50, 51, 52, 55, 57, 92
Alexander the Great	282
Alogi	207
Amos	173, 302, 305, 310
Andronicus	189
Antioch	205, 218, 228, 251
Antiquities of the Jews	213
apocalyptic prophet	30, 104, 108, 180
Apollonius of Tyana	112
apologetics	28, 36, 49, 82, 84, 85, 165, 181, 287
apostles	115, 116, 189, 203, 214
Aramaic	24, 118, 138, 196, 204, 218, 284, 303
Aramaic context	138
Argurion	240
Armilus	169
Arnal, William	127, 131, 146, 147
Asclepiodotus	190
Asia Minor	116, 305
Aslan, Reza	104

Assyrian	151
atheism	9, 10, 13, 21, 28, 29, 35, 37, 42, 62, 67, 111, 134, 140, 197, 282, 302, 353
Athronges the Shepherd	113
Attis	137, 144, 166
cult of	144, 166
Augstein, Rudolf	79
Augustine	209
authorship, problem of	38, 202, 203, 205, 327
Avalos, Hector	36, 45, 50, 52, 53, 54, 55, 57, 85, 90, 118, 123, 179, 197, 199

B

Bagatti, Fr B	155, 156
Barbour, Robin S	47
Bayesian analysis	134
Belfast Analogy	95
Beloved Disciple	205, 206, 222, 225
Berlinerblau, Jacques	37
Bethabara	185
Bethany	185, 236, 239, 291, 323
Bethlehem	149, 150, 151, 152, 154, 162, 229
Bethsaida	164
bias	36, 37, 50, 57, 90, 91
biblical historians	36, 38, 48, 57, 59, 62, 76, 78, 82, 100, 126, 179
biblical inerrancy	66, 71
biblical literalism	71
biblical scholars	9, 36, 37, 38, 42, 53, 57, 63, 77, 79, 82, 100, 117, 130, 151, 157, 167, 179, 196, 209, 210, 216, 235, 317, 325, *See*
biblical studies	35, 36, 38, 39, 45, 50, 52, 54, 57, 58, 59, 60, 65, 68, 73, 78, 82, 87, 90, 91, 118, 197, 201
BioLogos Foundation	66, 69, 70, 93
Blowers, Paul	67, 68
bluster	63, 79
Bocks, Susi	59
Brodie, Thomas L	77, 227, 250
Brown, Raymond	203
Buddha	80, 81, 92
bullying	63, 71, 78

C

Caius	*See* Gaius
Calvary	*See* Golgotha
Capernaum	152, 246, 291
Carabas	114, 263, 275, 293
Cargill, Robert	68, 93

Carrier, Richard 10, 11, 32, 39, 40, 41, 46, 52, 53, 54, 57, 78, 80, 83, 86, 97, 110, 118, 119, 120, 121, 123, 128, 129, 131, 132, 133, 135, 138, 139, 140, 142, 143, 144, 145, 160, 161, 166, 167, 169, 170, 171, 172, 175, 179, 192, 193, 194, 198, 199, 200, 210, 223, 224, 225, 227, 245, 251, 252, 259, 270, 280, 281, 282, 293, 294, 295, 302, 309, 310, 311, 314, 328, 330, 332, 333, 357
Casey, Maurice 197
Catholic Biblical Association 73
Catholic Theological 72
Catholicism 12, 72, 73, 95, 99, 154, 156, 182, 198, 274
Celsus 24, 121, 122, 174, 198
Cerinthus 207, 219
Charlesworth, James 107, 121, 206, 222, 251
Chilton, Bruce 121, 128, 129, 130, 146, 147, 175, 294
Christ Myth theory 27, 28, 29, 30, 38, 44, 54, 62, 90
Christian writings 11, 115, 116, 136, 153, 180, 183, 190, 212, 218
Christianity 10, 12, 21, 22, 24, 25, 26, 27, 29, 30, 31, 36, 37, 42, 43, 44, 45, 47, 50, 54, 63, 65, 66, 70, 79, 82, 84, 86, 90, 92, 99, 100, 104, 111, 112, 115, 123, 126, 127, 132, 134, 135, 142, 143, 145, 152, 159, 160, 161, 166, 167, 168, 169, 170, 180, 182, 186, 192, 194, 198, 203, 204, 214, 215, 223, 224, 244, 246, 251, 252, 309, 351, 357
Clement 188, 203, 221, 224
Cleomenes 308, 311
Codex Siniaticus 182
Codex Vaticanus 182, 191, 199, 327
coherence 134
Cohn, Haim 108, 121, 244, 252, 257, 258, 261, 264, 270, 271, 280, 294, 299, 300, 309, 332
Colani, Timothée 238
Collins, Francis 69
Colossians 189, 204, 205, 222
contextual plausibility 135, 136
Coptic 326
Corley, Kathleen 105
Council of Nicea 182
Court at Jamnia 212
Craig, William Lane 65, 157, 158, 159, 196
creationism 28, 42, 43, 44, 58
criterion of dissimilarity 134
criterion of embarrassment 10, 25, 108, 110, 134, 140, 141, 142, 143, 144, 145, 149, 156, 159, 161, 165, 229, 306, 320
criterion of heavy interpretation 140
criterion of inexplicability 139
criterion of repetition 140
Crossan, John Dominic 101, 107, 110, 179, 211, 227
Crucifixion 136, 165, 284
Cynics 101
Cyrenaics 282

D

Daniel	40, 41, 42, 168, 169, 170, 208, 232, 239, 259, 261, 317
Dark, Ken	155
darkness story	302
Darwin, Charles	11, 42, 43, 44
Davidson, Paul	198
Davies, Phillip	87, 88, 90, 97, 99, 179
Dead Sea Scrolls	107, 169
Dead Sea Scrolls Project	107
Decline and Fall of the Roman Empire	240
Deconstructing Jesus	101, 107, 121, 122, 267, 311, 316, 356
Deuteronomy	40, 203, 211
Dickson, John	84
Didakhê	117, 212, 219
Dionysius	207
disciples	24, 25, 104, 106, 109, 130, 131, 142, 157, 159, 160, 163, 164, 190, 204, 205, 208, 230, 231, 232, 233, 234, 235, 236, 237, 244, 245, 246, 247, 249, 255, 256, 257, 280, 286, 291, 299, 316, 319, 321, 322, 323, 324
discourse features	139
Docetist	188
double ending	328
Dreher, Rod	71
Droge, Arthur	85
Drury, John	210
Dykstra, Tom	86, 90, 97, 227

E

Ecclesiastical History	238
eclipse	301
École Biblique	74
Egypt	116, 218, 282, 305, 306, 310
Egyptian, the	113
Ehrhardt, Arnold	227
Ehrman, Bart	11, 49, 78, 83, 85, 86, 88, 97, 104, 108, 120, 121, 123, 142, 143, 180, 184, 187, 192, 196, 197, 198, 199, 200, 221, 295, 332, 333
Eleusinian	228
Elijah	140, 141, 228, 249, 251, 302
Elisha	229, 251
Emmanuel Christian Seminary	67, 68, 69, 93
Enns, Peter	65, 66
Ephphatha	164
Epiphanius	116, 152, 172, 186, 207, 223
epistles	38, 45, 131, 132, 135, 155, 187, 197, 331
Essenes	102
Eucharist	246, 247, 308

Eusebius	121, 189, 199, 223, 238, 284, 285, 295, 326
evangelical theology	69
Evangelists	141, 143, 144, 203, 207, 243, 255, 260
evolution, theory of	42, 45, 58, 219
exegesis	75, 82
explanatory credibility	135

F

fabrication	99, 137, 140, 149, 150, 157, 207, 275
false messiahs	237, 238
Farrer, Austin	210
feminism	105
Ferguson, Matthew	175, 201, 202, 222
fides quaerens indicium	89
Field of Blood	241, 242
Filson, Floyd	206
Fiorenza, Elizabeth Schüssler	105
First Jewish–Roman War	238
Fitzgerald, Timothy	38
forgery	86, 120, 192, 200, 333
Fox News	104
Funk, Robert W	20, 21, 110

G

Gaius	207, 271
Galilean	101, 102, 110, 130, 263
Galilee	21, 23, 111, 113, 130, 229, 232, 248, 291, 306, 319, 321, 329
Gandhi	107
Garden of Eden	44
Geisler, Norman	64
Genesis	42, 44, 71, 307
Gethsemane	136, 162, 248, 249, 317
Gibbon, Edward	240
Gnosticism	155, 283
Godfrey, Neil	13, 54, 82, 83, 91, 126, 127, 131, 145, 146, 216
Golgotha	284, 285, 290, 294, 295
Goodacre, Mark	87, 146, 210, 213

gospel 12, 22, 23, 24, 25, 38, 45, 53, 54, 63, 86, 90, 100, 101, 102, 103, 104, 107, 109, 110, 112, 114, 116, 117, 118, 119, 120, 126, 127, 130, 131, 134, 135, 136, 137, 140, 141, 142, 143, 144, 147, 149, 150, 151, 153, 154, 155, 157, 159, 160, 161, 180, 184, 185, 187, 194, 196, 197, 200, 201, 202, 203, 204, 205, 206, 208, 209, 210, 211, 212, 213, 215, 218, 219, 220, 221, 222, 223, 224, 225, 226, 227, 228, 229, 232, 235, 237, 239, 241, 243, 244, 247, 248, 250, 251, 253, 256, 257, 258, 259, 260, 262, 263, 264, 265, 267, 268, 270,

273, 274, 275, 277, 280, 283, 284, 289, 290, 291, 292, 294, 297, 302, 305, 306, 314, 316, 319, 321, 324, 325, 326, 327, 329, 330, 331, 332, 334, 351
apocryphal 112, 155, 283, 302
John 45, 104, 105, 106, 109, 110, 122, 135, 137, 144, 151, 154, 161, 163, 166, 171, 174, 185, 194, 195, 201, 202, 204, 205, 206, 207, 208, 214, 215, 217, 219, 220, 222, 224, 225, 229, 230, 239, 243, 244, 245, 246, 247, 248, 249, 251, 252, 255, 259, 261, 268, 283, 286, 287, 290, 291, 292, 297, 302, 303, 304, 307, 308, 313, 318, 323, 324, 329, 332, 333
Luke 23, 45, 103, 105, 106, 109, 113, 114, 122, 143, 144, 151, 155, 159, 164, 171, 174, 196, 201, 202, 204, 205, 206, 208, 209, 210, 211, 213, 214, 215, 218, 219, 223, 224, 225, 226, 230, 232, 239, 241, 243, 244, 246, 249, 252, 259, 262, 263, 268, 271, 273, 274, 286, 289, 290, 291, 297, 298, 299, 300, 301, 303, 304, 307, 313, 318, 322, 324, 328, 329
Mark 35, 45, 87, 102, 103, 104, 105, 109, 120, 132, 135, 137, 138, 141, 142, 143, 144, 146, 147, 150, 151, 152, 154, 157, 158, 159, 161, 162, 163, 164, 165, 166, 171, 174, 184, 185, 186, 193, 201, 202, 204, 205, 208, 209, 210, 211, 212, 213, 215, 218, 219, 220, 222, 223, 224, 226, 227, 228, 229, 230, 231, 232, 234, 235, 236, 237, 238, 239, 240, 243, 245, 246, 248, 249, 250, 251, 252, 256, 257, 258, 259, 260, 261, 262, 263, 264, 265, 266, 267, 268, 269, 270, 273, 274, 275, 277, 280, 281, 282, 283, 284, 286, 288, 289, 290, 291, 292, 293, 294, 295, 297, 298, 299, 300, 302, 303, 304, 305, 306, 307, 310, 313, 314, 316, 317, 318, 319, 320, 321, 324, 325, 327, 328, 329, 330, 332, 333
Matthew 23, 45, 64, 102, 104, 105, 106, 109, 131, 142, 143, 144, 150, 151, 152, 154, 159, 161, 164, 166, 171, 174, 185, 188, 196, 201, 202, 204, 207, 208, 209, 210, 211, 212, 213, 215, 217, 218, 219, 221, 222, 223, 226, 229, 230, 235, 236, 240, 241, 243, 244, 252, 258, 265, 267, 273, 286, 289, 290, 291, 294, 297, 300, 303, 304, 305, 306, 307, 313, 318, 319, 320, 321, 322, 329
Synoptic Gospels 211, 215, 290, 291, 292
Goulder, Michael 87, 210
Greek 24, 31, 40, 101, 103, 118, 138, 147, 152, 172, 181, 189, 199, 202, 204, 207, 209, 210, 218, 233, 235, 240, 245, 249, 255, 263, 282, 284, 297, 298, 301, 306, 314, 326, 327
Greek Context 138

H

hadith	80, 81
Hakeldama	242
Hamerton-Kelly, R G	237
Hanina ben-Dosa	102
harmonization	184
harrumphed	29
Hasid	102
hedonism	105

Helms, Randel	53, 174, 208, 223, 227, 235, 250, 251, 253, 259, 260, 263, 270, 286, 293, 294, 295, 310
Heracleon	217
heresy	28, 67, 152, 207
hermeneutics	203, 332, 333
Herod Antipas	23, 114, 129, 273, 274
Herod the Great	23, 24, 31, 113, 129, 150, 250, 273, 274, 275, 289
historical plausibility	136
historicity	9, 11, 14, 29, 36, 39, 64, 70, 78, 81, 83, 85, 86, 88, 89, 90, 91, 92, 100, 116, 118, 119, 122, 126, 127, 130, 138, 149, 156, 197, 264, 332
Hitchens, Christopher	149, 150, 156, 171
Holy Spirit	190, 229, 230, 241, 324, 330
homosexuality	69
Honi the Circle-Drawer	102
Hooker, Morna	47, 118, 132, 142
Horsley, Richard	107
Hosanna	237, 266
Huffington Post	67, 93
Hurtado, Larry	76

I

Iconoclast	102
Ignatius	212, 219
Iliad	314
Inanna	144
Industrial Revolution	43
Inside Higher Ed	68, 93
Intelligent Design	58
intercalation	211, 237
Irenaeus of Lyons	203, 228
Isaiah	152, 153, 166, 167, 168, 169, 170, 172, 184, 226, 228, 231, 236, 239, 260, 263, 273, 298, 299, 306, 310, 317
Iscariot	159, 160, 240, 245, 246
Islam	12, 80, 81, 99, 104
Israel	52, 53, 72, 75, 106, 107, 128, 130, 150, 151, 159, 160, 163, 165, 167, 169, 185, 241, 257, 269, 273, 298, 307

J

Jacob	39, 307
Jeremiah	185, 241, 277, 278, 284
Jeremy	185
Jerusalem	22, 23, 25, 64, 74, 94, 113, 114, 115, 128, 130, 156, 208, 235, 236, 237, 238, 241, 244, 245, 266, 267, 275, 276, 277, 278, 285, 290, 291, 292, 299, 302, 304, 305, 306, 322
Jesuit University of Marquette	75

Jesus
- arrest of   206, 231, 235, 249, 250, 255, 319
- as heir of David   106
- as king of the Jews   297
- as Passover lamb   245, 292, 307
- as political messiah   103
- as savior of Israel   106
- as savior of the world   106
- as son of David   169
- as Son of God   7, 21, 22, 26, 164, 168, 228, 230, 300, 324
- as son of Joseph   169
- as son of man 79, 159, 172, 238, 239, 246, 251, 252, 255, 261, 294, 316, 332, 356
- as stealth messiah   111, 117
- execution of   162, 165, 206, 235, 267
- historical Jesus 14, 27, 45, 54, 57, 76, 95, 96, 100, 111, 120, 121, 123, 125, 128, 145, 146, 147, 170, 179, 197, 224, 250, 294, 333, 353
- Jesus of faith   22, 26, 37, 99, 101, 196
- Jesus of history   22, 26, 99, 100, 101
- ministry of   174, 230
- Passion of the Christ   235
- resurrection of   63, 64, 110, 156, 157, 169, 196, 206, 235, 305, 306, 313, 332
- sources for   180
- trial of 23, 67, 108, 195, 235, 248, 250, 257, 258, 259, 262, 263, 264, 265, 266, 273, 291, 318

Jesus ben-Ananias   114, 263, 275, 276
Jesus Myth theory   12
Jesus of Faith   12
Jesus of History   12
Jesus of Nazareth   12, 14, 21, 22, 88, 125, 130, 149, 151, 277, 297, 319, 356
Jesus Seminar   110
Jesus studies   30, 46, 48, 51, 57, 82, 96, 117
Jewish law   23, 101, 102, 157, 257, 262, 264
Jewish priests   109
Jewish satire   153
Jewish Scriptures   168, 207
Job   39, 235
Johannine   215, 224
John of Gischala   115
John the Baptist   23, 45, 102, 112, 128, 130, 140, 161, 208, 228, 229
Jonah   39, 235, 236, 249
Jonathan   114, 116, 168
Joseph 31, 39, 151, 166, 167, 169, 224, 250, 262, 268, 289, 313, 314, 317, 318, 323, 332
Joseph of Arimathea   262, 313, 314, 318, 332
Josephus 25, 31, 103, 112, 113, 114, 122, 155, 173, 213, 214, 221, 223, 236, 275, 277, 284, 293, 294, 295, 304

Joshua	39, 42, 113, 121, 122
Judaism	102, 108, 127, 128, 134, 142, 147, 192, 212, 218, 219, 251, 252, 262, 309
ancient	86
Judaean	24, 262
Judas	113, 159, 160, 161, 165, 240, 241, 242, 243, 244, 245, 246, 250, 255, 314
Judas of Galilee	113
Judea	21, 23, 30, 107, 116, 127, 130, 132, 138, 150, 168, 220, 238, 253, 262, 266, 278, 291, 308, 314
Junia	189
Justin Martyr	116, 203

K

kabbalah	128
Kannaday, Wayne	142, 197
Käsemann, Ernst	47, 126, 227
keeper of secrets	153
Keith, Chris	48, 52, 54, 90, 123, 132, 146, 147
Kennard, J S	152, 153, 172
King James	184, 189, 298
King Jeroboam	231
King of Israel	300
Kingdom of God	104, 231, 232
Koester, Helmut	103, 107, 120, 223, 331, 334
Koresh, David	106
Kuhli, Horst	152

L

L	161, 196, 209, 215, 225
Lake of Genneseret	232
Laodicea	189
Lao-Tzu	80, 81
Lataster, Raphael	83, 85, 90, 96, 196, 197, 200
Latin manuscripts	186
Lazarus	24, 109, 206, 239, 268, 271, 291, 318
Le Donne, Anthony	48, 52, 54, 76, 90, 123, 132, 133, 140, 146, 147
least distinctiveness	137
Levensen, Jon D	38, 53
Levi	204, 230
Levin, Susan	154, 172
Levi-Strauss, Claude	20
Lewis, C S	227
Licona, Mike	63, 64, 65, 306
Lincoln Christian University	76
Little Apocalypse	237

logoi	210, 211
long ending	325, 327, 328
Lord's Supper	160, 246, 292
Ludd, Ned	80
Lydus, John	302, 309

M

Macarius Magnes	228, 234, 251
MacDonald, Dennis R	87, 97, 210, 211, 223, 224, 227, 250, 270, 314, 332
Machoveč, Milan	104
Mack, Burton L	101, 110, 111, 121, 122
Maclean, Jennifer	227
Magician, the	103, 113
Malachi	184, 228, 229
Malina, Bruce	104
Marcan Appendix	157
Marcion	214
Marco Polo	80
Markan Priority	38, 209
Mary Magdalene	110, 306, 307, 317, 318, 320, 322, 325
Mary the mother of James	306, 318, 322
Mary the mother of Joses	*See* Mary the Mother of James
Mary the wife of Cleophas	307
McBride, Dean	73
McGrath, James	82, 153, 172
Megiddo	156
Meier, John P	50, 141, 143, 147, 154, 159, 161, 165, 166, 174
Melchizedek Scroll	169, 170
Merovingian	110
messiah	26, 112, 113, 114, 115, 165, 166, 167, 168, 169, 170, 171, 236, 260, 266, 282, 287, 288, 299, 356
Messiah ben David	169
Messiah of Aaron	169
Metzger, Bruce	85, 96, 182, 186, 198, 199, 333
Micah	150, 151, 239, 273
miracles	24, 25, 26, 40, 100, 110, 115, 136, 170, 219, 230, 247, 304
Mishnah	23, 136, 152, 153, 310
Mithraism	228
moneychangers	24, 105, 109, 237, 244, 268, 291
moneylenders	235
Moreland, J P	65
Mormonism	14, 28, 99, 109, 354
Moses	39, 40, 42, 81, 96, 105, 113, 114, 141, 211, 246, 306
Mount Gerizim	114
Mount of Olives	113, 236, 237, 244, 248
Muhammad	80, 81, 91, 96

multiple attestations	135
Musonius Rufus	282
mythicism	10, 28, 35, 37, 44, 45, 58, 62, 86, 90

N

Nailed 4, 12, 27, 29, 31, 36, 57, 83, 85, 92, 96, 111, 116, 120, 147, 160, 165, 172, 174, 175, 190, 197, 218, 222, 223, 232, 251, 252, 257, 262, 265, 267, 269, 271, 283, 295, 314, 332, 333, 334, 353, 356, 357

natural plausibility	136
natural selection	44
Nazarene	150, 151, 152, 153, 154, 172
Nazareth	128, 149, 150, 151, 152, 153, 154, 155, 156, 172, 173, 229
Nazir	152
Nazoraean	151, 152, 172
Nazorean	152, 153, 154, 172
New International Version	198

New Testament 11, 13, 22, 24, 25, 44, 45, 49, 52, 59, 65, 66, 76, 82, 84, 88, 91, 96, 102, 103, 110, 112, 118, 131, 142, 152, 155, 161, 172, 180, 181, 182, 183, 185, 186, 187, 188, 192, 194, 197, 198, 199, 205, 207, 208, 215, 216, 222, 224, 225, 250, 270, 294, 298, 302, 330, 331, 333, 351

New Testament Apocrypha	82
Noah	39, 43, 44
Noll, Kurt	85
No-True-Scotsman	83
Numbers	152, 292
Nympha	189, 199

O

Old Testament 39, 40, 42, 44, 52, 53, 65, 67, 69, 70, 74, 75, 80, 105, 150, 155, 166, 203, 211, 227, 230, 235, 236, 238, 244, 248, 250, 259, 299, 317

Olivet Discourse	*See* Little Apocalypse
On the Origin of Species	43
oral preservability	136
oral source	140
Origen	24, 155, 185, 188, 228, 251, 284, 297
original ending	325, 327, 329
Orsini, Pasquale	216

P

Palestine	72, 79, 80, 128, 218, 275, 304
Papias	204, 210, 214, 242, 243, 252
paradidomi	160
paradigm shift	39, 44, 58, 87

Passover 24, 121, 239, 245, 247, 248, 258, 259, 267, 268, 270, 277, 290, 291, 292, 301, 307
Patmos 207
Patriarchs 39, 71, 74, 75, 80
Patripassianists 188
Paul 25, 45, 65, 104, 116, 117, 131, 132, 138, 143, 152, 154, 158, 160, 168, 188, 189, 192, 197, 198, 201, 204, 205, 207, 214, 227, 244, 245, 246, 256, 270, 292, 294, 304, 331, 333
Perrin, Nicholas 49, 54, 210
Perrin, Norman 227
Peter 9, 115, 116, 173, 204, 205, 206, 218, 222, 235, 243, 244, 245, 248, 262, 263, 274, 281, 283, 319, 322, 323, 327
Pharisees 101, 109, 110, 230, 239, 262, 267, 291, 318
Philemon 204, 205
Phillip 99, 153, 179
Philo of Alexandria 22, 114, 257, 265, 271, 275
Philostratus 112
Pickering, Wilbur 330
Plato 144, 256
Plutarch 144, 202, 308, 309, 311
Pontius Pilate 23, 114, 250, 264, 265, 266, 267, 268, 273, 274, 278, 279, 288, 289, 290, 307, 313, 317
Pope Benedict 72
Porphyry of Tyre 232, 234
Porter, Stanley 48, 54, 131, 132, 133, 143, 145, 146, 147
Pre-Christian 168
Price, Robert 11, 28, 31, 53, 83, 101, 107, 110, 120, 121, 122, 154, 172, 174, 179, 224, 227, 238, 243, 250, 251, 252, 267, 274, 283, 293, 294, 301, 306, 308, 309, 311, 313, 314, 316, 317, 318, 332, 356
Princeton Theological Seminary 107
prophecy 149, 150, 151, 152, 185, 208, 261, 286, 287, 292, 307, 308
Proverbs 255, 285
Psalm 106 235
Psalm 116 248
Psalm 22 164, 287, 288, 300, 303, 317
pseudohistory 35
pseudomedicine 35
pseudoscience 35
Pulpit Commentaries 234

Q

Q 161, 192, 196, 209, 210, 211, 213
Q+ 210, 211
Quaestiones Naturales 23
quest paradigm 126
Quirinius 24

Qur'an 81

R

Rabbi Hillel 101
Ratzinger, Joseph *See* Pope Benedict
Reformed Theological Seminary 70
Rollston, Christopher 66, 67, 68, 93
Roman Catholics 188
Roman empire 116
Romans 103, 108, 113, 114, 115, 131, 166, 188, 189, 201, 245, 253, 267, 268, 279, 292, 311, 317
Rome 115, 116, 121, 129, 144, 169, 203, 207, 208, 212, 214, 218, 219, 224, 265, 282, 297
Romulus 144, 169, 201
Rylands Library Papyrus P52 215, 220, 225

S

Salm, René 155, 156, 173
Salome 306, 307, 318
Sanders, E P 108, 130, 131, 201
Sanders, Jack T 132
Sanhedrin 23, 103, 109, 166, 250, 257, 258, 259, 262, 263, 264, 289, 313, 318
Satan 4, 117, 162, 230, 243, 244, 250
Schonfield, Hugh J 104, 121
Schröter, Jens 82, 132
Schweitzer, Albert 101, 104, 125
scribal alterations 183
scribal interpolations 186
scribes 109, 150, 183, 185, 186, 187, 188, 189, 190, 191, 193, 194, 220, 228, 230, 264, 267, 289, 291, 298, 299, 300, 308
scripture 49, 65, 66, 138, 150, 151, 166, 167, 168, 171, 180, 182, 184, 187, 192, 194, 237, 240, 241, 250, 256, 286, 299, 302, 307, 331
Sea of Galilee 232
secular biblical scholars 38, 100, 212
Seneca the Younger 23, 302
Sepher Toldoth Yeshu 153
Septuagint 138, 147, 229, 237, 249, 259, 263, 307
Shellard, Barbara 210
shorter ending 327
sicarii 113
Simon 103, 115, 116, 239, 280, 281, 282, 283, 290, 323
Simon bar-Giora 115
Simon Magus 115, 116, 122, 283
Simon of Gitta 115
Simon of Peraea 113

347

Simon Peter	281, 283
Simon the Magician	*See* Simon Magus
son of Zebedee	*See* John
Song of Solomon	239
Southern Baptists	63, 64
Southern Baptists of Texas	64
Star of Bethlehem	23
Streeter, B H	212
Sweeney, Michael	68
Swinbourne, Richard	196
Synoptic problem	38, 209, 213
Syria	116, 129, 218

T

Tabor, James	106
Tacitus	113, 202
Taheb	114, 116
Talbert, Charles H	201, 220
Talmud	153, 166, 167, 168, 170
Talmud Yerushalmi	153
targum	138
Temple	24, 73, 102, 103, 105, 109, 131, 208, 212, 243, 244, 252, 268, 269, 276, 277, 278, 284, 285, 288, 291, 292
textual variance	137
The Secular Bible	37
The Tower of Babel	44
Theissen, Gerd	48, 107, 143, 159
Theodotus	190
theological correctness	57
Theophilus	213, 228, 251
Thessalonians	192
Theudas	103, 113
Thomas	206, 251, 324
Thompson, Thomas	53, 71, 72, 73, 74, 75, 78, 83, 88, 94, 111, 120, 227, 251
Torah	102, 204, 270, 292, 307
Tosefta	153
Transjordan	218
Trinity	162
Twelve Disciples	159, 160, 204
Tyson, Joseph B	214

U

Urgemeinde	158, 159

V

Verenna, Thomas	67, 83, 88, 111, 120
Vermes, Geza	102, 108, 121
Virgin Mary	205, 307
Virginia Union Theological	73
vividness of narration	137

W

Waltke, Bruce	69, 70, 71
Wegner, Judith	157, 174
Westminster Theological Seminary	65
Widowfield, Tim	12, 83, 91
William Tell	80
Williams, C S C	142, 310
Williams, Jarvis	168
Winnie the Pooh	51
Wrede, William	37, 101, 212
Wright, N T	89, 126, 146

Y

Yeshu ha-Notzri	153
Yeshua of Nazareth	50

Z

Zealot	103, 104, 115
Zechariah	166, 185, 236, 240, 246, 248, 252, 307
Zindler, Frank	172, 173, 283

Jesus: Mything in Action
continues in volumes II and III.

In vol. II (chapters 13 – 18), we discuss the construction (and deconstruction) of the Gospels; how Jesus is presented in the rest of the New Testament; and examines the historical sources for Jesus outside of the Bible.

In vol. III (chapters 19 – 25), we engage in a bold thought experiment: a multi-chapter time travel expedition through the origin and evolution of Christianity. I call it "The Gospel According to H.G. Wells."

About the Author

David Fitzgerald is a writer and historical researcher who has been actively investigating the Historical Jesus question for over fifteen years. He has a degree in history and was an associate member of CSER (the former Committee for the Scientific Examination of Religion). He lectures around the world at universities and national secular events. He is the author of *Nailed* and *The Complete Heretic's Guide to Western Religion* series.

He has also been called "one of the busiest atheist activists in the Bay Area." In addition to serving on the board of San Francisco Atheists, Center For Inquiry-SF and The Garrison-Martineau Project, he was also the Director/Co-Founder of both the world's first Atheist Film Festival and *Evolutionpalooza!*, San Francisco's annual Darwin Day celebration. He has also been honored to work with the Secular Student Alliance. He lives in San Francisco with writer, producer and film actress (also his wife) Dana Fredsti.

I welcome your comments, criticisms and especially corrections. William Strunk has a useful motto that has guided me well while writing this book: "Understanding is that penetrating quality of knowledge that grows from theory, practice, conviction, assertion, error, and humiliation."

-DF

Contact me at: Everybodylovesdave@gmail.com.

If you like *Jesus: Mything in Action*, you'll also love:

**Because Religion isn't just wrong.
It's hilarious.**

The new book series by David Fitzgerald, award-winning author of *Nailed*

"Fitzgerald's writing is part sniper, part machine gun. In his newest book, Fitzgerald takes aim at Mormonism and exposes many of the religion's silliest and scariest tenets with precision and speed reminiscent of Harris' "Letters to a Christian Nation." After reading this book, you will be hoping (but not praying) for Mormon missionaries to ring your doorbell just so you can tear their religion apart for fun."

- David Silverman, President of American Atheists

If you like *Jesus: Mything in Action*, you'll also love:

Nailed

Ten Christian Myths That Show Jesus Never Existed at All

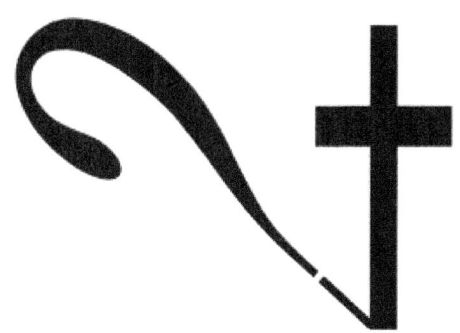

David Fitzgerald

Voted one of the Top Five Best Atheist/Agnostic Books of 2010
- About Atheism.com Reader's Choice Awards

Why would anyone think Jesus never existed?
Isn't it perfectly reasonable to accept that he was a real first

century figure? As it turns out, no. ***Nailed: Ten Christian Myths That Show Jesus Never Existed At All*** sheds light on ten beloved Christian myths, and with evidence gathered from historians all across the theological spectrum, shows how they point to a Jesus Christ created solely through allegorical alchemy of hope and imagination; a messiah transformed from a purely literary, theological construct into the familiar figure of Jesus – in short, a purely mythic Christ.

Praise for *Nailed*:

"Fitzgerald's is possibly the best 'capsule summary' of the mythicist case I've ever encountered …with an interesting and accessible approach."
—Earl Doherty, author of *The Jesus Puzzle*

"Fitzgerald summarizes a great number of key arguments concisely and with new power and original spin. I really learned something from him. Recalls classical skeptics and biblical critics. A surprising amount of new material."
—Robert M. Price, author of *Deconstructing Jesus and The Incredible Shrinking Son of Man*

"David Fitzgerald reveals himself to be the brightest new star in the firmament of scholars who deny historical reality to 'Jesus of Nazareth.' His brilliance would have been sufficiently established had he done nothing more than illustrate and explain traditional arguments with a clarity and transparency never achieved…But he has done more. He has developed new arguments and insights as well..."
—Frank R. Zindler, editor of American Atheist Press and author of *The Jesus the Jews Never Knew*

"Fitzgerald has hit the nail on the head…A nice, readable

introduction to the top ten problems typically swept under the rug by anyone insisting it's crazy even to suspect Jesus might not have existed."

—Richard C. Carrier, Ph.D., author of *Not the Impossible Faith: Why Christianity Didn't Need a Miracle to Succeed*, *Proving History* and *On the Historicity of Jesus*

Available from Amazon, Amazon.UK, Barnes & Noble, Smashwords and other online retailers.

See *Nailed's* **page on Facebook for more information.**

Printed in Great Britain
by Amazon